A BROKEN RECORD

A Broken Record examines economic reform in the Punjab in the period 1900–47 in an attempt to historicize theories of institutional change and community development. It advances the economic history of the region by analysing microeconomic reform in the province. A close examination of programmes of rural reconstruction in colonial Punjab reveals stark parallels with more contemporary prescriptions of development economics. Simultaneously, a study of the trajectory of legislative change sheds light on the institutional legacies of colonial rule.

The book engages deeply with the theoretical scholarship on development and rural uplift that emerges in this period and develops an intellectual genealogy that links colonialism to development studies. It questions the continued valorization of the 'community' despite a lack of supportive evidence and argues that one reason for the continued popularity of ideas of community development and institutional malaise is that both absolve the status quo from blame.

Atiyab Sultan is a career civil servant in the Pakistan Administrative Service, currently serving as Additional Deputy Commissioner, Lahore. Previously she has served as Assistant Commissioner in Gujrat, Jhelum, and Islamabad, as well as in the Planning and Development Board, Punjab, and the National Planning Commission, Islamabad. She holds MPhil and PhD degrees from the University of Cambridge, UK, and has taught Economics at the Lahore University of Management Sciences, Pakistan.

A BROKEN RECORD
Institutions, Community, and
Development in Pakistan

Atiyab Sultan

CAMBRIDGE
UNIVERSITY PRESS

University Printing House, Cambridge CB2 8BS, United Kingdom

One Liberty Plaza, 20th Floor, New York, NY 10006, USA

477 Williamstown Road, Port Melbourne, vic 3207, Australia

314 to 321, 3rd Floor, Plot No.3, Splendor Forum, Jasola District Centre,
New Delhi 110025, India

103 Penang Road, #05–06/07, Visioncrest Commercial, Singapore 238467

Cambridge University Press is part of the University of Cambridge.

It furthers the University's mission by disseminating knowledge in the pursuit of
education, learning and research at the highest international levels of excellence.

www.cambridge.org
Information on this title: www.cambridge.org/9781108832632

First published 2022

Printed in India by Avantika Printers Pvt. Ltd.

A catalogue record for this publication is available from the British Library

ISBN 978-1-108-83263-2 Hardback

CONTENTS

FIGURES

Tables

PREFACE

This book examines economic reform in the Punjab in the period 1900–47 in an attempt to historicize theories of institutional change and community development. Existing scholarship on colonial Punjab is preoccupied with either the rise of nationalist politics and the political transition to independence from the British, or the role of the military. The economic history of the region is meanwhile focused on large-scale changes such as the establishment of the canal colonies.

This book advances the economic history of the region by conducting an analysis of microeconomic reform in the province, thus providing an alternative way of studying the colonial impact on the Punjab. A close examination of programmes of rural reconstruction in colonial Punjab reveals stark parallels with more contemporary prescriptions of development economics. At the same time, a study of the trajectory of legislative change sheds light on the institutional legacies of colonial rule. The book situates the legal changes and microeconomic reforms in the political context to reveal the assumptions, ideological commitments, and underlying motives of the official and political actors involved. A study of the private papers and publications of the relevant officials, including Malcolm Darling and Frank Brayne, personalizes this account and humanizes a discourse on institutions, which otherwise might remain vague. The book also engages deeply with the theoretical scholarship on development and rural uplift that emerges in this period and develops an intellectual genealogy that links colonialism to development studies. It questions the ahistorical nature of development studies and the continued valorization of the 'community' despite a lack of supportive evidence. The book argues that one reason for the perpetuity and continued popularity of ideas of community development and institutional malaise is that both absolve the status quo from blame.

Acknowledgements

My greatest debt is to my late doctoral supervisor at Cambridge, Chris Bayly, without whose encouragement and support this project would have been neither conceived nor undertaken. Chris's intellect and affection created the ideal environment for embarking on an independent piece of research and navigating it through the quagmires of inaccessible archives, meandering ideas, and crippling self-doubt. The many conversations and supervisions with Chris became the crucible of this work, and it was an immense privilege to work in the shade of his scholarship and humanity for nearly three years.

Chris's untimely death in April 2015 was both shocking and saddening, and I owe a great debt of gratitude to my subsequent doctoral supervisor at Cambridge, David Washbrook. David's thorough and sharp critique of the book improved its content and level of clarity considerably. His eye for detail and witty questioning of assumptions also made the process of writing as relaxing and rewarding as it could be. After the completion of doctoral studies, David encouraged me to publish the thesis and it is a matter of lasting regret that he is not alive to see the finished product. I could not have asked for better guides than Chris and David on this journey, and the final output owes much to their labour, patience, and kindness.

I am extremely grateful to Ayesha Jalal whose scholarship, integrity, and thoughtfulness over the years have meant more than words can say. I would also like to thank Clive Dewey who guided me through the materials on colonial Punjab and answered countless questions, always very graciously.

I am grateful to Barbara Roe and Rachel Rowe at the Centre of South Asian Studies, Cambridge, for their efficient and friendly help on countless occasions; Ann Leonard at the Cambridge University Library for her kind assistance with numerous requests; Leigh Denault, Stephen Thompson, Kamal Munir, Mishka Sinha, John Slight, and Jagjeet Lally for their help and for being a constant source of advice and encouragement. I am also thankful to friends at the Centre for History and Economics at Cambridge for their critique on various aspects of this work and for numerous opportunities for an exchange of ideas.

I am grateful to the staff at the Punjab Archives, Lahore; the National Documentation Centre, Islamabad; and the National Archives, Islamabad, for their assistance and for ensuring a continuous supply of tea while I pored over archives. I would also like to thank Mian Kamal-ud-din who very kindly facilitated my research in Risalewala and Faisalabad in 2015.

I have the warmest gratitude for Alia al-Kadi who has been the sincerest of friends and a pillar of support for the past many years. I am also grateful to my cousin, Shermin Imran, and her family, and uncle Ijaz Bhatti and his family, for their hospitality and care during my years in England. For numerous kindnesses and general camaraderie, I am grateful to Sahar Alamgir, Nazish Afraz, Mahreen Mahmud, Sarah Khan, Sara Zubair, Asmah Hyat, Sophiya Anjum, Saumya Saxena, Sana Siddique, Mashaal Mahnoor, Sana Waheed, Amna Baig, and the list goes on.

I am thankful to Qudsiya Ahmed at Cambridge University Press for her interest in this work and for ably steering it to publication. I am also grateful to the two anonymous reviewers who made many useful comments and suggestions.

I owe a debt of gratitude to Abdullah Sumbal, Chairman, Planning and Development Board, Government of the Punjab, who kindly allowed me to use an image of Anna Molka Ahmed's painting of the Punjab Civil Secretariat on the cover of this book.

My brothers, Haider and Hashir, have been witty critics of this work – I am grateful for their engagement and comments. My mother has been quietly loving and supportive at each step of the way, while also calmly ensuring that I did not dawdle too much during the terminal stages of writing this book. There are not enough words to thank my father, who embraced the project and made many useful comments and suggestions, sat with me in archives and pored over documents, travelled cities and opened doors – this book would not have been possible without him. My daughters, Samar and Ariana, and husband, Omar Hayat Gondal, have enlivened the final stages of revision considerably, and I owe much to their patience and support.

This book is lovingly dedicated to my parents, Nayyara Malik and Ather Sultan.

INTRODUCTION

Institutions, Debt, and the Deadweight of History, Punjab c. 1900–47

The myth of eternal return states that a life which disappears once and for all, which does not return, is like a shadow, without weight, dead in advance, and whether it was horrible, beautiful or sublime, its horror, sublimity and beauty mean nothing. We need take no more note of it than of a war between two African kingdoms in the fourteenth century, a war that altered nothing in the destiny of the world, even if a hundred thousand blacks perished in excruciating torment.

—Milan Kundera, *The Unbearable Lightness of Being*[1]

In *The Unbearable Lightness of Being*, Milan Kundera discusses the problem of 'eternal return': he writes that in life everything would be cynically permitted if it were seen as happening only once, never recurring, and disappearing into a vacuum after occurrence. History is sometimes viewed as an account of events and things long past, a recital that may be interesting, dramatic, and tragic, but with little consequence in the long run. However, the discourse on institutional development is one that rakes the graveyard of history and raises a spectre haunting current day attempts at economic development. 'Institutions' are seen as almighty and eternal, and the post-colonial state as a corrosive inheritance of imperial rule that negatively affects progress by structuring the rules of the game and making any real welfare gains impossible.[2] Simultaneously, the field of development studies has emerged as one that is ahistorical and forward-looking, constantly in search of innovative cures to lead poor countries to prosperity. This book is an attempt to historicize both the discourse on colonial institutions and prescriptions in development studies through an examination of economic reform in colonial Punjab.

The central argument of this study emerges from a dialectical engagement with the economic history of the Punjab on the one hand and theories and practices of development studies on the other. Existing scholarship on colonial Punjab views it either as a leading beneficiary of empire and the site for some of its greatest achievements, or as a victim of planned social and economic engineering that has perpetuated extractive institutions and poverty for successive generations in the region. This book argues that both these accounts of the colonial impact in the Punjab are preoccupied with macroeconomic and large-scale changes, such as the establishment of canal colonies, and ignore a history of microeconomic reform in the province that does not admit as reductive an assessment of empire as the two dominant and conflicting accounts. Therefore, the first contribution of the book is in unearthing a forgotten history of economic reform in the Punjab and its implications for assessing the immediate and long-lasting impacts of colonialism.

The second contribution this book makes is in challenging two key strands of thought in development studies. The first of these concerns institutional explanations of underdevelopment which argue that post-colonial economies remain poor due to extractive colonial institutions inherited by the independent states.[3] 'Development' is then seen as a way of shaking off this imperial inheritance through various types of ameliorative strategies, including community development programmes undertaken by the post-colonial states. An important implication of taking a sequential view of 'institutional formation' and 'economic development' separated in time by the exit of the imperial state, is the overlooking of attempts at 'economic development' *during* a period of colonial rule. This book demolishes such a chronology and suggests that, in colonial Punjab, macroeconomic processes of 'institution building' co-existed with microeconomic practices of 'economic development' and the tendency to engage in the latter is not the nationalist assertion of post-colonial states alone. Socio-economic development was, in words and practice, part of the colonial administrative agenda in the Punjab and went hand in hand with the large-scale structural reforms that the provincial government was enacting. Furthermore, this study unearths the colonial roots of community development and its implications at length.

In order to engage with this theoretical and historical scholarship, the issue of peasant indebtedness in the Punjab is studied where both structural change and economic reform meet, at macro and micro levels. By focusing on what was (and remains) a grave socio-economic issue engendering poverty and underdevelopment,[4] I trace how 'institution building' and 'economic development' were two *simultaneous* processes in colonial Punjab. Existing historiography of the region is dominated by the study of centralizing processes and macroeconomic reforms with the task of economic development falling to the independent states after 1947. This book argues that the scourge of indebtedness led to reform initiatives, information gathering, and attempted ameliorative practices undertaken by the colonial government in a period where institutional structure was also changing. The issue of indebtedness crystallized the two strands of governance: the structural changes that some historians believe caused mass indebtedness among the peasantry, and the enthusiastic reform agenda pursued by some colonial officers to provide relief to the peasant. In fact, it may be argued that peasant indebtedness in the Punjab was exaggerated to facilitate the construction of various tropes (including the usurious moneylender) and to create room for colonial cures and reforms.

If the processes of institutional development are largely associated with the erstwhile colonial empire in South Asia and economic development is mostly linked with post-colonial government, the two become linear and mutually exclusive, with the analysis of institutions becoming time-warped, reducing them to an ever-fixed mark. 'Weak' institutions are then seen as the legacy of an extractive colonial system which, despite the most well-intentioned plans, still pave the way to hell for the progressive independent state today. While such an approach automatically neglects the innovation and impact of post-colonial rule on institutional structure, it can also absolve present day executors and policymakers by laying the blame on an inherited system. Institutionalist explanations of underdevelopment remain popular even as 'institutions' remain a black box whose definition is yet to be agreed upon. Such an approach has also facilitated a reductionist view of colonialism: encouraging broad generalizations to be made on the institutional legacies of British versus French colonialism, for instance, while diminishing the role of local context. The book probes and develops these themes.

A Statement of Claims

The main contentions of this book are as follows: first, it challenges the perception that 'economic development' is largely a post-colonial preoccupation and presents a case study to unveil the close similarities between colonial and post-colonial attempts at understanding and alleviating underdevelopment. Second, it presents a fine-grained account of the academic and practical ways in which 'development' was attempted in the Punjab, presenting a new articulation of the economic history of the region that is at variance with existing macroeconomic accounts of the history of the province. Third, it highlights the present situation in the Punjab, both in terms of economic life and continued attempts at development to observe the close parallels between colonial efforts to achieve economic development and current schemes, in the context of community development programmes. It argues that colonial efforts, which failed to produce significant results, have been largely forgotten and that current attempts recycle the same ideas to similar ineffectual ends. Debt is the 'specific problem of underdevelopment' which allows this book to probe the discourse in a concrete manner, both the institutional strand which makes claims on how indebtedness spread and the micro-development strands which were initiated in the colonial period to combat it.

The book is divided into six main chapters and a postscript. The chapters are divided into sections focusing on the *problematique*, the remedies, the officials, the politics, and the discourse respectively. The first chapter details the 'problem' under study and why the Punjab was selected for this project. I begin by examining the existing scholarship on the province and contrast the stark binary in views among academics: one group, including Clive Dewey, views the Punjab as an economic success overhanging with the fruit of colonialism. The other, including Imran Ali, sees the growth as accompanied by and causing underdevelopment. The first chapter compares and contrasts these two divergent accounts of the Punjab by exposing the assumptions and constraints embodied in each understanding of the history of the province. The second chapter begins with a description of indebtedness and how that provides a useful lens for constructing an alternate understanding of the Punjab. It examines the extent and nature of peasant indebtedness in the province and how reform efforts aimed at alleviating the same involved both institutional and microeconomic changes.

The third chapter studies the problem of credit and indebtedness in greater detail. The nature and spread of indebtedness in the province are examined, and the legal innovations introduced to combat the scourge are studied as an instance of macroeconomic or institutional change. It also discusses the political context in the province at the time and examines the policies of the major parties, especially the Unionist Party. The interests of the political elite and the challenges they face from officialdom are examined to build a more nuanced understanding of the political economy of reform in the province.

The fourth chapter focuses on microeconomic efforts in the form of the cooperative credit movement undertaken by the colonial state to alleviate indebtedness among the peasantry. Development is seen to work at macro and micro levels in these two chapters, through institutional or legal changes and microeconomic cooperative efforts respectively. The latter widened into a general movement of 'rural reconstruction' which shares close similarities with more contemporary programmes of community development and microfinance initiatives.

The fifth chapter engages with the individuals spearheading the attempts at alleviating indebtedness and their varying perspectives on the issue. It focuses on the life and works, professional and academic, of Sir Malcolm Darling. Using his private papers, a detailed account of his engagement with the issue of rural poverty is presented. He is both the embodiment of the institutional change ushered in by colonialism and also the microeconomic practitioner who took an active interest in finding a cure for indebtedness, becoming an expert on rural poverty in the Punjab in the process. The chapter further includes a discussion of the discourse on development among the colonial bureaucracy, along with its limitations. Darling's views on indebtedness are contrasted with those of Frank L. Brayne, another official in the Indian Civil Service (ICS), with a markedly different approach to indebtedness. Brayne was the architect of the 'Gurgaon experiment', a community-based programme of rural development which inspired his more general work in 'village uplift' characterized by missionary zeal.

The sixth and final chapter examines the direction of economic research and how that impacts development policy in the Punjab in the early twentieth century. The publications and methodology of the Punjab Board of Economic Inquiry are studied in detail, alongside a survey of other economic literature being produced in the province in this period. Parallels between this scholarship and trends in academic inquiry in the post-colonial period are drawn to reaffirm how the colonial economic experiment in the Punjab can be viewed as a precursor of development studies.

A concluding postscript examines the continued popularity of community development programmes and the ahistorical nature of development studies. The book ends with a discussion of the salient themes and the new questions they raise in the economic history of the Punjab.

Notes

1   Milan Kundera, *The Unbearable Lightness of Being* (New York: Harper and Row, 1984).
2   See, for instance, the scholarship of Douglass North, Daron Acemoglu, Geoffrey Hodgson, and Simon Johnson on institutions discussed in Chapter 1.
3   See, for example, D. Acemoglu and S. Johnson, 'Unbundling Institutions', *Journal of Political Economy* 113, no. 5 (2005): 949–95.
4   For a discussion of the continued hold of the moneylender on rural credit see Anita Gill, 'Interlinked Agrarian Credit Markets: Case Study of Punjab', *Economic and Political Weekly* 39, no. 33 (2004): 3741–51.

1 | GLASS HALF FULL?
Two Views of the Punjab

Colonialism hardly ever exploits the whole of a country. It contents itself with bringing to light the natural resources, which it extracts, and exports to meet the needs of the mother country's industries, thereby allowing certain sectors of the colony to become relatively rich. But the rest of the colony follows its path of under-development and poverty, or at all events sinks into it more deeply.

—Frantz Fanon, *The Wretched of the Earth*[1]

His speech is mortgaged bedding,
On his kine he borrows yet
At his heart is his daughter's wedding
In his eye foreknowledge of debt.
He eats and hath indigestion
He toils and may not stop
His life is a long-drawn question
Between a crop and a crop

—Rudyard Kipling, *The Masque of Plenty*[2]

Robert Tawney famously described the vulnerable state of the Chinese peasantry in the early twentieth century as follows: 'There are districts in which the position of the rural population is that of a man standing permanently up to the neck in water, so that even a ripple is sufficient to drown him.'[3] James Scott later used this description to draw an evocative account of peasant rebellion in Southeast Asia in his seminal *The Moral Economy of the Peasant*.[4] Scott discussed the destruction of what he termed as the 'moral economy', the worldview and practices of the peasants premised on the subsistence ethic, due to colonialism. Scott's description of the Vietnamese peasantry was in contrast to Samuel Popkin's account of the Southeast Asian peasant in *The*

Rational Peasant.[5] Popkin stressed that peasants behaved rationally and benefited from market practices that were ushered in with colonialism. The test of time has seen Scott's scholarship remain a more convincing account of how peasant societies experience colonialism with Popkin's explanation marginalized. This may well hold for Vietnam where the pernicious effects of colonialism were more pronounced, leading to numerous peasant rebellions and famine, but for the Punjab the academic discourse remains deeply divided.

In many ways, the discussion of a peasantry driven to starvation in Vietnam and perpetually dealing with food crises is only peripherally relevant to the Punjab. The Punjab was the richest province of colonial India where the British established a vast canal irrigation network and consequently inhabited 'canal colonies', converting thousands of acres of barren land to some of the most fertile and productive tracts in the region. It was the granary of the empire, noted for the mass increases in agricultural output and also for its sword-arm as the major recruiting ground for the imperial army. And yet the large-scale achievements were accompanied by widespread poverty and indebtedness in the province. How do we assess the contrasting images of agricultural growth and military prowess on the one hand, and an impoverished peasantry and entrenched elites on the other? Most of the scholarship on the province is preoccupied with political developments leading up to 1947[6] or the economics of the canal colonies. The peasant, who remained economically unimportant and politically passive, was hardly the agent of change or revolution as in Southeast Asia. However, by studying the colonial discourse and the politics around the peasant in the period 1900–47, one can gain valuable insights not only into the economic history of the region but also into the history of development studies.

Scholars of the Punjab have taken diametrically opposed positions on the economic impact of colonial policies on the province. Some like Clive Dewey have highlighted the many transformative and large-scale achievements of the British government that saw Punjab emerge as the poster child of empire in India. It became a site for economic growth and opportunity and also remained relatively calm and loyal to the British. The setting up of the canal colonies brought large increases in agricultural production and yield as well. On the opposing side, Imran Ali and others have argued that these changes were geared towards revenue extraction and led to led to socio-economic underdevelopment and large-scale indebtedness in the province with damaging long-term consequences.[7] This chapter unpacks these two divergent theses on colonialism in the Punjab, unveiling the respective assumptions and limitations of each argument. The following chapter presents an alternate way of constructing the economic history of the Punjab. Instead of viewing structural change in the Punjab from a macroeconomic perspective, it is suggested that the forgotten history of microeconomic reform and legal and institutional innovations offer a fruitful and novel way of conceptualizing the colonial impact on the province.

The chapter is structured as follows: I discuss four major themes along which the current explanations of economic change in colonial Punjab differ. The four themes are: changes in the property rights and revenue extraction regime; the position of the military in the Punjab, the role of landlords, *pirs*, and other elite groups in the province; and lastly, general developments in the bureaucratic and administrative structure of the province. I then discuss the limitations of theories of institutional development and economic reform and how these relate to the Punjab.

Two Views of the Punjab

It was the best of times, it was the worst of times.

—Charles Dickens, *A Tale of Two Cities*[8]

At the time of annexation by the British, the Punjab was a vast region of the Indian subcontinent stretching from Peshawar to Delhi, spanning a terrain as diverse in geography as it was in ethnicities and communities. After the fall of the Mughal empire, the dynamic Sikh leader Maharaja Ranjit Singh had conquered and consolidated this kingdom, whose rise would be as meteoric as its sudden and precipitated decline from colonial conquest. Following Ranjit Singh's demise in 1839, the Punjab fell prey to intrigue and political squabbling over the question of succession. Simultaneously, the British, through calculated contracts and agreements with the Sikh nobles, slowly stretched their influence across the wealthy province, finally conquering the entire region after two Anglo-Sikh wars. The annexation was complete in 1849, and soon afterwards, strategic, economic, and political concerns made the province one of the most important and lucrative from the imperial point of view.

The Punjab was one of the last regions to be annexed by the British in South Asia and conquered, during what Ian Talbot claims, was a 'mature' imperialism.[9] The motivations and modus operandi of the British in the Punjab differed substantially from their initial skirmishes and conquests in India. Company rule had been dictated overwhelmingly by economic considerations and myopic ravaging and looting. This had engendered much resentment among the locals, culminating in the rebellion of 1857. The Punjab, by contrast, was conquered by an imperial power that was now establishing itself as the ruler of India, not just a passing plunderer. Considerable time and energy were devoted to ensure successful annexation of the province, and the telegrams, plans, and foibles of British administrators prior to wresting complete control of the province are testament to that. More importantly, subsequent British rule of the province can be looked upon as planned, deliberate, and, perhaps, more enduring, indicating why some believe that colonial rule in the province still impacts welfare outcomes in the region today.

The administration of the Punjab was initially dominated by two ambitious British administrators – the brothers Henry and John Lawrence. While Henry Lawrence was more instrumental in the annexation of the province, his brother John had a greater role in crafting the administrative rubric of the province, a process that gave rise to a distinct 'Punjab school of administration' (further emphasizing the peculiar nature of the imperialist endeavour in the province). In the years immediately following annexation, the primary goal of British policy in the Punjab was 'the accumulation and exercise of political power' and a 'deliberate weakening of those social groups who might otherwise have shared power with the British'.[10] However, scholars have viewed the political, administrative, and economic changes ushered in by the colonial state differently. The reforms included changes in the property rights regime, and the role of the military, landlords, and local elite. This section traces the divergent accounts of these initiatives and exposes the limitations of each perspective.

Property Rights and Revenue Administration

The fixed revenue demand placed by the British state in the Punjab was crucial from the point of view of the colonial government for it ensured a steady stream of income into state coffers. The colonial state therefore invested heavily in establishing an efficient and effective system of collecting land revenue in cash, which was the major source of income for the government. The new method of revenue collection and administration entailed a detailed examination of the existing distribution of land holdings and property. By commissioning a wide range of documents that became the basis of the new revenue system, the colonial state became a modernizing agent that made the rural landscape legible, certified claims to land holdings, and created nodes of power and influence that would impact socioeconomic development in the region. Second, this system of revenue generation also became the foundation on which institutional change in the Punjab was predicated, as discussed in the following section. This was accentuated in the canal colonies which were irrigated and 'settled' by the British, leading to large-scale social and economic engineering.

After the British presence was firmly established, John Lawrence laid out an ambitious plan of administrative reform in the province. The province was divided into 27 districts under district commissioners, in turn merged into seven divisions headed by commissioners. The top three levels of administration – provincial, divisional, and district – were reserved for British officers and the Indians were only admitted to low-level jobs such as Assistant Commissioners and *tehsildars*. Initially, the posts for Indians were dominated by non-Punjabis. John Lawrence,[11] on his part, wanted district officers to be dynamic and actively involved in their work, being tireless, 'omniscient and omnipresent'.[12] To this end, the British appointed some of their best officers in the Punjab, and in 1851 the Board of Administration described the reform programme as 'an imperial experiment, imperially conducted'.[13]

The development of the administrative system occurred in two distinct phases: the first from 1849 to 1862 was characterized by 'personal rule' administered by individual district officers who were sympathetic to Punjabi customs and indigenous institutions. The second phase, introduced by the enactment of the Punjab Code of Civil Procedure in 1862 and the Punjab Laws Act of 1872, was marked by increasing centralization and formalization of law and bureaucratization.

In order to assess the revenue demand and to establish ownership of the land, a range of 'teleological documents' were commissioned, which helped map the villages and districts.[14] Together these defined land ownership and revenue payments in the Punjab, establishing the formal legal connection between the peasants and the state.[15] Such documents were important in making the rural landscape of the Punjab 'legible' and open to efficient assessment for revenue collection by the state. While the *patwaris* in charge of property documents assumed almost legendary prowess and influence in the process, no such fine-grained understanding of rural society was attempted with regard to improving the quality of life. Altruism cannot be expected of the imperialist state but given the rhetoric of developing Punjab as an example for the rest of empire, it is interesting to note that the vision was premised on the financial stability of the state first.[16]

By cataloguing and formalizing claims to property, the intention of colonial administrators was to preserve village structures as they had found them, but paradoxically enough the very act of codification of law and formalization of property rights irreversibly altered the rural landscape. The flexibility and informality of pre-colonial property arrangements was replaced by a legal concretization of claims and ownership.[17] The colonial state thus became an agent of modernization and structural change in a way that froze a particular moment in rural relations in the Punjab as a permanent legal distribution. While some individuals were empowered as a result, there were many other features of a traditional system, notably its flexibility and ability to give the relatively powerless more negotiating power, which were weakened through the bureaucratization of rural relations. Writing in 1910, Sir James Wilson, an officer in the Indian Civil Service (ICS), wrote how under the colonial regime 'for a few pennies, any peasant can obtain a map of his fields and a clear statement of all the rights relating to them'.[18] However, the mere acquisition of such a map did not confer any political power or social capital to the peasant who now had a new set of masters in the local bureaucracy and legal system to contend with if he ever needed to validate his claim on the land.

In the early years of British rule in the Punjab, changes in the property rights and revenue regime created widespread resentment due to other factors. The colonial aim was to implant the same revenue system that it had previously implemented in the North-West Provinces of India, and which had been successful there. The chief principles of this system were a moderate *jama* (revenue demand), a limited recognition of property claims except those of major cultivators, and, in some cases, revenue collection on a community level. However, in the Punjab, the revenue demand turned out to be quite excessive – perhaps unwittingly so. Crop prices had been very high in the years 1844–46 and the British, basing their assessment on the figures from these years, had ended up demanding an exorbitant share to be paid in cash, a policy that was highly resented by the cultivators.

While the revenue demand was later adjusted, the policy of imposing fixed cash assessments was a mainstay of the reforms in the revenue system. The cash assessments were imposed for periods lasting up to 30 years with the government pocketing half of the net produce. Corruption among low-rank officials and political quarrels among the British administrators further undermined this system. One class of low-rank officials, the *patwari*s, in particular played a very damaging role. Entrusted with the task of determining the size of land holdings and keeping records of property ownership, they were offered high salaries in the hope of ensuring efficiency in revenue collection. Together with the *lambardar*, the *patwari* formed the interface of the colonial state for the peasantry. *Lambardar*s collected the tax from the proprietors and adjudicated disputes regarding revenue collection and the contestation of the same in court. However, the excessive powers vested in them led to widespread corruption and the *patwari* often assumed a particularly manipulative role in the rural landscape. From the earliest days of assessment and revenue collection, they assumed a negative role with a settlement officer in 1863 noting:

> [T]he time of *patwari*s is now almost wholly taken up in preparing their annual papers ... the details ... are nearly all fictitious and untrustworthy, so that really these *patwari*s are employed for years in adding up imaginary sums, for which they are paid by the *zamindars* (with a percentage of the government demand).[19]

These issues would become exacerbated over the years and lead to the *patwari* assuming excessive powers in rural Punjab and becoming a node for corrupt practices.[20]

The administrative changes in revenue extraction discussed thus far led to an efficient collection of the various taxes. Both Imran Ali and Clive Dewey have differing views on the benefits and limitations of the reformed system of revenue assessment and collection. Imran Ali's central argument in his seminal work *Punjab under Imperialism* is that despite the façade of macroeconomic achievements and growth, colonialism in the Punjab led to long-run underdevelopment. He argues that British rule in the province was dominated by three major themes: political entrenchment, revenue extraction, and military requirements.[21] His assessment is in sharp contrast to Clive Dewey's which views colonialism in the Punjab as creating opportunities for many communities and individuals, allowing them chances of social mobility denied in the earlier feudal system. The system of property rights and revenue collection established by the British was key in their administration of the province and allows these divergent theses to be examined more closely.[22]

After annexation, the British undertook revenue assessments in each district, drawing up settlement reports which enabled the determination of the agricultural tax to be levied. This tax was the most important source of income for the state. While this demand was lower than the earlier Sikh percentage, the fact that it was collected with more regularity and efficiency made it a more onerous obligation for the peasantry. The land tax collections can be calculated as a percentage of the net income of the farmers: in 1906–07, this percentage was 32.5, in 1916–17 it rose to 42.3, in 1932–33 it became 148.3, and it remained at high levels in subsequent years, for example, in 1936–37 it was 116.1 per cent and in 1938–39 it was 79 per cent.[23] Revenue settlements also formalized the claims to property ownership in the province, a process which led to 'individualization' in property rights, marking a shift from the more collective and complex forms of property ownership in the pre-colonial era.[24]

The establishment of the canal colonies, which were set up by irrigating erstwhile barren land, allows these divergent views held by Ali and Dewey to be analysed quite sharply. In some ways, the canal colonies represent the height of social and economic engineering by the British in the Punjab, as these tracts were populated through allocation of land by colonial officials. Specific communities were given preference in this exercise, and while there is a degree of similarity in how the colonies were established, there were some key differences over time. This section discusses the establishment of the colonies (a process referred to as 'colonization') and the various effects it produced, which have led to a binary discourse.

The control of the colonial government on resources in the province was absolute, especially in the canal colonies where both land and water distribution was explicitly in the hands of colonial offices. This allowed a high degree of discretionary authority and micro-management of land and water (the key inputs in agriculture) by the state. Ali notes: 'State policy determined matters both great and small, ranging from the formulation of the general principles governing land distribution to the implementation of measures in the minute circumstances of the local arena. Here was an interventionist imperialism, extensively engaged in demographic and economic change.'[25]

The official reports for the canal colony projects articulate the aims of the colonial government. In the case of the Chenab colony, the two major stated aims of colonization were:

1. to relieve the pressure of population upon the land in those districts of the province where the agricultural production has already reached or is fast approaching the limit which the land available to agriculture can support, and
2. to colonize the area in question with well-to-do yeomen of the best class of agriculturists who will cultivate their own holdings with the aid of their families and the usual menials but, as much as possible, without the aid of tenants and will constitute healthy agricultural communities of the best Punjab type.

A third objective added to the two above was to create 'villagers of a type superior in comfort and civilization to anything which had previously existed in the Punjab'.[26]

Imran Ali argues that the distribution of land in the canal colonies had far-reaching political and economic effects of which the 'British were fully aware'.[27] Land grants were awarded to those allied with the colonial state. Revenue considerations remained important, as only those projects were sanctioned whose profitability was ensured. In later colony projects, the needs of the military were given preference, as discussed in a following section.

Clive Dewey views the colonization of land as a positive development, which created opportunities for land ownership and social mobility, while Imran Ali stresses that the income generated from these lands were used to increase the size of the bureaucracy and the military instead of being used for social and economic uplift. The generation of large amounts of tax from the colonies also allowed the British not to extract heavily from the larger landlords, which ensured the continued support of the latter for the colonial government.[28]

Ali criticizes the increase in the size of the bureaucracy that stemmed from the system of revenue collection, which employed different officials for collecting the various types of taxes. The revenue system in the canal colonies was on a fluctuating basis, unlike other parts of the Punjab where the taxes were collected through a fixed assessment where rates were fixed for a period between 10 and 30 years. Fluctuating assessment in the colonies entailed more work for the bureaucracy, which evaluated the situation at each harvest. This also provided numerous opportunities for corruption among the lower level of the bureaucracy, and a double staff of *patwaris* had to be maintained, one from the Revenue department (for maintaining land records) and one from the Irrigation department (for assessing water and land revenue rates). The alternative view would be to see these as opportunities for government service that provided income and social respectability.

Colonial officials posted in the canal colonies criticized this complex system of revenue collection and the many opportunities for corruption that it created. F. L. Brayne, an ICS officer known for his efforts in rural reconstruction that are detailed later in the book, was disappointed with the failed attempts to introduce a fixed assessment system in the canal colonies. In 1933, Brayne wrote that the fluctuating assessment was intended to be temporary but had instead become permanent with evil results. Brayne remarked that 'one has only to tour in these areas to realize the demoralizing influence of the fluctuating assessment. The complaints, the bitterness, the jealousies, the uneasiness, and the lack of any corporate sense in the villages are very striking'. He also felt that agrarian conditions in the canal colonies were more stable than the *barani* tracts, so there was no practical necessity to justify the fluctuating assessment.[29]

Clive Dewey, however, notices the agricultural advances through the irrigation of erstwhile barren land. Many of these gains were linked closely with the advancement of military aims as discussed in the following section. He also points out that the migration of groups from overpopulated districts of the Punjab to the canal colonies and the large increases in food production averted a population explosion and food scarcity. This is in sharp contrast to Ali who contends that the movement of people from overpopulated tracts of the Punjab into the canal colonies meant that no technical innovations were undertaken to fight the population pressure but instead people were just shifted to new colonies. By focusing on the large-scale changes and movements, both groups of scholars glean a partial truth into the colonial economic impact in the Punjab. The same dichotomy in views can be seen in how they both view the role of the military.

Many colonial officers writing about the Punjab also extolled the achievements of the empire in the region. Sir James Wilson wrote in 1910 that land in the Punjab rose in value under colonial rule with 28 million acres of cultivated land rising in value from 50 million sterling to 150 million sterling over a period of 20 years. The canal colonies in particular were lauded as a massive colonial success and Wilson wrote:

> In fifteen years nearly a million people migrated from their old homes and settled down permanently amid surroundings of great comfort and prosperity. Altogether about 2.5 million acres of what was formerly

wasteland have been allotted to nearly 100,000 fortunate individuals, the usual form of allotment being a square plot of 28 acres and arrangements being made to provide irrigation to each plot from the state canal. Roads were aligned all over the area, villages laid out on the most approved sanitary plan, and everything done to help the settlers to begin their careers in the new country.[30]

He further wrote: 'In 1907–08, the largest of them, the Chenab colony, was able to feed itself and export over 2 million worth of wheat, cotton and oil-seeds' and 'What wonder if they, as they themselves say, pray night and day for the Government that has conferred such benefits upon them, and are confident that the necessary steps will be taken to remove any reasonable cause of grievance.'[31]

Military Benefits

Existing scholarship on the Punjab highlights it as a militarized province that also provided half the recruitment of the imperial army. The British kept as many as 59,000 soldiers in the Punjab after 1849 to subjugate the province, disbanding the former Sikh army and disarming the people. These measures ensured that the Punjab remained coercively loyal to the empire in the rebellion of 1857, though there is historical evidence of the British burning down villages in case of revolt.[32] When the Punjab became the recruiting ground for the army, military personnel were given land grants, large pensions, and other allowances after retirement. Clive Dewey and Imran Ali view the accruing of these benefits to military personnel differently – one stresses the opportunities for social and economic mobility and stability that these provided, while the other focuses on the impacts this had on subverting the socio-economic advancement of non-military groups in Punjabi society, in the short and long terms.

The process of colonization also reflected a preference for advancing military aims over provincial or agricultural concerns. When the Jhelum colony was settled between 1902 and 1906, there was a marked departure from the stated imperial aims for colonization as discussed in the previous section for the Chenab colony. In the Jhelum colony, a large percentage of the land irrigated by canal irrigation was reserved for the military and new provisions were introduced to encourage horse breeding for the army. Instead of the agricultural aims (or demographic concerns), which underpinned earlier instances of colonization, military aims were paramount in the Jhelum colony.

One way in which this was achieved was through the award of land grants to those who could provide horses for the imperial army, and these tended to be landholders of means much above the lower peasantry usually given land grants. Even if small landholders applied to obtain land, very often they could not afford the cost of buying branded mares that met the army cavalry requirements. Such mares were a necessary prerequisite for obtaining land grants but were limited in number, so the price of mares rose sharply, making them unaffordable for a large section of the agricultural population. Horse breeding also entailed the necessary skills and experience, which ordinary farmers did not often possess. The net result of these considerations was that the size of grants remained large and they were given to the wealthy, leading to a less egalitarian distribution.[33] When some officials raised objections to this preference accorded to the military at the expense of agriculturists, the financial commissioner remarked:

> The main object will now be an Imperial one, namely, to encourage horse breeding and to create a reserve of horses fit for service with troops. It is difficult to combine the Imperial with the original provincial aim … as to the policy of the change, the land belongs to Government and it is for Government to decide what use to make of it. If an Imperial purpose can be efficiently served, my personal opinion is that the Provincial objects should not be allowed to stand in the way.[34]

The extent to which horse breeding determined land allocation in the Jhelum colony and the subsequent allocation of other lands to military personnel. Despite protests from the peasantry and local bureaucracy (as horse breeding went against agricultural interests in general), grants were given on this basis. The British also believed that the larger landowners would make more successful colonists than the peasants (though in following years these expectations were not met). In addition to land grants, eight large stud farms were established with a requirement of maintaining 50 mares. Seven of these farms were allocated to elite landlord families of northwestern Punjab and the eighth to a professional horse breeder. While in the Chenab colony the British had explicitly wanted to allot land to peasants, believing them to be more hardworking and enterprising and wanting to curtail the power of local 'squires', the aims were reversed in the Jhelum colony where military aims took precedence. The change in thinking was justified by the settlement commissioner as follows:

> In its favour it might be argued that as the wealth of the Jhelum colony will be concentrated in fewer hands it will possess more elements of progress than the Chenab colony where there will be a dead level of dull prosperity.… Perhaps we have in India too many peasants, prosperous and admirable though they are, and should now aim at raising a class of more wealthy and

more intelligent land-holders, who might combine with the virtues of the peasantry a higher standard of comfort and a greater readiness to make an advance in civilization.[35]

An astonishing 54.1 per cent of the land in the Jhelum colony was allotted for horse-breeding purposes and a further 9.49 per cent in grants to military personnel for other purposes. Grants included the allotment of large areas, ranging from 25 to 50 acres in size, to ex-soldiers and commissioned and non-commissioned officers. In many cases the areas allotted to army men were the most fertile, and many who felt they had been given less fertile areas would file formal applications to get alternate, more productive tracts. In total, the Punjab government allotted about a 'third of a million acres of prime irrigated crown land' to military grantees in the interwar period, worth around 370 million rupees in 1945–46 prices.[36] In fact, over time the preference given to the military resulted in financial losses for the government, which could have earned more from agricultural taxes on the same areas of land.

Military recruitment was also tied in with the demand for land revenue, with the districts providing the largest number of recruits benefiting from lower instances of the tax. For instance, while land revenue as a percentage of net income for holdings in Jullundur and Ludhiana rose as high as 17.8 per cent and 22.2 per cent in 1928–29, the highest corresponding figure for the recruitment districts of Jhelum was 8.4 per cent.[37] This supplemented the other benefits to military recruits and their families discussed by Ali. Ali shows how canal colonies that contributed a large proportion of the military force were less profitable for the government in terms of annual net revenues than those colonies that were not that significant for military recruitment. So, for instance, in 1915–16 the Sidhnai Canal generated a net revenue of 51.55 per cent and a net profit of 48.18 per cent, compared to the Lower Jhelum canal that generated a net revenue of 20.07 per cent and a net profit of 17.37 per cent. However, Ali also shows that the major benefits to recruitment-rich districts was not in terms of a decreased levy of taxes but in the form of land grants, horse-breeding grants, camel grants, and so on.[38]

Clive Dewey views the military in the Punjab from a different perspective. He argues that defence spending 'galvanized the economies and flattened the societies of the areas on which it was concentrated'. He analyses the three districts of the upper Sind Sagar *doab* – Rawalpindi, Attock, and Jhelum – which were the primary recruiting ground for the army and also home to 'the largest cantonment and the densest network of strategic railways in South Asia'. Dewey says that the Indian army converted 'a particularly backward and inaccessible tract into the natural heartland of the second largest successor state'.[39]

Between 1855 and 1881, the population of the three *doab* districts increased by 140 per cent, but Dewey argues that the income of the peasantry increased at an even faster rate. Dewey describes how the fortunes of the *doab* districts had improved as a result of large-scale recruitment in the army:

> An immense influx of pay and pensions derived from military service swamped agriculture as the great determinant of consumption and investment. The profits of cultivation and carriage soared as military expenditure generated new markets. A century of military town building culminated in the designation of the largest cantonment city as the provisional capital of Pakistan. The doab acquired one of the best networks of railways and roads in India, because of the strategic importance of communications. There was even a show of industrialisation, heavily concentrated in the building trades and extractive industries. As a result, the inhabitants of the doab were better-fed, better clothed, better-housed and better-educated at independence than they had been at annexation. They were also comparatively free. All the [peasants'] natural masters – landlords, moneylenders, traders, officials, kulaks – were weakened when their erstwhile dependants obtained access to resources provided by the army.[40]

Landlords and Local Elite

A key aspect of British rule in the Punjab was the patronage of landlords and local elites. This included the award of land grants, support for the Punjab Unionist Party (a political party composed almost entirely of large landlords), and other forms of official patronage that allowed the landlords to maintain their superior position in the Punjab. Ali believes this led to a long-term shift in Punjabi society that privileged the large landlords:

> In bolstering landlordism through additional economic resources, the British helped to perpetuate a stratum that was receding in importance in other parts of South Asia during the twentieth century. This partnership found political expression in the Punjab National Unionist Party, which continued to dominate the provincial legislature till the final months of British rule. Its repercussions continued to affect the political economy of the region after 1947, for the landlords remained a strong force in Pakistan. They have to date succeeded in preventing the implementation of an effective land reform. They have also helped to abort the functioning of a democratic political system, for fear that it might erode their privileged

position. Moreover, they have found in military rule a useful substitute for
the protective rulership provided by the British prior to 1947.[41]

Ali stresses that hierarchical caste patterns were preserved under colonial rule – for
example, the Jats continued to be the most influential class in the new colony villages
while other castes continued to provide labour and other petty services. The menial
class also retained its status so there was only limited social mobility. Dewey, on the
other hand, believes that while overall the percentages of different classes may have
remained constant, there was a lot of 'churning' in Punjabi society so that enterprising
and motivated individuals within a caste were able to advance economically through
the new opportunities that colonial rule provided. They could escape the shackles of
feudalism which had oppressed them for generations in the rural context. Ali stresses
that even in the physical layout of the newly inhabited canal colony villages, the social
hierarchy was preserved, with the richer classes given spacious residential compounds
separated from the dwellings of the poor. More significantly, the denial of proprietary
rights to the poor was an official policy as confirmed in a press communiqué in 1914:

> It appears however to Government a sound principle that in making
> selections of grants of Government waste, tenants, labourers and
> other landless men should not be as a rule be chosen, as their selection
> involves the aggravation of the difficulty, already acutely felt, of obtaining
> agricultural labour and it is obviously undesirable that Government should
> use its position as the proprietor of large tracts in such a way as to upset the
> existing social and economic order.[42]

Apart from the denial of proprietary rights, the landless poor also did not get voting
rights even in 1935 when the franchise was at its widest. At the same time, the already
landed classes were given generous land grants for various services – for example,
aiding the recruitment of soldiers during the World Wars. In the case of a *pir* from
the Attock district, he was given

> a personal landed gentry grant of ten rectangles in 1916 along with the lease
> of 15,000 acres of land in his home district ... the *Pir* was thanked by the
> lieutenant governor for his services 'in the sure knowledge that you will not
> relax your efforts as long as the army needs man'.[43]

General Administration

Several other changes in the Punjab have also been the subject of scholarly examination
and determined the political economy of the region in the colonial era. One key aspect

was the explicit reluctance of the British government to implement any major plans for fostering economic development. These included proposals for the improvement of agricultural conditions. For example, a scheme was proposed under which 3000 acres would be utilized for experiments in sugarcane cultivation and a further 20,000 acres set aside for cultivators who would supply a sugar factory with the necessary cane. But the governor of the Punjab, Sir Malcolm Hailey, refused to agree to the proposal even on a reduced scale, and eventually the scheme was dropped altogether.[44]

There was also a lot of debate, criticism, and resentment over some of the legislative changes enacted in the Punjab. Starting from the Punjab Alienation of Land Act (1901), which was initially passed to curb landlessness among the Punjabi peasantry, there were numerous pieces of legislation relating to land ownership, tenancy, debt, and colonization of lands in the newly irrigated tracts which proved to be controversial and have been viewed differently in later scholarly analyses. The Punjab Alienation of Land Act was hailed as a symbol of the government's commitment to the peasantry who were losing their land en masse to urban moneylenders when they failed to pay their debts. However, later scholarship, for example, by N. G. Barrier, takes a less sanguine view of the matter. Barrier suggests that the Act was passed not to save the peasant from the clutches of the moneylender but to allow the larger landlords to assume the role of the moneylender as the Act only prohibited the transfer of land from an agricultural to a non-agricultural caste. So the issue of peasant indebtedness remained and the landlords were able to increase their land holdings when the peasant defaulted. This is discussed in greater detail in the following section.

Apart from the legislation relating to land alienation, the laws introduced for the colonization of land also created much controversy. In 1906, a bill was introduced in the Punjab Legislative Council for the Colonisation of Government Lands. It was meant to supersede the earlier Government Tenants Act (Punjab) of 1893, which was found to be inadequate for the allotment of land in the canal colonies. The bill created great controversy in the canal colonies for it threatened to consolidate the very relations with the state from which the grantees sought relief. The bill was opposed in the Punjab Legislative Council by the nonofficial members, and even the most loyal of these, Malik Umar Hayat Khan Tiwana, spoke out against it. It was passed in the Council with the support of the official members, however, and was then sent to the Centre for the Governor General's assent. At that level it was vetoed, one of the rare instances of this kind in the constitutional history of British India.[45]

Dewey stresses the many benefits that the formalization of property rights and the establishment of a modern bureaucracy led to in the Punjab. Apart from gains in agricultural productivity and the opportunities for entrepreneurship and social mobility through joining government service or the military, he discusses the urbanization of the province and its spillover benefits. He mentions the case of Rawalpindi, which developed from a small town into one of the major cities of the area due to military expenditure and needs:

> It is always difficult to disentangle the contribution which military expenditure makes to the development of a town from all the other sources of urban growth: trade, industry, administration, religion. Fortunately the only city in the Sind Sagar doab – Rawalpindi – was so completely a creation of the Indian army that the role of military expenditure is beyond question: the defence budget dictated the pattern of its growth. At annexation it was nothing special: just another Sikh fort with a bazaar at its gates, commanding an important crossroads in the middle of a fertile plain. The army soon changed all that. Once British strategists realised that Rawalpindi was the perfect base for expeditions all along the northwest frontier – far enough along the Grand Trunk Road to be within easy reach of the full range of the passes, and far enough in the rear not to be overrun by the first invader – the construction of the biggest cantonment in India was only a matter of time; and the cantonment turned the village of the Rawals into the third largest city in the Punjab, second only to Lahore and Amritsar.[46]

Dewey also points to the increased purchasing power of the Punjabis and how that affected their consumption and living standards. The report of the Punjab Provincial Banking Inquiry Committee estimated that the peasants spent at least 35 million rupees on gold and silver jewellery in the 1920s, the majority of this being part of dowries.[47] There was a tendency to acquire property among the former military men – many soldiers spent their pensions and other payments at the time of retirement to pay back mortgages or to buy more land. They also sometimes became mortgagees themselves. Dewey argues that between 1900 and 1940

> … competition from peasant moneylenders drove professional creditors – Hindus belonging to the commercial castes – out of the rural mortgage market. As long as they got the use of additional land, 'agriculturist moneylenders' were prepared to lend larger sums on easier terms than *sahukars* because they were comparatively indifferent to the financial returns on their investment. The factors which dictated the *sahukars'* willingness to invest in land – rent levels and the profits of farming – were irrelevant to a set of mortgagees who were only interested in self-cultivation. Outside the belts of suburban market gardening and the handful of high farming zones, neither rents nor profits were high enough to attract most

sahukars; they had better things to do with their hard-worked capital. As a result, agriculturist moneylenders held five sevenths of the mortgages with possession in Jhelum in 1940; and the amount of peasants borrowed from *sahukars* fell by 75 percent in the course of a single settlement. For the first time in recorded history, the Muslim peasants of the western Punjab were meeting their own borrowing requirements.[48]

For Imran Ali, the situation is more sobering. He recognizes that the canal colonies represented one of the most extensive attempts at social and economic engineering by the British in South Asia, but he underlines that it was determined by the following considerations: the distribution of land was determined by the official imperative to consolidate the position of the British and to advance military interests while maintaining an extractive revenue collection system to finance governance. Second, land grants were given to military personnel or allocated to others to meet military requirements, for example, in the case of horse-breeding grants. Third, the resources and associated revenues generated from the irrigation, revenue, and police departments were transferred to the central administration. Fourth, corruption among lower levels of bureaucracy remained rampant and unchecked; and last, capitalist forms of agriculture were not encouraged and did not emerge on any substantial scale. The existing social hierarchy and feudal system were maintained in these shifts, leading to Ali's conclusion that the province experienced growth without development.

The Limitations of the Two Approaches

The two divergent perspectives espoused by Imran Ali and Clive Dewey each have their limitations. At the very least, the starkness with which they differ points to the multi-faceted nature of colonial intervention in the Punjab and its shifting short- and long-term impacts. Imran Ali focuses on extractive institutions, especially in the canal colonies and their relationship with long-run underdevelopment. Dewey focuses on the fruits and opportunities of colonialism, which facilitated social mobility and better market practices. Ali bemoans the fact that there was no state push towards industrialization or any attempt to enable a more egalitarian distribution of resources. Dewey lauds the extensive irrigation and communications networks that created multifarious spillover effects. Both therefore focus on *macroeconomic* or *large-scale* interventions and how they impacted individual lives and social outcomes, arriving at opposing conclusions regarding the colonial administration of the province. A key limitation in both perspectives is that they neglect *microeconomic* efforts at development. For Ali, the idea that the extractive colonial state might be undertaking schemes to benefit the poor is contradictory in itself, and, for Dewey, the limited success of these efforts leaves him looking for more convincing evidence on the benefits of colonial rule.[49] However, important microeconomic interventions were undertaken by the colonial government and I suggest that studying these offers a fresh perspective on understanding economic development in the Punjab, one that allows us to link the divergent theses presented by Ali and Dewey and also provides an alternative view of colonial rule in the province.

Peasant indebtedness in the Punjab was a microeconomic issue that became an endemic problem in the late nineteenth and early twentieth centuries. The colonial government undertook various surveys and inquiries, introduced legislative changes, and also initiated several schemes to battle the scourge of indebtedness throughout the first half of the twentieth century. For these reasons, it allows the interrogation of a different kind of economic rationality and its expression in the Punjab, one that is absent from the analyses presented by Ali and Dewey.

On the one hand, the issue of debt can be traced to the institutional transformation of the Punjab that Ali and Dewey study. Those siding with Ali – for example, N. G. Barrier – blamed peasant indebtedness on the high revenue demand placed by the colonial state on the Punjabi peasantry. They argue that the high demand forced the peasant to borrow from usurious moneylenders, and the power of colonial courts enabled the implementation of contracts: millions of acres of land were transferred to moneylenders when the peasant failed to repay the loan. Arguably the story retains important parallels with other regions under colonial rule – for example, James Scott's description of Southeast Asia under French and Dutch colonialism sounds eerily familiar:

> [F]ar from shielding the peasantry against the fluctuations of the market, colonial regimes were likely to press even harder in a slump so as to maintain their own revenue. The result was something of a paradox. In the midst of a booming export economy, new fortunes for indigenous landowners, officeholders and moneylenders and occasionally rising average capita per income, there was also growing concern with rural indebtedness and poverty and an increasing tempo of peasant unrest. It was not unlike the discovery of pauperism in the midst of England's industrial revolution.

Dewey, and those who view the Punjab as a crowning success of empire in India, argue that the peasant was wasteful and lacked the financial discipline to enjoy the fruits of prosperity provided by colonial rule. They believe that unnecessary loans were taken to fund weddings and funerals, and other 'unproductive expenditure', causing the peasant to become indebted and ultimately forced to give his land to his debtors. Malcolm Darling, an ICS officer who rose to the position of Financial Commissioner of the Punjab and authored the monumental *The Punjab Peasant in Prosperity and*

Debt,[50] conducted investigations into peasant finance and budgets. His writings lay the blame at the peasant's own mismanagement of funds borne out of his unfamiliarity with financial transactions and an adherence to customs and social obligations for which he borrowed liberally and injudiciously.

However, the exploration of indebtedness in colonial Punjab allows an advance beyond the theoretical perspectives presented by Ali and Dewey. The various 'cures' and efforts employed by the provincial government were meant to battle this scourge. Apart from legislative changes, there were microeconomic schemes, which encompassed a wide-ranging movement of cooperative credit and rural reconstruction, a culture of 'economic research' and data-gathering at individual and household levels. The writings and papers of officials involved in solving the problem and their failure present a narrative that does not fit neatly into the broad analyses by Ali and Dewey. Instead, a more complex understanding of structural change and economic reform in colonial Punjab emerges, which not only questions the existing historiography but also challenges contemporary notions of economic development. It is a ubiquitously convenient 'solution' to argue that the 'institutional' legacies of colonialism engender long-run malaise in post-colonial economies, but a searching look at the Punjabi economy and society in the early twentieth century questions these assumptions. By studying the emergence and cures for indebtedness as a practical example of colonial ameliorative policies, parallels can be drawn with more contemporary notions of economic development.

Interestingly, both the explanations can be categorized as a primitive application of a binary perspective in development studies, namely modernization and dependency. Dewey's views subscribe to the modernization perspective that sees the colony or developing country as lacking in inputs (including technology, administrative techniques, seeds, and so on) that a modern state can provide and sees capitalism as the economic system best designed to achieve this. Dependency theory, on the other hand, views international capitalism and colonialism as the cause of ruin of the third world. According to dependency theorists, 'the economic growth of the world's rich countries is … dependent on the accumulation of capital, and to a large extent, this assimilation came either directly or indirectly from the third world'.[51]

While modernization and dependency theories were only formulated in the 1950s and 1960s, it is interesting to note how explanations of the colonial impact on the Punjab can also be viewed retrospectively as a precursor of these theories. While Dewey views the Punjab as a beneficiary of empire and its modern ways, Ali sees it as a site of exploitation and extraction that benefited the imperial centre. How does the plethora of reform initiatives allow us to gain a fresh perspective on the economic history of the Punjab? The following chapter attempts to answer this question.

Notes

1   Frantz Fanon, *The Wretched of the Earth* (London: Penguin, 2001 [1961]), p. 129.

2   Rudyard Kipling, 'The Masque of Plenty', *The Collected Poems of Rudyard Kipling* (Ware: Wordsworth Editions Ltd,1994), p. 41.

3   Robert Tawney, *Land and Labour in China* (London: George Allen and Unwin Ltd, 1932), p. 77.

4   James C. Scott, *The Moral Economy of the Peasant: Rebellion and Subsistence in Southeast Asia* (New Haven: Yale University Press, 1976).

5   Samuel L. Popkin, *The Rational Peasant: The Political Economy of Rural Society in Vietnam* (Berkeley: University of California Press, 1992).

6   This scholarship is discussed in detail in Chapter 4.

7   This view echoes nationalist critiques of imperial economic policies and the drain of wealth, for example, in Dadabhai Naoroji, *Poverty and Un-British Rule* (London: S. Sonnenschein & Co., 1901); Paul A. Baran, *The Political Economy of Growth* (New York: Monthly Review Press, 1957); Hamza Alavi, P. L. Burns, G. R. Knight, P. B. Mayer, and Doug McEachern *Capitalism and Colonial Production* (London: Croom Helm, 1980); and Amiya Kumar Bagchi, *The Political Economy of Underdevelopment* (Cambridge: Cambridge University Press, 1982).

8   Charles Dickens, *A Tale of Two Cities* (New York: Barnes & Noble Classics, 2004 [1859]), p. 1.

9   Ian Talbot, *Punjab and the Raj* (New Delhi: Manohar Publications, 1988), p. 10.

10   Andrew J. Major, *Return to Empire: Punjab under the Sikhs and British in the Mid-Nineteenth Century* (New Delhi: Sterling Publishers, 1996), p. 168.

11   The agency and distinctive flair that Lawrence brought to the province was considerable. There was a statue of Lawrence in the city of Lahore, holding a sword in one hand and a pen in the other, asking 'By which will you be governed?'

12   R. J. Roseberry, *Imperial Rule in Punjab: The Conquest and Administration of Multan, 1818–1881* (New Delhi: Manohar Publications, 1987), p. 111.

13   Major, *Return to Empire*, p. 126.

14   The first of these was a detailed 'village field map'. This map formed the basis of the revenue documents, which included details of each village owner, cultivator, field, and seasonal crop, and a 'running account', known as the *jamabandi*, describing the ownership and revenue due from each specific plot of land. In the late nineteenth- and early twentieth-century colonial Punjab, this was perhaps the most crucial document in the collection of revenue. In addition to the *jamabandi*, a *shajra nasb*, or a genealogical tree tracing the lineage of male owners in the village, was also drawn up (effectively cataloguing male inheritance) as well as a *darkhwast malguzari* (official contract with the revenue payers), a *wajib-ul-arz* (village administration paper), and a *riwaj-i-am* (digest of tribal custom).

15   See David Gilmartin, *Empire and Islam: Punjab and the Making of Pakistan* (Berkeley: University of California Press,1988); and Matthew Nelson, *In the Shadow of the Shariah:*

Islam, Islamic Law and Democracy in Pakistan (New York: Columbia University Press, 2011), p. 22.

16 Later on even the popular press would criticize the system. See, for instance, the article 'A Greater Punjab', *Civil and Military Gazette*, Lahore, 8 July 1916, which described the administrative system of the Punjab as that of a 'little grocer'.

17 This is discussed in length in Tom G. Kessinger, *Vilayatpur, 1848–1968: Social and Economic Change in a North Indian Village* (Berkeley: Columbia University Press, 1974), p. 83.

18 From James Wilson, *More Truths about Land Records and Land Revenue in the Punjab* (London: University of California Press, 1910), p. 2.

19 Quoted in Nelson, *In the Shadow of the Shariah*, p. 28.

20 *Patwaris* were widely lambasted in the popular press. See, for instance, criticisms in the following newspaper articles: 'Patwarion ka halat-i-zar' ('The state of patwaris'), *Zamindar*, 12 September 1912; and 'Naak mein dam hai mera gaon ke patwari se' ('The entire village is bothered by the patwari'), *Zamindar*, 18 October 1912.

21 Imran Ali, *Punjab under Imperialism, 1885–1947* (Princeton: Princton University Press, 1988), p. 5.

22 See a discussion of colonial land revenue policies and how they were geared towards extraction in Irfan Habib, 'Colonisation of the Indian Economy', *Social Scientist* 3, no. 32 (1975): 23–53; Bipan Chandra, 'Colonialism, Stages of Colonialism and the Colonial State', *Journal of Contemporary Asia* 10, no. 3 (1980): 172–85; and Mridula Mukherjee, 'Some Aspects of Agrarian Structure of Punjab 1925–47', *Economic and Political Weekly* 15, no. 26 (1980): 46–58.

23 Mridula Mukherjee, *Colonialising Agriculture: The Myth of Punjab Exceptionalism* (New Delhi: SAGE Publications, 2005), p. 6.

24 Ali, *Punjab under Imperialism*, p. 4.

25 Ali, *Punjab under Imperialism*, p. 10.

26 Report of Punjab Colonies (Baillie) committee 1907–8 (Lahore, 1908), London, British Library India Office Records, IOR/V/26/315/1, ch. 1, para 16.

27 Ali, *Punjab under Imperialism*, p. 14.

28 Ali, *Punjab under Imperialism*, p. 168.

29 Quoted in Ali, *Punjab under Imperialism*, p. 174.

30 Wilson, *More Truths about Land Records*, p. 7.

31 Wilson, *More Truths about Land Records*, p. 8.

32 Major, *Return to Empire*, pp. 135, 189.

33 Ali, *Punjab under Imperialism*, p. 26.

34 'Note on annexing brood mare conditions to peasant grants in Jhelum Colony', quoted in Ali, *Punjab under Imperialism*, p. 27.

35 Quoted in Ali, *Punjab under Imperialism*, p. 28.

36 Ali, *Punjab under Imperialism*, p. 98

37 See, for instance, M. Mukherjee, *Colonializing Agriculture*, p. 8–9.

38 Ali, *Punjab under Imperialism*, pp. 112–25, 160–09.

39 Clive Dewey, 'Some Consequences of Military Expenditure in British India: The
    Case of the Upper Sind Sagar Doab 1849–1947', in *Arrested Development in India:
    The Historical dimension*, ed. Clive Dewey, pp. 93–169 (Delhi: Manohar Publications,
    1988), p. 93.

40 Dewey, 'Some Consequences of Military Expenditure in British India', p. 95.

41 Ali, *Punjab under Imperialism*, p. 84.

42 Press Communiqué, Punjab Government, 8 December 1914, in 'Grant of land to the
    depressed classes in Lower Bari Doab Colony', BOR J/301/1179 A, quoted in Ali,
    Punjab under Imperialism, pp. 193–95.

43 Ali, *Punjab under Imperialism*, p. 106.

44 Note on the colonization of the Nili Bar by Sir Malcolm Hailey, Governor Punjab, 21
    August 1925, para 7 in Colonisation of Nili Bar BOR 301/1/C9/3 B KW, quoted in
    Ali, *Punjab under Imperialism*, p. 57.

45 See N. G. Barrier, 'The Punjab Disturbances of 1907: The Response of the British
    Government in India to Agrarian Unrest', *Modern Asian Studies* 1, no. 4 (1967): 353–83;
    and Ali, *Punjab under Imperialism*, p. 68.

46 Dewey, 'Some Consequences of Military Expenditure in British India', p. 123.

47 Dewey, 'Some Consequences of Military Expenditure in British India', p. 103.

48 Dewey, 'Some Consequences of Military Expenditure in British India', p. 113.

49 Critiques of development economics have also focused on critiquing macroeconomic
    policies and nation-centric approaches such as planning and a growth focus. See,
    for instance, William Easterly, *The Tyranny of Experts: Economists, Dictators and the
    Forgotten Rights of the Poor* (New York: Basic Books, 2014). Easterly terms the World
    Bank as nation-centric in its approach, pushing developing countries to have over-
    planned economies.

50 Malcolm Darling, *The Punjab Peasant in Prosperity and Debt* (Bombay: Oxford
    University Press, 1925).

51 John Isbister, *Promises Not Kept: Poverty and the Betrayal of Third World Development*
    (Hartford: Kumarian Press, 2003), p. 47.

2 | AN ALTERNATIVE ECONOMIC HISTORY OF THE PUNJAB

Ah, then again greed touched your greedy soul
And you began to fine us, a simple folk,
For every little thing, done or undone.
If ridges of a field were small,
Or if someone dug some mud to make a wall,
Or if the cattle yard was unclean,
Or if some water course was merely crooked,
There was a fine for each and everything.
Though fines unmentioned were in agreement,
The rule of Patwaris is hard to bear,
Their mouths we cannot sweeten everyday
They stop our cultivation, if we go
To see a friend, who happens to be ill
We are not school boys to ask for leave
For every little thing we wish to do
We have not taken voluntary exile
That we should never cross the bounds of Bar.
We undertook to cultivate the soil;
You cannot say that we failed in that.
More than our parents we have cherished you,
We thought you always good and kind,
We thought you wished us well and never will
Allow such things to happen very long
But is this true? We cannot think it is
That you are thinking of passing a law
To legalise the robbery of Ahalkars
And make that legal which was not before.[1]

An alternative strategy for studying economic development in the Punjab is by
examining the problem of indebtedness in relation to institutional change and

economic reform. The Punjab was the richest province of colonial India, its breadbasket as well as the major recruiting ground for the Imperial army. For these reasons, the political and financial stability of the province were key objectives of the colonial state. Indebtedness in the province was also conceptualized by officials in a way that maintained the status quo and did not threaten the maintenance of law and order or the payment of land revenue. To the official mind, the chief economic issue for the Punjab peasantry was that of indebtedness. Not only did peasant indebtedness propel legal changes and administrative action but particular colonial officers also became heavily involved with initiating reforms to combat it. In some ways, indebtedness emerged from the commissioning of the range of property documents mentioned earlier that made land holdings in the Punjab assessable. Once the appropriate revenue demand had been assessed, the tax was levied, and by 1900, indebtedness and landlessness among Punjabi peasants reached epidemic proportions. Malcolm Darling, a civil servant who spent four decades serving in the Punjab, became the leading expert on rural poverty in the province in the first half of the twentieth century. Darling's monumental study on the Punjab peasant's poverty, first published in 1925, remains a key source for studying the various dimensions of the problem. While Darling shies from identifying the extractive revenue payments as the major cause of indebtedness (blaming instead the peasant's social obligations and his lack of prudence and thrift), he lays bare the seriousness of the issue and the vicious grip of the moneylender on thousands of peasants. Talking of the moneylender, he mentions how he 'rarely charges less than 18, and often demands more than 50 percent' as interest and in case of default, 'he exacts compound interest'. Fraud was common, which further added to the misery of the peasant. Darling succinctly remarks: 'Nowhere has moneylending been brought to a finer or more diabolical art than in India. The result ... is that millions of cultivators are born in debt, live in debt and die in debt.'[2]

Carrying out a detailed statistical survey of thousands of proprietors, Darling discovered that only a mere 17 per cent of peasant proprietors were free from debt in 1918–19, a figure that had reduced to 13 per cent by 1930. Average debt per proprietor in the first survey was 463 rupees in 1919 and 600 rupees in 1930. In 1921, the total agricultural debt was 90 crore rupees (equivalent to 60 million pounds at the time), which was 15-and-a-half times the amount collected in land revenue. The figure increased to 120 crore rupees by 1930 and total agricultural debt stood at 140 crore rupees (105 million pounds), which was 22-and-a-half times the land revenue.[3] The system of land revenue, so painstakingly grafted by the British, continued to be beset with inefficiencies and widespread corruption, well into the twentieth century. Simultaneously, the issue of peasant indebtedness and landlessness aggravated over time.

A brief discussion of the method of the moneylender, or *sahukar* as he was known, is relevant here. In the first two decades of British rule when the new system of property rights and land allocation was still nebulous, land had not yet assumed any monetary significance. The moneylender was therefore interested in the crop, from which he aimed to extract a double profit, at the expense of the cultivator and the purchaser respectively. Under these conditions, 'the lion's share of the produce went to the moneylender instead of the State'.[4] After 1870, however, land itself became valuable and the moneylenders developed a vicious system of holding the land as collateral, which overwhelmingly resulted in the ouster of the cultivator from the land. Some cultural references to the moneylender, generally known as Khatri, highlight his place in Punjabi society:

Je Khokha sir khe pawe, to bhi Khokha khat liawe
(If a Khatri puts ashes on his head, even then he will make some profit)
Char chor te chare thug, char suniar, te chare thathiar
Char chauke solah, solah dune batrih
Ek mara jia Khatri
(Four thieves and four thugs, four goldsmiths and four workers in brass
Four times four is sixteen, twice sixteen is thirty two
One poor creature of a Khatri is equal to them all in deception)[5]

Interestingly, while in gross terms, the Sikhs demanded more land revenue during their rule (generally between 33 and 40 per cent of produce), the debt was significantly lesser. Revenue collected in kind was not oppressive generally, as it automatically depended on the financial circumstances and surplus the peasant had reaped in that particular season. Darling observes that 'the fact that in the Lahore district there were more wells in the fifties [1850s] than there are now shows that people found it worthwhile to sink capital in the land'.[6] Under colonial rule, however, land holdings shrank and the manner of division made it impossible for the peasant to survive without accruing debt, unless he had other sources of income (which happened infrequently). Add to that the vagaries of losing cattle due to epidemics, crop losses from droughts, and heavy expenses on weddings, and the situation became quite desperate. Another factor causing the peasant to live in straitened circumstances was the levy of local cesses and municipal taxes which had been almost negligible under the Sikhs. Under British rule, peasants had to pay the land revenue in addition to 20–30 per cent of the revenue for public goods like education, police, and 'community projects'. What made the colonial demands harder to comply with was the unfailing regularity with which the taxes were collected, compared to the more flexible regime under the Sikhs.

According to colonial officials, the peasants who enjoyed relative prosperity under colonial rule dissipated their advantage by reckless borrowing, which entrapped

them in the debt cycle.[7] It was commonly observed that a peasant proprietor limited
his borrowing not by his needs but by his opportunities to borrow. Some scholars
have blamed neither the character of the peasant nor the colonial state for the
impoverishment of the peasant but instead pointed out that the climate of the region
is unsuited to industriousness and initiative.[8]

The first indication of rising indebtedness among the peasantry was the large
increase in debt litigation after 1860. Between 1866 and 1874, 231,000 acres of land
were transferred in sales and mortgages annually, usually from the cultivators to non-
agricultural castes like the moneylenders. Darling notes that while moneylenders had
been present in India since times immemorial, it was only under the colonial state that
they became masters and not servants of the village. The ethnic and demographic
composition of the moneylenders also changed. While previously, rich cultivators
or local merchants had lent money to the poorer peasants, the creation of the land
market and the designation of land as a valuable asset attracted a new trading and
moneylending class from outside the farming community.

In the first 50 years of colonial rule in Punjab (1849–99), the increasing transfer of
land to the moneylenders and the rapid impoverishment of the peasantry occasioned
little action from senior colonial officials, even as some district-level officers expressed
grave concern at the situation. While John Lawrence privileged the rights of the
peasants over non-agricultural castes in small disputes and claims, the moneylender
was still able to manipulate the system and the illiterate peasant to his advantage.
Lawrence sought to put checks on the powers of the moneylender and his account
books, but subsequent governors abandoned the practice.[9]

As the peasant's lot gradually worsened, colonial officers showed particular
unwillingness to entertain the idea that the revenue demand may be excessive. In 1871,
Lieutenant Governor Robert Henry Davies defended the levy and said reducing it
'will change our peasant proprietors from being, as at present, thriving and industrious
cultivators of the soil, into petty landlords of the worst type—idle themselves and
rack-renters of others'.[10] Succeeding Lieutenant Governors, R. E. Egerton and C. U.
Aitchison, also denied that the issues of indebtedness and the transfer of land was
serious. Egerton dismissed them as 'a natural process of competition, which is both
wholesome and necessary'.[11]

Writing in the 1930s, Hubert Calvert, an Indian Civil Service (ICS) officer who
became deeply involved with the issue of rural indebtedness, said:

> It is customary to blame the cultivator for improvidence but it is not
> explained why this characteristic developed after 1849 and has been
> practically confined to owners, especially to the owners of the best lands

... the charge of extravagance on marriage expenses was reduced to relative unimportant limits by the Deccan Ryots Commission and Mr Thorburn, Mr Keatinge and Mr Datta have corroborated their finding ... it thus became clear that the active factor in peasant indebtedness has been the desire of the village usurer to get hold of the produce.[12]

The situation on the ground worsened and in 1884, S. S. Thorburn, a revenue officer in the district of Dera Ismail Khan, sent an uncommissioned report on the matter to the financial commissioner describing the extent of damage in his district: 80 per cent (86,000 acres) of the cultivable land in his district had been transferred from Muslim cultivators to Hindu moneylenders in the last five years, and Muslims were paying 2 lakh rupees per year as interest to the Hindus whom they disdained and looked upon as social inferiors. Aitchison summarily rejected Thorburn's findings and recorded his opposition to any interference in the situation in a minute thus: 'So far as the evils complained of are inherent in the character and traditional habits of the people, or in the gradual extension of law and systematic government over a country hitherto governed more or less irregularly (and this His Honour fears is at the root of the evil), little, if anything, can be done to improve the position of the agriculturalists.'[13] Aitchison sent the debt correspondence to Calcutta with a note that the entire discussion be dropped. Thorburn on his part was undeterred and wrote his findings in a book *Musulmans and the Moneylenders*, sending copies to the India council and England, and criticizing the 'dead weight of the system' for the deteriorating situation.

Meanwhile, J. B. Lyall, the new Lieutenant Governor of the Punjab, also dismissed the issue as unimportant and advocated *laissez faire*, blaming the peasant for his debt: 'Only a minority of these men have proved fit for the improved status we gave them; the majority will descend in time into the position which suits them – of mere tillers of the soil.'[14] Lyall was soon forced to retract as in 1886–87, 1,200,000 acres of land were transferred and in the succeeding year, it increased to 1,300,000 acres. Almost 500,000 acres of this were transferred to urban traders and there was an increase in crime and unrest during this period. Communal rioting flared up and often took the form of a direct attack on the moneylender. Lyall was forced to commission another inquiry into the matter, which produced extremely divergent opinions from the local officers on the situation, some still vehemently opposed to any reform or protection for the peasant.

Lyall reluctantly introduced the earlier practice instituted by John Lawrence, of examining the accounts of moneylenders and empowering the judiciary and revenue officers to consider the facts of a situation in repayment claims. He was later also forced to request the central government for remedial legislation that culminated in the Punjab Alienation of Land Act of 1900. The peasant's lot remained precarious after the introduction of the Act, however. Though the land transfers to non-agricultural castes virtually ceased, some large landowners assumed the role of moneylenders and continued to charge the peasant exorbitant rates. The only recourse open to the government was to provide alternative means of finance to the peasants with lower interest rates.

While colonial accounts of indebtedness in the Punjab blame the moneylender for the impoverishment of the peasantry, N. G. Barrier finds a more sinister explanation for the passage of the Punjab Alienation of Land Act. Contending that the Act was passed a decade after the worst peasant riots and alienations, he suggests that the legislation was intended to benefit the landlord elite of the Punjab by allowing them to replace the urban moneylending caste. Indeed, in the years following the passage of the act, the landlords started to lend money to the peasants. In other studies, moneylenders are seen as less oppressive as the colonial accounts suggest.[15] In one of the first village surveys conducted in the Punjab by E. D. Lucas, a former principal of the Forman Christian College in Lahore, he writes:

> The moneylender is not altogether the bloodthirsty creature he is often painted, but is often the means of saving the farmer from complete ruin since there are no banks in the villages and the Cooperative Credit Societies have only recently come into existence. The farmer is always in need of money. Sometimes a marriage, funeral or some other ceremony has to be celebrated; often seed is required at the time of sowing; when the crops fail, the farmer who has just managed to make both ends meet during the prosperous years, has to borrow money to keep alive and the only person from whom he can get it is the moneylender. In rural economy the moneylender is a necessity. Many a peasant admits that though he has to pay heavily for what he borrows, that often times his very existence is due to the help received from him. A Punjabi proverb says: *Shah bina pat nahin, Guru bina gat nahin:* There is no respectability to man without a banker; no heaven for one who has not a guru.[16]

It is pertinent to note that the Punjab was more indebted than other parts of India. The surveys of the Provincial Banking Enquiry Committee in 1929–30 found that 87 per cent of proprietors in the Punjab were indebted compared to 54 per cent in Uttar Pradesh, 50–65 per cent in Bihar and Orissa, and 59 per cent in the Central Provinces.[17] Peasants had to contend with both the usurious moneylender and the merchant moneylender. The former, typified by the *Pathan*, was concerned with earning as much interest as possible, while the merchant moneylender was more interested in controlling the prices in the market. Both types of moneylending, however, worked against the interest of the peasant.[18] Mufakhrul Islam challenges the notion that the Punjab Alienation of Land Act wiped out moneylenders from the market, arguing that notwithstanding the decline in its annual rate of return, the non-agriculturists in general and the merchants or moneylenders in particular would continue to compete with the agriculturists for a sizable share of the land available for purchase and that, despite the restrictions imposed by the Act of 1901, purchase from the agriculturists would constiture a significant part of their total purchase.[19]

Having acquainted oneself with these salient themes in the economic history of the Punjab, one can begin to imagine an alternative, microeconomic account based on an analytical discussion of the emergence of and proposed solutions to indebtedness. The following section discusses how indebtedness emerged in the Punjab and its importance in policy and political circles. It also discusses the reform strategies in greater detail and highlights aspects of the colonial footprint that are not discussed in the existing, macro-based analyses.

Debt as the Central Problem

> If history shows anything, it is that there's no better way to justify relations founded on violence, to make such relations seem moral, than by reframing them in the language of debt—above all, because it immediately makes it seem that it's the victim who's doing something wrong.
>
> —David Graeber, *Debt: The First 5,000 Years*[20]

No rural problem in colonial Punjab preoccupied the official imagination like peasant indebtedness in the late nineteenth and early twentieth centuries. Whether it was the high priests of officialdom in the nineteenth century who viewed it as an inevitable phase in the monetization and liberalization of the Punjabi economy or the passionate junior officials who were moved by the plight of the landless peasantry to petition for remedial legislation, peasant indebtedness remained a burning policy issue throughout colonial rule in the province. Despite this, however, there was little success in combating the scourge of indebtedness. Even after the passage of the landmark Punjab Alienation of Land Act in 1900, senior officials remained reluctant to endorse an active role for the state in alleviating indebtedness. Indeed, the Act itself can be considered less as an instrument benefiting the peasantry and more in line with the interests of large landlords in the province. However, the early twentieth century witnessed an outpouring of reforms championed by junior officials. At the same time, local politicians, particularly those belonging to the Unionist Party, introduced a series of laws aimed at curbing indebtedness. Both types of reform, the legal-institutional changes ushered in by the politicians and the microeconomic community-based movement favoured by the state, were predicated on varying conceptions of what caused indebtedness and what could be done to alleviate it.

In some ways, indebtedness was a convenient social ill to focus on, providing scapegoats outside the state machinery and existing power structures. This allowed for comfortable prescriptions, whether legal or in the establishment of cooperatives, that did not threaten the influence of rural politicians or the bureaucracy. One must unravel the various discourses of debt and the paths of remedy to expose the underlying assumptions and commitments of the agents of change. The first step is an acknowledgment of failure: neither the laws nor the cooperatives ultimately rescued the Punjab peasantry from debt, but in their wake they left a proverbial lesson from history and a fine account of how bureaucratic stasis and political self-interest operate. The legal changes introduced represented an instance of institutional change that built on the earlier colonial endeavour to formalize property rights and provide a judicial avenue for resolving cases of indebtedness in court. The cooperatives, on the other hand, represented a microeconomic experiment bearing close similarities to contemporary ideas on community development or the popularization of microfinance. This furthers the central argument of this book by drawing parallels between contemporary theories and practices of development and the colonial economic policy agenda in the Punjab.

In 1884, Thorburn published his statistical study of indebtedness in the Punjab discussed earlier. This led to passionate advocacy for the introduction of legal measures by the government to provide relief to indebted peasants and, after a decade of policy discussions and peasant riots, the Punjab Alienation of Land Act was passed in 1900. This Act prohibited the outright transfer of land from agricultural castes to non-agricultural castes and was therefore intended to check the power of urban moneylenders. It soon became apparent that the Alienation of Land Act was not a panacea for indebtedness, as landlords started lending out larger sums themselves, thereby supplementing their own land holdings when the indebted peasant defaulted. The condition of the poorer peasants remained just as precarious.

This scenario provided the perfect opportunity for the youthful enthusiasm of particular colonial officials to be translated into innovative policy cures, and the cooperative movement in the Punjab may be seen as an example of such remedial measures. However, the movement met an inglorious fate despite the passionate exertions of these officers. In some ways, it reflected the larger failure of 'developmental policy' in the Punjab, which had arguably caused the scourge of indebtedness in the region in the first instance. Indeed, as discussed in the first chapter, some of the existing literature on the Punjab reverberates with accounts of the malign state structure benefitting the parasitic landed elite, military officials, and the colonial coffers.[21] However, there is value in plucking the eye of cooperation from this malfunctioning leviathan and examining this failed exercise in closer detail, because of the intimate way cooperation touched the everyday economic lives of individuals in the Punjab. This also allows us to think beyond the meta-narrative of 'institutional and state-level weaknesses' to examine a tangible example of attempted redress and reform at a microeconomic level. What are often ossified as *institutional weaknesses* are instead analysed for their precise role in altering incentives and decision-making for individuals, the specificity allowing us to pierce the often vague discourse on 'institutions'. I argue that despite the loaded rhetoric, which imbued cooperation with transformational properties, including the cultivation of 'thrift and good character' among Punjabi peasants, the movement was poorly financed by the government, opposed at the highest levels, and used as a 'palatable' form of communism to accommodate and absorb socialist sentiments before being ultimately neglected and left to collapse.

More importantly, the movement is a perfect microcosm for the examination of development policy in the Punjab under colonial rule. While existing scholarship focuses on the impact of large-scale economic changes, a study of microeconomic policy and its impact allows an alternative way of understanding the nature of the colonial impact in the province. This throws up many loci of debate even within the official machinery as the various tiers of bureaucratic machinery differed over the meaning and purpose of economic reform in the province. It also complicates the binary view of the Punjab government as either benevolent or mercenary, instead revealing the internal conflicts and how these affected the everyday implementation of ameliorative policies.

Despite the rich rhetoric, which referred *inter alia* to the brotherhood of men, social equality, and inculcating better farming and living habits, the cooperative movement remained peripheral and marginal in its impact. There were several reasons for this, but perhaps the most significant sprang from the official machinery itself where there was a plethora of meanings attached to the word 'cooperation' and what it entailed. A central question was whether it was a philanthropic device or a financial institution. Many officials were vehemently opposed to the idea of engaging with the peasant at such a deep and intimate level, considering it an unnecessary millstone for the government. Others were passionate about the movement, but with both types of officials manning the administration at various levels, schemes were started and then abandoned when left in the hands of a less committed officer. A major impediment was the cultural stereotyping involved, which looked upon the peasant as inherently wasteful and incapable of redemption. Ultimately, the movement failed to alleviate indebtedness in a real sense in the province.

Notes

1   This poem (translated from Urdu) was anonymously published in *Zamindar*, 8 March 1907.

2   Malcolm Darling, *The Punjab Peasant in Prosperity and Debt* (Bombay: Oxford University Press, 1925).

3   Darling, *The Punjab Peasant*, p. 5.

4   Darling, *The Punjab Peasant*, p. 179.

5   These are common Punjabi proverbs about the moneylending castes.

6   Darling, *The Punjab Peasant*, p. 219.

7   For a rebuttal of cultural arguments against peasants, see Eric Stokes, *The Peasant and the Raj: Studies in Agrarian Society and Peasant Rebellion in Colonial India* (Cambridge: Cambridge University Press, 1978), pp. 234–36.

8   E. D. Lucas, *The Economic Life of a Punjab Village* (Lahore: Civil and Military Gazette Press, 1935), p. 94.

9   Punjab Administration Report, 1849–51, Lahore, Punjab Archives, pp. 227–34.

10 Punjab Administration Report, 1872–3, Lahore, Punjab Archives, p. 7–8.

11 Punjab Administration Report, 1880–1, Lahore, Punjab Archives, p. 22.

12 Hubert Calvert, *Wealth and Welfare in the Punjab* (Lahore: Civil and Military Gazette Press, 1922), pp. 249–50.

13 H. C. Fanshawe, secretary to the Punjab government to J. A. Grant, secretary to the financial commissioner, 23 May 1885, quoted in Norman G. Barrier, *The Punjab Alienation of Land Bill of 1900* (Durham, NC: Duke University Press, 1966).

14 Quoted in S. S. Thorburn, *Mussalmans and the Moneylenders in the Punjab* (Edinburgh: William Blackwood & Sons, 1884), p. 87.

15 For a discussion of the demonization of the moneylender in the colonial period and the varying images of moneylenders in development studies, see S. Sharma and S. Chamala, 'Moneylender's Positive Image: Paradigms and Rural Development', *Economic and Political Weekly* 38, no. 17 (2003): 1713–20.

16 E. D. Lucas, *The Economic Life of a Punjab Village* (Lahore: Civil and Military Gazette Press, 1935), p. 30.

17 'The Punjab Provincial Banking Enquiry Committee Report, 1929–30', Chapter 4, Cambridge, Cambridge University Library.

18 Neeladri Bhattacharya, 'Lenders and Debtors: Punjab Countryside 1880–1940', *Studies in History* 1, no. 2 (1985): 305–42.

19 M. Mufakharul Islam, 'The Punjab Land Alienation Act and the Professional Moneylenders', *Modern Asian Studies* 29, no. 2 (1995): 271–91.

20 David Graeber, *Debt: The First 5,000 Years* (New York: Melville House Publishing, 2011), p. 5.

21 A vivid account of this is in Imran Ali, *Punjab under Imperialism, 1885–1947* (Princeton: Princeton University Press, 1988).

3 | COMBATING INDEBTEDNESS I
Laws and Institutions

They realise at last that change does not mean reform, that change does not mean improvement.

—Frantz Fanon, *The Wretched of the Earth*[1]

The link between the formalization of property rights and access to credit has been the subject of serious academic inquiry in recent decades. Perhaps most notably, the Peruvian economist Hernando de Soto[2] has analysed the relationship between the two in post-colonial and fragile contexts. However, the debate has a much longer history of informing policy, especially in colonial contexts where the desire to increase revenue collection by the colonial power hinged on the prior registration of property. The fact that this formalization of property rights also enabled experiments involving access to credit in the Punjab is a later development, and one that echoes in scholarship such as de Soto's till today.

In the Punjab, the architecture for combating indebtedness had two major parts: legal changes and reform initiatives. This chapter interrogates the legal and institutional changes starting with the Punjab Alienation of Land Act of 1900. It then discusses the various pieces of legislation pushed by the Punjab Unionist Party, especially in the period 1937–46 which came to be known as the period of 'golden laws'. By critically evaluating the preoccupation with indebtedness, it shows how the issue was a convenient one to focus on. It begins by discussing some of the theoretical literature on institutions to allow a full appreciation of the impact of these legal changes.

Institutions and Economic Development

In his seminal work on institutions and institutional change, the economic historian Douglass North defined institutions as humanly devised constraints that structure political, economic, and social interactions, and are a primary determinant of the economic performance of a state.[3] The extensive social and economic engineering in the Punjab meant that the administrative or institutional structure in the province was in large part constructed by the British.[4] It is therefore possible to question some theories of institutional development that posit that colonial institutions are responsible for long-run underdevelopment, by examining the history of the Punjab. In particular, the ideas of institutional theorists who believe that secure property rights and cheap credit must be the foundations of a sustained strategy of economic reform[5] can be tested. Such an engagement also allows us to unpack the concept of 'institutions' and conceptualize more fruitful ways of engaging with the historical roots of underdevelopment. This section develops each of these points individually.

North's pioneering scholarship on institutions emerged in the 1970s and 1980s and became a forerunner among theories of long-run economic development. The core principle of this new school of thought was that institutions created the incentive structure of the economy and 'as that structure evolves, it shapes the direction of economic change towards growth, stagnation or decline'.[6] As scholarship on the subject broadened, the problem of collective action and the 'tragedy of the commons' emerged with a realization of the importance of individual property rights in a market economy. It was believed that if property rights were 'not well-defined, when they are ill-enforced, or when a collective of agents rather than an individual agent holds ownership rights, basic individual incentives that in competitive markets would lead … to efficiency results instead fail, and the efficiency results vanish with them'.[7] Individual property rights were regarded as a prerequisite for the functioning of a market economy and the absence of the same hailed as a key 'institution' that causes long-run underdevelopment. Instead of a free and independent individual reaping the fruits of a capitalist system, economists theorized on the many obstacles that constrained choice in the economy and 'institutions' emerged as the catch-all term for describing these. A leading economist Kenneth A. Shepsle noted: 'Standing between the individual qua bundle of tastes and available social choices are institutions … frameworks of rules, procedures and arrangements – that prescribe and constrain … the way in which business is conducted'.[8] This also underlined the need for economists to analyse the political economy of a society, as competitive markets could not operate in a vacuum, with political actors deciding many of the rules of the game or 'institutional constraints'.

Following the concern with the uncertainty and instability that political structures introduced into society, North's first intuition was that 'the major role of institutions in society is to reduce uncertainty by establishing a stable (but not necessarily efficient) structure to human interactions' and he formally defined institutions as 'the rules of the game in a society or, more formally, as the humanly devised constraints that shape human interaction'. Thus, he emphasized that institutions, in consequence, 'structure incentives in human exchange whether political, social and economic'.[9] Building on these ideas, North investigated path dependence and institutional structure, extending his ideas to developing economies. Development economists in the 1960s and 1970s had obsessed over technological change and capital accumulation as the prerequisites for growth, ignoring historical antecedents. The growth models popular during this period assumed that property rights were enforced. The new institutional approach to development economies pioneered by North posits that enforcement of property rights has a cost that affects the allocation of resources and thus has an effect on growth. Hence, the institutions that assure those rights become a relevant piece in the economic architecture that the process of growth and development is built on, and their comparison provides a fundamental explanation of differences in growth and development between different contexts.[10]

Scholarship on institutions has since burgeoned and institutionalist explanations of underdevelopment remain a dominant discourse. However, most of the scholarship is ahistorical even while making historical claims – for example, the emphasis on individual property rights and cheap credit were 'institutional' strategies tried by the colonial government in the Punjab but did not produce high or stable incomes. This section discusses some of the claims and assumptions of institutionalist theorists and how these can be challenged by a study of indebtedness and related legal changes and relief measures in the Punjab.

Property Rights and Cheap Credit

An examination of institutional change and colonial economic reforms in the Punjab can allow the emphasis on property rights and cheap credit as the key institutions for fostering long-run development to be challenged. Institutional theorists regard contracting institutions – for example, those vesting secure property rights in the individual – as vital in enabling an individual to invest in himself and his family, as the title deed allows him to use his land as an asset against which to borrow. The availability of cheap credit is another institution widely regarded as essential for sustained economic development, as credit empowers the individual to improve his human capital and economic prospects.[11] The faith in cheap credit is evidenced in the recent popularization of microfinance as a panacea for underdeveloped countries, while the World Bank, among other multilateral institutions, is pioneering a movement to digitize land records in the developing world to solidify the claim of the individual on his assets. Indeed, a new strand of scholarship is emphasizing the importance of having 'control' and not just 'ownership' over land assets.[12]

While the faith of liberal thinkers and multilateral organizations in individual property rights has been questioned by scholars like Elinor Ostrom who find group property rights as more efficient, the dominant discourse remains couched in a political economy that overshadowed the grant of property ownership under colonial rule, that is, vesting property rights in the individual.[13] This emphasis on first providing secure property rights and then enabling access to cheap credit automatically suggests that the Punjab may be an ideal case study to put this faith in these institutions to test. The fact that the formalization of property rights in the Punjab and the monetization of the economy were also accompanied by mass landlessness and indebtedness suggests at the outset that the faith in these institutions may be misplaced. But it provides a good hypothesis to test – that is, does an excavation of evidence from a province in which secure property rights were established and cheap credit was available verify the contemporary prescription of development economists that the key institutions for sustained economic development are individual property rights and the availability of cheap credit?

It is possible also to delve deeper into the importance of property rights. The liberal conception is that all rights rise out of property. One can assume that colonial efforts at the formalization of property rights in the Punjab were less an ideological promotion of liberalism and more driven by the economic imperative to effectively assess and collect land revenue. Nevertheless, the introduction of individualized property rights was not just an economic project but also a political and social one. Nor was it devoid of having long-run consequences. In a paper studying land tenure systems in colonial India, Abhijit Banerjee and Lakshmi Iyer contend that differences in types of property rights help explain long-run economic growth. They find that in the present day, areas in which property rights were typically given to large landlords by the British lag behind in welfare outcome to those in which the rights were given to small-scale peasant proprietors. The former have significantly lower agricultural investments and productivity in the post-Independence period compared to areas in which these rights were given to cultivators. These areas also have significantly lower investments in health and education.[14] However, this and similar studies are based on econometric data, that is, the use of instrumental variables instead of actual historical evidence. Evidence from the Punjab can challenge this conception by providing historical accounts of economic life in areas where property rights were formalized and cheap credit provided. The subsequent sections of this book develop the argument further by narrating how attempts to individualize property rights and provide cheap credit only dragged the peasantry further into debt, a historical episode that remains forgotten amidst the continued support for similar policies today.

Unpacking Institutions

'Weak' institutions are constantly held up as the reason for long-run underdevelopment in South Asia. The theoretical literature on institutions makes many claims about the relationship between property rights and welfare outcomes, and about bureaucratic and legal changes. However, there are numerous gaps and assumptions in a literature that lacks historical depth and nuance even while making historical arguments. There are significant ways in which the theoretical literature on institutions can be advanced through a study of economic development in the Punjab, and this section discusses a few relevant themes.

Much of the academic evidence on institutions and their impact on development relies on econometric studies that use proxies for capturing their effect. For example, in a famous study by Acemoglu and Robinson,[15] the mortality of European settlers in colonies is used to proxy for institutions. Other studies have used rainfall and latitude as proxies for them. The economic historian is likely to be skeptical about the usage of climate and geography as instrumental variables for the state of institutional development in a region, and the scholarship on institutions stands to advance by a closer engagement with the history of specific institutions, instead of the ambition to quantify them in a variable. Much of the nuance and variety in institutional change is lost by the crass generalization of institutional set-ups, with the distinctions drawn being fairly wide-ranging. At the same time, the idea that institutions are the cornerstone for sustained welfare gains has lost none of its currency and has become an almost catch-all concept for whenever a policy intervention fails: the 'system' or the 'bureaucracy' are held as ultimately responsible and pernicious enough to undo the best-laid schemes of the development economist. It is doubly surprising therefore to find that the scholarship on institutions and their relationship with economic development is so patchy in historical depth and context. This lacuna can be filled through a narrative history of institutional change in the Punjab, which exposes how the colonial bureaucracy operated, especially while seemingly implementing an agenda of economic welfare. Indebtedness in the province and the ensuing remedial measures provide a classic case for studying how a development intervention fails during a time when institutional structure was also being envisaged.

There are other theoretical contributions to be made as well. Following North's proposition that institutions – that is, the social, economic, legal, and political orderings of a society – are a primary determinant of its economic performance, there have been some attempts at distinguishing between different types of institutions. For example, a distinction has been made between contracting institutions (that is, institutions that support private contracts) and property rights institutions (that is, institutions that constrain government and elite expropriation). Such a distinction may be arbitrary, and a case can be made for the confluence of both types of institutions; nevertheless, this binary links various types of institutions with different types of academic literature – for example, contracting institutions are linked with the literature on contract theory, while elite expropriation has been the subject of socialist critique as well as theories of political science. Some studies find a robust link between property rights institutions and long-run economic growth, investment, and financial development.[16] This result is explained by suggesting that individuals have greater power to negotiate contracts with private parties by opting for alternatives or negotiating the terms but less so with the state and elites. A more conventional understanding of institutions will see them as determining the legal and fiscal capacity of a state. This capacity allows the state to levy and collect taxes and support markets. Some scholars argue that this capacity is increased by fighting external wars, and political stability and inclusive political institutions bolster this capacity.[17] State capacity was built in response to waging wars, which required raising revenues through taxation. Both these perspectives are relevant for the Punjab where property rights were being explicitly formalized by the British and contracts were being enforced through colonial courts. However, these functional institutions were producing indebtedness and other negative consequences, which is at odds with the theoretical literature on institutional change and suggests the need for a deeper examination of these negative effects and their causes.

Aside from distinguishing between types of institutions, an important departure in the critical analysis of institutions is to unveil them as resulting from a cumulative and incremental process rather than a static instrument devised at a certain point in time. The model of a constant institutional set-up sees it as a discontinuous change, like a critical juncture to be replaced only when there is an institutional breakdown, emphasizing the persistence and durability of institutions. An alternative way is to view institutions as the result of an *incremental process*, one that is evolving and altering not only with a replacement but through everyday performance. Such a view also highlights the role of individuals manning institutions at particular points in time and humanizes terms like the 'bureaucracy' and the 'legal system' for their malleable and fallible everyday existence. It also opens up institutions to myriad possibilities of partial reform instead of a dramatic overhaul. Technological progress and demographic change can also be captured within such a framework. The task then is to navigate between the Scylla of structural determinism and the Charybdis of unbridled agency. This is captured evocatively in a study of debt and reform in colonial Punjab where the early twentieth century was replete with legal and administrative changes continually debated and undertaken. A discussion of the debates around the passage of key legislation, including the Punjab Alienation of Land Act and its many subsequent revisions, the Debtors Act, the Colonization bill, and the private papers of officials, allows an examination of the differing viewpoints and ideas reflected in these outcomes. By acknowledging which ideological positions 'win' in policy debates, it is possible to gain a better understanding of the ideological roots and intended impacts of the laws and remove their apparent modern muteness. Similarly, the institutional changes in how property rights were awarded in the Punjab and who enforced them are all laden with normative assumptions about the state and its role in society, as well as the rights of the citizen or subject. By tracing the everyday trajectory of institution-building, a granulated understanding of their constraints and limitations can be developed, which opens the door for incremental change and reform.

Apart from the immediate and topical effects of colonial policies, as seen in the rising indebtedness and landlessness of the Punjabi peasantry in the late nineteenth century, the long-run impoverishment of the people is sometimes attributed to the *quality* of institutional changes brought by the British. While overtly centralizing and modernizing administrative functions, colonial institutions privileged personal connections and nepotism and retained all the drawbacks of the traditional feudal system cemented with the apparatus of the modern state.[18] At the same time, colonial accounts of South Asian society are replete with frustration at the predominance of friendship, nepotism, and the abuses of discretionary authority these allow. At heart is an argument about 'South Asian culture', which privileges family and friendship over the impartial state structures that colonial governance introduced. Advocates of empire will blame South Asian culture for the failed institutional transplant of British bureaucratic laws and institutions. Conversely, critics of empire argue that blaming South Asian culture is a racial argument, and the institutions set up under colonial rule were geared towards maximizing discretionary authority. By the same token, discretionary rule can also be more benevolent as the potential to effect positive change, if one is inclined to undertake it, is greater. In the Punjab, these concerns allow one to understand both the emergence of debt and the enthusiasm of officers keen to provide solutions for it. While senior officials and policymakers retained a high degree of vertical authority, more junior officers repeatedly had their schemes and ideas quashed through various bureaucratic loopholes or stasis.[19] Institutional structure in the Punjab therefore retained a downward dynamism (to facilitate the implementation of any directive from the centre or senior officials) while possessing an upward inertia that counteracted against any change in the status quo.

Indebtedness and Economic Development

Finally, by studying an active and enthusiastic attempt at microeconomic development (through the various cures colonial officers suggested and implemented to reduce indebtedness), it is possible to study an instance of the contemporary practice of economic development but with an important difference: colonial officers were undertaking these schemes when institutions were not as ossified and established. In other words, the 'system' or 'bureaucracy' was comparatively more flexible due to the fact that the British were still creating the administrative and legislative structures for the governance of the province that would later become the 'colonial legacy'. There is also an explicit paternalist rhetoric in the governance of the Punjab that favours a more 'benevolent' rule. Why then do the schemes to reduce indebtedness still fail? More importantly, are contemporary attempts at economic development following the same lines of research, information gathering, and output that the colonial schemes did? I suggest that they are, and therefore their failure is neither surprising nor should it be unexpected. In fact, it is proposed that contemporary cures (for example, microfinance) echo the colonial attempts to reduce indebtedness (for example, cooperation) and are as doomed to fail as the latter. While this provides evidence for the limited historical memory of economic development as a field of inquiry and practice, it also challenges the proposition that 'economic development' as we know it is a subject of study and practice that only emerged with post-colonial governments. Similar efforts were occurring under colonial rule and the evidence from the Punjab testifies to that. This is the third reason for studying debt in connection with institutional change in the Punjab.

There were different schools of thought when it came to addressing the problem of rural poverty in the Punjab. Those of an evangelical disposition like that of Frank Lugard Brayne believed in ideas of thrift, blaming the peasant for his wastefulness and lack of financial discipline. Only through managing his finances better could the peasant lift himself out of debt and poverty and build the secure and prosperous future the colonial state envisioned for him. More nuanced prescription offered by, for example, Malcolm Darling, sought to understand the social context of the peasant before prescribing for him. Darling believed in the potential of cooperatives in freeing the peasant from debt and improving his thought, character, and habits. To the official mind, cooperation represented the golden mean between the individualistic hedonism of capitalism and the collective impositions of communism.

Subsequent chapters analyse both the academic analysis offered by Darling and the brute enthusiasm of Brayne. But before prescription comes diagnosis. The viewpoints of various colonial officers and local economists are studied to develop a finer understanding of this. For example, C. F. Strickland, another Indian Civil Service (ICS) officer stationed in the Punjab, published an article on the rural problem of India in 1929 and described the main issues as debt, illiteracy, lack of hygiene, and fragmentation of land holdings.[20]

This chapter focuses on the relationship between institutional change and economic development in the Punjab. Institutional change in this context occurs through debt legislation, while microeconomic reform discussed in the next chapter begins with cooperative credit movement and intensifies in the campaign for 'rural reconstruction' and 'village uplift'. Large-scale economic reform is seen to coincide with microeconomic welfare programmes, and a new rationality of 'development' emerges that became a harbinger of 'community development' programmes and more recently 'microfinance' initiatives.

Legal Changes to Combat Indebtedness

The first and probably the most significant piece of legislation introduced by the British to combat indebtedness in the Punjab was the Punjab Alienation of Land Act, passed in 1900 by the Imperial Legislative Council. This was in response to the large-scale transfer of land from peasants to moneylenders in the event of default. Since Thorburn's publication of *Mussulmans and the Moneylenders* in 1884,[21] the issue of peasant indebtedness had figured prominently in official debates. The eventual passage of the Act in 1900 was viewed differently by the various concerned parties. While the official narrative hailed it as a boon for the peasantry, some felt that it benefited the large landowners, as the wording of the Act only barred the transfer of land from an agricultural to a non-agricultural caste. Though this was a blow to the power of mostly urban Hindu moneylenders, the large landowners could now lend to a greater extent and increase their own land holdings if the peasant defaulted. Opponents of the Act also suggested that it was framed to ensure goodwill among the landlords in rural areas where most of the imperial army was recruited. Furthermore, it was said to sharpen the urban–rural divide in the Punjab as well as to fan communalism. Lord C. M. Rivaz[22] left little doubt as to the motives of the Bill when he introduced it on 27 September 1899, saying that it was for those 'who furnish the flower of the native army'.[23]

The Punjab Alienation of Land Act, 1900, remained a focal point of legislative reform in the province and was revised multiple times.[24] This signalled the various problems thrown up with each amendment of the Act and the potential to revise it for the better. At the same time, it showed how debt remained a pressing economic issue for the Punjabi rural populace throughout the period 1900–47. Indeed, in 1922 when the Act had been in operation for over two decades and the cooperative movement was gaining influence, Hubert Calvert, a colonial officer, wrote that 98 per cent of the Punjab peasantry was in debt.[25] The all-India ratio of moneylender to population was 1:367, but in the Punjab it was 1:100. Although the population of the province was one-tenth that of India, one-fifth of all moneylenders in the country were in the Punjab.[26] In 1917–18, the North West Railway earned 764 lakh rupees, the major irrigation works earned 267 lakh rupees, while the moneylenders in the Punjab earned about 500 lakh rupees (the actual figure may have been higher as these figures tended to be under-reported).[27]

Some of this lack of results can be attributed to deficiencies within the Alienation of Land Act and its implementation. Annual reports on its functioning relate the problems on the ground and the ambivalent reception of the Act among officials. Some issues were quite elementary. For instance, the report for 1901 details how the word 'agriculturist' cannot be translated adequately in local parlance:

> The general opinion seems to be that the ordinary *zamindar* has not yet come to appreciate the significance of the expressions 'agriculturist' and 'member of an agricultural tribe' and consequently no common vernacular rendering of the two expressions appears to have gained a footing among the people ... the commissioner of Jullundur notes that some native officials do not grasp the difference between 'agriculturist' and 'member of an agricultural tribe' and ascribes their failure to unsatisfactory translation in the Urdu version as it seems to them a contradiction in terms to refer to a Brahman or Mahajan as a *zera'at pasha shaks*.[28]

Furthermore, the government reports reflect some of the apprehensions of the critics regarding the benefits the landlords stood to gain from the Act while the moneylenders moved swiftly to claim debts before it was implemented:

> The Act has generally been well-received by the well-to-do agricultural community. It is difficult, however, to give any useful appreciation of the feelings of the people because in the first place the erroneous and exaggerated impressions which people of all classes formed regarding the Act ... the moneylending community thoroughly disapprove of the Act. This however was in a great measure to be expected. The effect of the Act was apparent long before it came into force and may have operated differently in different places. The general opinion is that moneylenders exerted themselves to the utmost to acquire all the land they could before the Act came into force and this is borne out by the statistics of transfer which are contained in the Land Revenue Report.[29]

This was reinforced in the conclusions of the report: 'The chief points which have struck the Financial Commissioner in connection with the commencement of the Act are ... the absence of all excitement, amounting to apathy in some cases on part of the people.'[30]

The passage of the Act also led to political and legal developments. A key piece of subsequent legislation that impacted agrarian society significantly was the Reforms Act of 1919 that led to the creation of the first Legislative Council elected in 1920. It was the 'Rural Block' in this council that was later renamed the Punjab National Unionist Party in 1923 and became known popularly as the Unionist Party. Dominated by large landowners, most were skeptical of the extent to which Unionist politicians would champion land reforms or any law that threatened a fundamental overhaul of agrarian relations. However, one Unionist politician who hailed from a poor peasant family, Chhotu Ram, became the leading voice on peasant welfare and pushed numerous pieces of legislation in the Punjab Legislative Council for peasant amelioration. Chhotu Ram, though later knighted for his services, was viewed with suspicion by officialdom as he tended to take a more radical line than most of the loyalist Unionists.[31] Between 1937 and 1946, Ram was crucial in passing several laws in favour of the peasantry, a period which came to be known that of the 'golden laws'. Another Unionist leader who was actively involved in introducing laws to combat indebtedness was Sikandar Hayat, who later became premier of colonial Punjab.

The Act continued to be a focal point of discussion in the subsequent decades, as it underwent multiple revisions. Most of these revisions were introduced at the initiative of politicians from the Unionist Party. In 1938, an amendment of the Punjab Alienation of Land Act, called the Punjab Alienation of Land (II) Amendment Bill (Act X of 1938), was introduced. This was popularly known as the 'Benami Bill'. *Benami* transactions, through which non-agriculturists engaged in fictitious transactions instead of land transfers to avoid the strictures of the Alienation of Land Act, were recorded in the name of agriculturist friends or relatives of the non-agriculturist in question. *Benami* transactions negated the very spirit of the effort to end indebtedness and prevent the sale of land from small peasants to moneylenders. This Bill was passed by the Assembly on 16 July 1938 and received the governor's assent on 23 February 1939. The main provisions of the Bill included the powers to detect illegal transactions and declare such transactions void with retrospective effect. By March 1940, 41,000 such *benami* transactions had been detected; the amount relating to these transactions was about 16 crore rupees. The Act could have proved even more beneficial, but its effective implementation was greatly hampered because the basic infrastructure required for its stringent and effective implementation, such as revenue staff records and manpower, did not exist. Once again the Unionist policy suggested that most of its legislative measures were actually directed towards protecting the interests of big landholders. Between 1901 and 1938, it is estimated, for example, that two-thirds of the land alienated away from the small peasant was in favour of the large landowners.[32]

In 1938, there was another amendment to the Land Alienation Act 1900. It was termed as the PALA (III) Amendment Bill. In common usage, it came to be known as the 'Zamindar Sahukar Act'. The Bill was introduced by Sikandar Hayat and sought to protect agriculturist debtors from agriculturist moneylenders. To discourage underhand transactions, the Act provided that even after a debtor had paid off his dues he could not alienate (transfer) his land in the name of his former creditor. This was important because in many cases creditors declared the debtors free to avoid the provisions of various laws and later on, by mutual agreement, had the debtor's land transferred in the creditor's name. The Bill introduced a three-year period after the debtor was said to have repaid the debt during which transfer of land to the creditor was not allowed. This showed the many informal ways in which the Act was ineffective in policing alienations of land and borrowing as many transactions were still being conducted on the side. While the Act failed to relieve indebtedness in a substantive way, it did lead to several other political developments that had far-reaching effect.

Peasant indebtedness remained at the forefront of Unionist economic policy and, apart from the Alienation of Land Act, various other laws were put forward by the party. An important law passed in this regard was the Punjab Moneylenders' Bill in 1924. The provisions of the Bill demanded the statutory maintenance of account books. The Bill generated much controversy as it was viewed to be detrimental to urban interests, while rural members supported it. Lala Lajpat Rai, a leader from the urban Hindu community, called it 'mischievous', Gokul Chand Narang, another member of the same group, said it would destroy legitimate trade.[33] It was later reintroduced as the Punjab Borrowers Protection Bill in December 1925. This time it was attacked as a communal measure. The Unionists defended it, saying it had no bias against any community and was a long overdue economic and political necessity. The Bill had to be, once again, reframed as the Punjab Regulation of Accounts Bill before it was finally passed by the council on 7 July 1926. Even then, the Governor of the Punjab vetoed it, saying he would enforce the important provisions of the Bill in some other way.[34] Even though it could not be implemented, the Unionists gained popularity in the rural areas by backing it. The episode shows the various constituencies that politicians in the Punjab were aiming to please: both the peasantry with the rise of nationalist politics, as well as the officials who continued to be the real source of power and patronage in the province.

A key assumption of agrarian policy in the Unionist Party was the belief that the revenue demand led to indebtedness among the peasantry. This was in contrast to the official narrative that blamed the peasant squarely for his own lack of thrift and wasteful expenditure on social occasions leading to destructive borrowing. In 1928, Sikandar Hayat moved a resolution that called for an abolition of land revenue on very small holdings and *barani* areas. This proposal was, however, defeated in the council by one vote, after a prolonged and enthusiastic debate.[35] Soon afterwards, the Punjab Land Revenue (Amendment) Bill was introduced in the Punjab Legislative Council by the government. This Bill had been vetoed by the governor in a previous council. The Bill proposed a reduction in land revenue from 33 per cent to 25 per cent of the value of the produce. Chhotu Ram wanted to add a provision that would exempt small farmers from paying revenue. However, it was rejected by the big landowners in the council, including Fazl-i-Husain. The Bill was passed on 11 May 1928 and secured the governor general's assent on 12 February 1929 after a strong recommendation by the Punjab government.[36]

A further piece of legislation, which had been rejected by the governor earlier, was passed in December 1929 and enforced in July 1931. This was the Punjab Regulation of Accounts Bill, which regulated the activities of moneylenders. It was followed by legislation designed to combat the effects of the Great Depression, which had led to a decrease in crop prices and increased debt. There was also an increase in the sale and mortgage of land. Chhotu Ram pushed for remedial measures in the council, the most important of which was the Punjab Relief of Indebtedness Bill, passed in November 1934.[37] By 1934, debt among the Punjab peasantry had reached 92 rupees per head, the highest in the country. This Bill called for a reduction of interest rates, proposing that in no case could interest exceed the principal amount of the loan. The Act also provided that the temporarily alienated land of debtors could not be auctioned for recovery nor could a debtor be arrested for non-payment. Additionally, the word 'agriculturist' under the Act was to include all landlords, labour, and owner-tenants. While this important Bill was sponsored by the government, it was strongly supported by the Unionists, with Chhotu Ram making an impassioned speech in its favour.

The Relief of Indebtedness Bill came into force as the Punjab Relief of Indebtedness Act on 8 August 1935. Under the provisions of this Act, Debt Conciliation Boards were to be established in each district of the province. The objective of the Boards was to settle debts fairly and amicably.[38] At first, five Debt Conciliation Boards, each consisting of one chairman and two members, were set up in the districts of Karnal, Hoshiarpur, Amritsar, Rawalpindi, and Jhang. Subsequently, one Board was constituted in each district with the exception of Jhang and Simla. In the Jhang district two Boards were set up, while no Board was established in the Simla district.[39] At the end of December 1939, 29 Boards were functioning in the province. In all 67,780 applications were referred by debtors and creditors to the Debt Conciliation Boards in the Punjab up to 31 December 1939. Out of these, 40,720 applications involving a debt of 56,242,216 rupees were instituted by debtors and 27,060 covering a debt of 27,100,434 rupees by creditors. Out of a total of 67,780 applications referred to

Debt Conciliation Boards, 46,399 were disposed of and the total debt settled amicably amounted to 20,426,008 rupees. It was conciliated for 8,677,351 rupees.[40] In some cases, the differences were quite large. For example, in Jullundur, a debt amounting to 5,203 rupees was settled for 100 rupees, while in Lyallpur the amount claimed was 7,406 rupees for a debt, but it was settled for 660 rupees, that too to be paid in annual instalments of 40 rupees only.[41]

Another law passed in this regard was the Debtors Protection Act, 1936, which was a supplement to the Relief of Indebtedness Act, 1934. The Act was again strongly championed by Chhotu Ram and opposed by business and urban interests.[42] Despite these measures, by 1937, rural debt in the province amounted to 200 crore rupees, moneylending being the second largest industry in the province after agriculture.

In subsequent years, the Unionists continued to introduce more and varied legislations to combat various aspects of indebtedness. For example, in 1938, the Restitution of Mortgaged Land Bill was introduced. This Bill proposed to terminate mortgages of land contracted by members of the agricultural tribes before 1901. This fanned communal divisions in the province, and in an article published in 1939, Raja Narender Nath showed that due to the provisions of the Bill, 200,000 Hindus and Sikhs had to return land to the original owners compared to 84,167 Muslims.[43] The Bill was passed in July 1938 and led to the return of around 756,131 acres of land to its original owners. The law affected large landlords as well, including Sikandar Hayat and Khizr Tiwana who lost 5.5 lakh rupees and 1.5 lakh rupees, respectively. In June 1939, the Unionist Party introduced the Registration of Moneylenders Bill, which required moneylenders to obtain licences. A moneylender without a licence could not take a debtor to court, and licences were subject to suspension in case of fraud. The Act was applicable to non-agriculturist and agriculturalist moneylenders alike, but only 8,232 people got themselves registered under the Act out of an estimated 55,000 moneylenders in Punjab. The Bill came into effect in June 1939 and was strongly opposed by moneylenders as well as the Congress party.[44]

Two other laws in the same period were also significant. The Punjab Agricultural Produce Markets Act, 1939 (Act V, 1939), more popularly known as the 'Mandi Act', was passed by the assembly on 2 February 1939 and was one of the most influential pieces of legislation passed by the Unionist Party. The Act led to widespread protests, especially by grain traders, which delayed its implementation till 1941. The Bill was designed to ensure fair prices and dealings between farmers and traders and led to the formation of the All Punjab Non-Agriculturist Association. A Black Week and series of protests were observed by traders against the Act till it was passed in April 1941 and implemented in December the same year. The second law, The Relief of Indebtedness (Amendment) Act, 1940, stated that interest of above 7.5 per cent for secured debts and 12.5 per cent for unsecured debts would be treated as usury and no debtor could be imprisoned or arrested in execution of a decree for debt. This did not apply to banks or cooperative societies. Furthermore, milch and transport cattle and personal dwellings of the debtor were protected under provisions of the Act. Additionally, any false documents prepared by the creditors could be challenged as a criminal offence. Finally, the Act declared that no decree or claim could be passed against an agriculturist debtor for any sum more than twice the original amount.

The trajectory of legislative reform which focused on indebtedness in the Punjab demonstrates several things. Firstly, it highlights the continued preoccupation with indebtedness as a major socio-economic issue that interested the politicians and the officials in the Punjab. Both sides had their own narrative on the emergence of debt, with the state blaming the peasant and his wasteful habits while the elite politicians targeted the revenue demand. However, the focus for both the bureaucracy and the political elite remained a convenient demonization of the Hindu moneylender. By framing the issue of indebtedness in these terms, the politicians and the state evaded any structural change in rural relations that would affect existing hierarchies of power. If anything, the legislations further cemented and benefited the landed elite.

Secondly, the truly revolutionary legislations, mostly pushed by Chhotu Ram, were opposed or delayed by senior officials as discussed earlier in the section. For example, in 1925, the Punjab Agricultural Marketing Bill was introduced to combat unfair trade practices in the agricultural sector. The governor of Punjab vetoed this, and it was only passed as the 'Mandi Bill' more than a dozen years later in 1937. The delay occurred despite evidence from the official Banking Enquiry Committee, which found that 49 per cent of weights and 69 per cent of scales used by grain merchants in the Punjab were fraudulent.[45] Unionist leader Fazl-i-Husain also accused the British government of nominating ministers to the legislative council to fan communal tension and to prevent the spread of nationalist ideas. He wrote: 'As soon as government officials found an Indian wielding influence, the tendency is to counteract his influence. This has come to be a government policy. Ministers cannot really be useful if their position is no better than that of a glorified Tehsildar, to do the bidding of the government.'[46] The rural public was wise to the situation and signalled its support for Unionist politicians like Chhotu Ram and Sikandar Hayat in rallies and conferences held throughout the 1930s. During this period, both the Congress and the Muslim League had very limited influence in rural Punjab. This was clearly demonstrated in 1938 when the Congress party organized a *kisan* conference at the same time as the Unionist Zamindari conference in Lyallpur. While over 150,000 people came to listen to Chhotu Ram and Sikandar Hayat at the Zamindari conference, Congress leader Jawaharlal Nehru only attracted an audience of around 15,000.[47] However, at various points, the politicians were also content with gaining popular support rather than effecting legal changes in the face of bureaucratic opposition.

There was a close link between the everyday experience of debt and how politicians, especially Chhotu Ram and Sikandar Hayat, sought legal remedies continuously throughout this period. Peasant indebtedness was no longer an issue to be taken to London (as Thorburn had done in the late nineteenth century), but it was now a chief means of assuring popularity among the electorate for the Unionist Party. The period of the 'golden laws' (1937–46), at the tail end of imperial rule in the region, was also possible, as official opposition to introducing institutional changes to debt relations lessened. Ironically, it was the indigenous leadership that was therefore responsible for a thorough 'legal and institutional' response to indebtedness, while the government hovered between opposition and indifference and instead promoted a different prognosis and remedy: that indebtedness resulted from certain character traits of the Punjabi peasant that could only really be altered through the silver bullet of cooperation or 'rural reconstruction'. In this sense, the narrative on the institutional inheritance of the colonial state needs to be revisited, as indigenous actors were actively shaping the legal system that the later independent, post-colonial state would inherit. As the colonial state became more invested in community-level change through cooperatives, it was left to the politicians and local elite to forge the legal legacy of colonialism in this regard. This may help explain why ineffective legal systems were perpetuated as local actors and elite politicians framed socio-economic issues in terms that maintained their privilege while gaining them popular support. Ultimately, this may help explain the perpetuity of extractive institutions better, as it points to a dynamic process of manipulation and consciously maintained hierarchies, which was set into motion in the colonial period. The following chapter details the cooperative movement in the Punjab, which became the official response to the problem of debt and rural backwardness in general.

The Politicians and Indebtedness

> There could be no greater slur inflicted on our capabilities: we are nincompoops, we are unable to ensure a local supply of exploiters, the process of exploitation has to be initiated elsewhere ... this itself is neocolonialism of a sort.
>
> —*Economic and Political Weekly*[48]

The persistent focus on peasant indebtedness in the Punjab owed as much to the usefulness of the issue to official and political interests as to its relevance for socio-economic prosperity. The official response in terms of cooperation and rural reconstruction and the laws introduced by politicians from the Unionist Party to combat the issue signify an important duality. With the government championing a low-cost grassroots initiative and the politicians seeking to effect long-run legislative change, these initiatives signalled the larger transition to representative government in this period. At the same time, both the state and the politicians were motivated by their own interests rather than an ameliorative impulse to aid the peasantry. This section interrogates the various dynamics at play, beginning with a discussion of the emergence of the Unionist Party and the passage of the Alienation of Land Act. It then examines the attempted transformation of the party from an elite coterie to a grassroots movement and also discusses the alternative political forces vying for popularity during this period. None of these alternatives, including the Congress and the Muslim League, made indebtedness the mainstay of their agenda the way the Unionists did, signalling there were political compulsions and benefits to the Unionist Party for championing this cause above others. Indebtedness and debt legislation were central in this period for electoral politics while at the same time ensuring legitimacy and continued power for the elite.

The Punjab Alienation of Land Act and the Formation of the Unionist Party

> The Unionists seem to believe that the Land Alienation Act is to them what the Vedas and the Holy Quran are to the Hindus and the Musalmans.
>
> —Raja Narendra Nath[49]

Throughout the period 1900–47, the Punjab Alienation of Land Act and attendant laws formed a focal point of discussion among the political parties. This is particularly true for the Unionist Party that emerged as a champion of rural interests and dominated the council and legislature in the Punjab. The Act was passed ostensibly to rescue indebted peasantry in the Punjab from the clutches of the usurious moneylender, but it signified a contradiction in British policy.[50] It ran counter to the *laissez faire* doctrine of the colonial state and was instead an interventionist measure, by no means supported by all members of the government.[51] Landlords in the Punjab supported the measure, as it allowed them to assume the role of the moneylender: the Act only prohibited transfer of land from an agricultural to a non-agricultural caste. The language and terms of the Act opened it for debate, as discussed earlier, with a controversy raging over which castes qualified as an agricultural caste. However, more importantly, as David Gilmartin has shown, it signalled a solidification of categories of caste and tribe in the province that the British had developed since the nineteenth century.[52] The development of the tribal idiom enabled the hierarchies that justified imperial rule in the Punjab and rested on a firm bedrock of administrative convenience. The Punjab Alienation of Land Act was a legal expression of the same hierarchies and categories and also provided the context in which the rural elite in the Punjab claimed political legitimacy in the legislative council.[53]

The Alienation of Land Act was praised widely by the rural elite, as evident in the debates of the legislative council of the province. In 1907, Sir Umar Hayat Tiwana, while addressing the Punjab Legislative Council, said: 'I am emphatically of the opinion that no act has done or is calculated to do more good to the agricultural community of the Punjab than the Land Alienation Act.'[54] At this time, there was no political party advancing rural interests in the council, but it was dominated by members of the rural elite favoured by the British. The opposition to the Act came from the urban, non-agriculturist Hindu lobby, the Hindu Sabha, which was also represented in the council that viewed the Act as detrimental to its interests. In 1909, the Sabha declared:

> [T]he practical working of the Act has been extremely detrimental to the Hindus in as much as, while almost all Muhammadan castes have been notified as agricultural tribes, the high caste Hindus have been scrupulously kept out, even where they have held land and followed agriculture as a profession for several generations ... the concessions granted to Syeds and *mujawars* [persons receiving offerings of a shrine] have been refused to the Brahmans, the privileges conferred on Pathans and Mughals have been denied to Khatris.[55]

Subsequently, the rural elite organized themselves into the Rural Block, which became the Punjab Unionist Party in 1923. The leading members of the party during the period after the passage of the Montagu–Chelmsford reforms, 1919–47, were Fazl-i-Husain, Chhotu Ram, Sikandar Hayat, and later Khizr Tiwana. All four used the Alienation of Land Act and the embedded language of castes and tribes to claim political representation and mass appeal. In 1928, Fazl-i-Husain declared the Act was seen by the rural people as the '*magna carta* of their political and economic life.'[56] In the council and legislature, it remained the bone of contention with their main political rival, the Hindu Sabha. The criticisms continued for decades and, in 1926, Pandit Nanak Chand, a Brahman in the Punjab Legislative Council, termed the Act 'an attack on the Hindu religion.'[57] Critics of the Act declared it a communal measure and one that ran counter to British policy in the province.[58] Writing in the *Tribune* newspaper, Chajju Ram, a non-agriculturist lawyer, said:

The bill is against the principles of political economy acted upon in this province since the commencement of the British rule. It strikes like a strange and backward step in the history of legislation in India. It is objectionable as a piece of legislation favouring certain classes of the community at the expense of the interest of another class which is an important factor in the present system of the village communities of the province.[59]

The Unionists used the Act to define their political ideology, establishing themselves as a secular political party protecting the interests of the backward.[60] Gilmartin declares that 'the structural foundations of the Unionist ideology were rooted not in the protection of the class interests of landlords but in the logic of the British colonial system itself' and that the Unionists used the 'Act and idiom of tribe to establish a popular ideology, justifying in indigenous terms the existing structure of hierarchical authority in their bid for democratic political power'.[61]

During the 1920s, the Unionists were engaged with supporting the government on the one hand (emerging as a 'loyalist' party) and opposing the urban Hindu lobby on the other. The Punjab disturbances in 1919–20 and the subsequent martial law had led to a heightened sense of paranoia on the part of the British who wanted to ensure stability in the province. The Unionists toed the official line, and the British intervened heavily in the allocation of seats to ensure that loyal voices were represented in the council. Some Unionist leaders maintained a position of independence, with Fazl-i-Husain accusing the government of fanning communalism and critiquing the bureaucratic nature of British rule. At the fifth Provincial conference in 1917, Fazl-i-Husain spoke in favour of communal harmony and also said:

What we object to is the bureaucratic system. The government of India is too wooden, too iron, too inelastic, too antediluvian to be of any use for the modern purposes we have in view. It has proved to be of too much rigidity.... It is the evil system which converts an irresponsible servant into an insolent master ... we are deeply grateful for the maintenance of internal peace, and for a very large number of blessings that the administration claims to have conferred upon us, but is that any justification for perpetuating the system which is mechanical, irresponsive, doctrinaire and absolutely impervious to public opinion?[62]

Despite these occasional criticisms, the party remained quite loyal to the British and derived its legitimacy from the political economy of colonial rule. Indeed, the primary audience for the party was also officialdom, as well as rival interests in the council. It was only in the 1930s that the Unionist Party, under a strategy developed by Fazl-i-Husain, sought to have a more grassroots appeal. Many large landlords in the

Punjab such as Mushtaq Gurmani were indebted and used the issue of indebtedness to popularize the tribal idiom on which Unionist power rested. In some cases, landlords led protests and actions against moneylenders, including the burning of property.[63] Gilmartin summarizes the situation thus: 'At the heart of the Unionist position was the desire to establish political control over the forces of the market … the spread of popular concerns about indebtedness, and the escalating potential for rural conflict, provided the foundations for the enunciation by the Unionists of an ideological defense of the whole structure of political power in rural Punjab couched in the Land Alienation Act's language.'[64] It also led to canvassing on the ground and legislation became a form of political assertion. During the 1930s, the Unionists ushered in a period of the 'golden laws' discussed earlier that sought to reform the original Act and also included other acts for debt conciliation and registration of moneylenders. Despite the rhetoric, however, the Unionists continued to favour the interests of the landed elite over those of the peasants if these conflicted.[65]

One leader who was pivotal in the transition of the Unionist Party from a lobby block in the council to having a more popular appeal was Sir Chhotu Ram, the only leader of the party hailing from a poor Hindu peasant family. Chhotu Ram emerged as the leading voice of remedial legislation, but his politics merits closer attention to gauge the underlying impulses. Ram was a member of the Punjab legislature for around 14 years and was leader of the party in the legislature from 1926–31. In the Unionist ministry of Sikandar Hayat established in 1937, he was initially appointed as Minister for Development (1937–41) and later took the portfolio of revenue (1941–45).[66] He started his political career as a vociferous critic of the rural moneylender, whose oppression his own family had endured in the Rohtak district of eastern Punjab. In one of his early speeches, he said: 'There is the much abused, much-dreaded, and much-despised *bania*. Servility, selfishness and greediness are his characteristics. He is the incarnation of Shylock in our own times.'[67] During the 1920s, he spoke against the moneylenders in the legislative council and was criticized by the Hindu Sabha for supporting a pro-Muslim legislation despite being a Hindu.[68] In 1916, he started publishing a newspaper, the *Jat Gazette*, for addressing rural problems and he later established the Zamindara League in 1923 in his home district Rohtak. He was the force behind the passage of remedial legislations during the 1930s. However, despite the popular image, he was a favourite of the British, who gifted him hundreds of acres of land and regarded him as an important loyalist politician.[69]

However, Chhotu Ram earned the displeasure of British authorities during the interwar period. This related mostly to his work for the Zamindara League and his writings in the *Jat Gazette*. In 1921, the deputy commissioner of the Rohtak district wrote: 'As you are aware there is little difference now between the Congress and the

Zamindar League of Chowdhri Chhotu Ram. His newspaper *Jat Gazette* is carrying on practically the same propaganda against the government as the Congress.'[70] In 1933, the deputy commissioner of the district declared Ram's work to be 'communist' in nature. Most of these criticisms related to a series of articles that Ram published in the *Jat Gazette* in 1933, titled 'Bechara Zamindar', literally meaning 'Abject Farmer'). In this series, Ram questioned the government's ownership of land and wrote: 'Forgive me if I ask you how this land belonged to you and how we are the tenants.'[71] The deputy commissioner felt that Ram deliberately wrote on the inequities of land revenue in order to create 'disaffection in the minds of the *zamindars*'.[72] The following passage written by Ram earned the most censure:

> Nobody can put off the revenue demand. It is like a messenger of death which must have its toll. There is the fear of attachment and sale. The property both moveable and immoveable is in danger. There is an apprehension of arrest. There is the fear of the arrest of the *lambardar*. There is the fear of forfeiture. Evidently when the non-payment of a demand is full of such terrible consequences, it is much more unbearable than death itself. The demand is made without having regard to the produce. Remission is almost nil. Suspension is not a blessing but has often proved a curse for in *barani* land the crops are average once in three years. For these reasons the land revenue has been the chief source of the indebtedness and the ruin of the zamindar.[73]

In a later series titled 'Thagi Bazar ki Sair' (literally, 'A Walk through the Market of Fraud'), Chhotu Ram described and criticized corruption in various government departments.[74] Later, as minister, he established a Peasants' Welfare Fund. However, many of these writings and actions were not intended to be drastic changes. For instance, one 'revolutionary' law that Ram wanted to introduce in 1928 would forego the land revenue demand from proprietors with very small holdings.[75] The proposal was rejected by the government but not before Chhotu Ram had earned a great deal of popularity in the press. However, when questioned about the scheme, Ram said what he had in mind was a 40-year programme that would gradually move to the point where the small proprietor would not pay.[76] Generally speaking, the legislations introduced in the 1930s by Chhotu Ram, while seemingly attempting to improve the lot of the peasant, also benefited the landlords directly. The laws introduced to regulate activities of urban moneylenders essentially allowed landlords to assume a greater hold over tenants and also bolstered their claims to political representation. This was symptomatic of the general politics of the Unionist Party that derived legitimacy from the colonial state and the categories it had introduced, while at the same time it capitalized on the policies of self-representation by using colonial laws and policy debates to gain popularity among the electorate. This was also the downside, as it meant that with the rising tides of nationalism and communalism, Unionist power would be dealt a deadly blow, and the party members either crossed over to the nationalists or gradually lost relevance in the changing political scenario.

One set of challenges to the Unionist Party came from the government itself and the internal dynamics of the party. During the 1920s, Fazl-i-Husain was the leader of the Unionist Party and envisioned it as a secular party that would champion agriculturist interests. Sensing his popularity and based on some anti-government views mentioned earlier, Sir Malcolm Hailey, the governor of the Punjab, had him placed on a reserved seat to prevent him from becoming a popularly elected leader in the legislative council.[77] The other challenge was due to the way in which the party operated. The Unionist Party started as a rural lobby in the legislative council and did not have any organized support on the ground. In the subsequent elections, it faced challenges from factional politics within the party as well as candidates in the constituencies that had greater appeal on the local level.[78] Additionally, with the rising popularity of the Muslim League during the 1930s, the Unionists faced criticisms from intellectuals and politicians that were supporting the demand for a separate Muslim homeland. Critics included Muhammad Iqbal, the poet-philosopher, and leading landlords like Mian Nurullah, an erstwhile member of the Unionist Party who joined the Muslim League and was one of the biggest landlords in the Lyallpur district.[79] The Unionists also clashed openly with Muhammad Ali Jinnah in the lead-up to Partition.[80]

Political Alternatives

The more formidable challenge to Unionist power came from the other political parties and movements active in the Punjab in the interwar period. These include the Muslim League, the Indian National Congress, the Ahrar movement, the Ahmadiyya sect, the Communist party, and the Khaksar movement in the Punjab.[81] By the late 1930s, the rise of nationalist parties and the popularity of the Muslim League meant that the Unionists faced difficulties in maintaining popular support. The Unionist Party's relations with the Muslim League and the Congress have been documented extensively. Indeed, much of the historiography on the politics of the Punjab relates to this issue.[82] This section focuses on social and political movements that were more directly engaged with economic issues and also discusses nationalist politics. The primary sources are secret files of the Punjab government during the interwar period that have not been used before. The secular stance of the Unionist Party in particular came into conflict with parties based on religious identity. In this scenario, the politics of indebtedness and economic reform became even more important for the Unionists as the basis of their political legitimacy and the mainstay of their agenda. Nevertheless, the party was weakened greatly by the challenges from the other political players.

The Indian National Congress and the Muslim League

The rural wing of the Congress was particularly weak in the Punjab in part due to the extensive popularity and efforts of the Unionist politician Chhotu Ram discussed earlier in the chapter. Chhotu Ram had initially supported the Congress in the province before parting ways in the early 1920s after the first Non-cooperation movement. Ram then became a staunch critic of the Congress. In general, the economic programme of the Congress was inspired by early nationalist thinkers like Dadabhai Naoroji, who had focused on the 'drain of wealth' in the Indian economy and the transfer of capital from the colony to the colonizer. By the 1930s, the Congress economic vision was a socialist one. In the Punjab, the Congress represented the interests of the urban Hindu moneylender, another reason why it did not develop a critical programme of rural reform. It remained a largely urban party and the economic vision was centred on nationalist demands, including a push for industrialization. It commanded a limited level of support among the poorest peasants and untouchables in a few districts of the Punjab – for example, Rohtak and Hissar. However, this never reached any substantial heights, and the party continued to be associated with urban mercantile and trading interests in the province.[83]

The Muslim League similarly did not have a well-developed economic agenda, a fact bemoaned by scholars in their study of the Pakistani economy in its initial years. The League was a latecomer in Punjabi politics and did not have a mass organizational base or a comprehensive economic programme attuned to the rural poor.[84] A few leaders, such as Muhammad Iqbal, expressed economic concerns in their critique of western capitalism and the poverty of the peasant, but these did not assume centre stage in League politics that focused on religious identity. So, for instance, Iqbal believed that the implementation of the *sharia* would lead to an improvement of the economic lot of Muslims.[85] By 1941, however, the need for an economic agenda had become obvious, and Jinnah called for a five-year plan for the economic and social advancement of the Muslim community. A committee was appointed to develop this vision, but a lack of funds led to its dissolution after a single gathering. It took a couple of years before a subsequent committee could be established and, when it was, it was dominated by capitalist interests though rural and cottage industries were also included. By 1945, a draft plan had been formulated at the national level, but it contained no clear economic vision and did not focus on indebtedness. Instead, it criticized the *zamindari* system in the Bengal, as well as capitalist interests while advocating the alleviation of poverty. However, it was riddled with errors of calculation and also rejected the Soviet model.[86] Both the Congress and the Muslim League did not have a well-defined economic programme and instead based their politics on anti-imperialism or religion predominantly.

The Ahrar Movement and the Ahmadiyya Sect

The Ahrar movement in the Punjab in the 1930s aimed at the social, political, and economic advancement of the Muslims. The ways to achieve these ends, as outlined in their pamphlets, included political mobilization and economic progress. Some of the ways outlined for the achievement of aims stated in their constitution included the establishment of branches of the Majlis-i-Ahrar throughout India, the organization of Jaish-i-Ahrar-i-Islam, the organization of peasants and labourers on economic principles, the advancement of indigenous industries, and the propagation of the Swadeshi movement.[87]

There was a conscious attempt to link economic progress with the movement as well as a call for more holistic economic development, including the advancement of industry. While the movement was initially born out of reservations among the Muslims about the potential of the Congress party to represent their interests, it soon developed an independent character. It was established in 1929 with the aim of creating an Islamic state in the subcontinent. At the same time, it was inspired by socialism with its leader declaring that 'the unjust distribution of production is the real root cause of all maladies and social injustice'.[88]

The Ahrars also became important because of their conflict with the Ahmadiyya sect. The Ahmadiyya sect, which originated in Qadian, included many influential members. However, the sect was also involved in tensions with Sikhs and orthodox Muslims who did not accept them as Muslims. In January 1935, tensions between the Sikhs and the Ahmadis flared up in Qadian:

> At an Ahmadiyya meeting at Qadian on the 23rd January, the district officers and the police were abused by the crowd. The meeting created a dangerous atmosphere and non-Ahmadis were in considerable danger of violence. The tension between the Sikhs and Ahmadis became acute on account of the repeated assertions of the Ahmadis that Guru Nanak was a Muslim and that the Sikhs ate beef.[89]

Tensions continued in the following years when

> bricks were thrown from the houses occupied by Ahmadis at a Hindu-Sikh meeting held on a plot of land overlooked by those houses. Complaints and counter-complaints were filed by the various communities of alleged assaults by the Ahmadis on Ahrars and Sikhs. Addressing a congregation at the meeting held in connection with the death anniversary of the founder of the Ahmadi sect on the 26th May, Mirza Bashir-ud-Din Mahmud delivered an intemperate speech asserting that even their enemies admitted that the Ahmadis were masters in Qadian and proclaiming that the Ahmadis would not rest until the Ahrars were completely crushed.[90]

The high-water mark of Ahrar–Ahmadi tension was reached in 1935. The appearance of an Ahrar publication entitled the *Mazhabi Daku* caused considerable resentment among the Ahmadiyya community, and the pamphlet was proscribed by the government. Propaganda against the Ahmadi community was intensified during March, and resolutions were passed that no Ahmadis would be given burial in a Muhammadan graveyard. Later, the Ahrar leader Pir Faiz-ul Hassan Shah declared in 1936 that any claimant to Prophethood or the Khilafat after the Prophet of Islam was liable to assassination. One major point of controversy was the Shahidganj incident in 1935 when Sikhs demolished the Shahidganj Mosque in Lahore, a property that was claimed by both Sikhs and Muslims. Fazl-i-Husain, in keeping with his secular views, wanted the Unionist Party to remain distant from the affair even as protests erupted all over Lahore and a curfew had to be imposed. In his diary entry for 14 January 1936, Fazl-i-Husain wrote: 'Various people came to me about the Shahdiganj mosque. I advised them to drop the matter, and then something may transpire to improve matters, but that there was no advance possible at this stage.'[91]

Fazl-i-Husain also regarded the Ahrars as the 'dangerous unemployed' who were out to 'create disruption in the Muslim community and thus injure its solidarity'.[92] The Ahrars staged demonstrations over the Shahidganj incident and criticized the Unionist position. This increased their following, especially in the rural areas where they held meetings criticizing both the government and the Unionists. Meanwhile, the governor of the Punjab advised Sikandar Hayat not to take on a pro-Ahrar position. The latter complied and his loyalty was acknowledged by the British.[93] During the same period, the urban Hindu lobby criticized Sikandar Hayat for the laws against moneylenders, terming them 'black laws'. But with official support, Hayat was able to withstand the opposition. In this way, the laws on indebtedness served an immediate political purpose for the Unionists, allowing them to maintain their political legitimacy vis-à-vis their rivals, and provided them with the veneer of autonomous politics that their loyalist position on communal issues did not.

The Communist Movement

The communist movement in India was directly concerned with social and economic reform and was also vociferously opposed by the colonial state. Confidential and secret files reveal the extent to which the imperial bureaucracy was preoccupied with ensuring the limited impact of the movement.[94] In one confidential note circulated by the Punjab government, it was mentioned:

> The Communist movement is an arsenal in which are weapons of attack on every phase of national life – an arsenal controlled by an enemy Power, to which human life is of no account and which is as immune from religious control as from all restrictions imposed by a civilization which it refuses to acknowledge.... Realistically viewed, Communism is an international criminal conspiracy and it is as such, rather than as a political movement, that the Security authorities of every country must treat it.[95]

Such a view necessitated surveillance of the activities of communists in the Punjab:

> In the absence of legal instruments by which the movement can be effectively sterilized, the alternative would seem to be the exercise of ceaseless vigilance over its every branch and phase.... It must not stop short at recording the organisation, public policy, utterances and activities of the so-called legal side, but must be especially directed to elucidating and keeping track of its 'illegal' counterpart, the underground courier and relay systems, and the various 'apparatuses' responsible for military training, sabotage, espionage and the 'disintegration' of the Armed Forces. Nor again should this surveillance be confined to the *organisations*, but must identify and keep track also of their *individual members*. Since communism knows no frontiers, yet it is centrally directed it follows that no detail, whether organisational or personal, whatever the country or the sphere, can be safely ignored as irrelevant to any one of the countries affected by the general conspiracy.[96]

Organizations like the Kisan Sabha in Amritsar were observed closely for their communist connection and the utmost secrecy was maintained.[97] The report from which the above extracts are taken was circulated among police and administrative officers in the Punjab with the instruction that:

The Governor in Council therefore attaches considerable importance to the need of exposing the tactics of the Communist International and of encouraging counter-propaganda in the rural areas by the most suitable methods and channels, etc. [T]he contents of the pamphlet should not be given to the Press in any form; they are intended to help officers to interpret the activities of Communists in India in their true light.[98]

The ensuing correspondence details notes from various district officers on the situation in their respective areas. For example, the deputy commissioner of Gujranwala district wrote in response:

There is no activity of the Communists party in this district at all. There is one nominal body at Gujranwala (Kirti Kisan Party) which is not active.... So the best course in my opinion would be to make no propaganda at present in this district, but we will remain on the alert to start it at once, if occasion arises.[99]

Labour unions were the object of special scrutiny and concern, and officers were directed to monitor their activities:

Indications exist of the intention of Communist agitators to further their propaganda through the medium of Trade Unions.... Other Communist creations of the current year are the Press Workers Unions of Lahore and Amritsar, the Young Workers' League of Lahore and the Masons' Union, Tarn Taran. In the second category, the most important is the Punjab Motor Drivers' Union which is now largely controlled by well-known Communist agitators who hope to extend its influence by the creation of new branches under its banner.[100]

Close surveillance of communist organizations continued throughout the 1930s and 1940s. This included student bodies and universities. The Commissioner of the Lahore Division wrote:

The fact that Zamindars are not at present likely to listen to Kisan agitation does not seem to be a very obvious reason for allowing communists to attempt to get a hold upon the Zamindars ... the communists appear to have had steady influence upon the students. My own experience is that we can handle the students without communists' assistance. It may seem somewhat brutal to say so but time and again it has been our experience in Lahore since the 18th August 1942 that what the students really dreaded is a police *lathi* charge. They would not mind going to jail but they know fully well that they would not go to jail until after the charge and they have a great dislike of being beaten up. Then the police entered D.A.V. College last year and gave the students a lesson, this one act was the biggest the steadying influence upon the student community.[101]

Among the Unionists, Chhotu Ram was accused of being a communist during the 1930s as mentioned earlier for his criticisms of land revenue policies. In 1936, Chhotu Ram wrote to Fazl-i-Husain: 'I am only half a socialist and our Party also has a fairly distinct tinge of socialism about it.'[102] However, the politics of the Unionists remained loyalist, and with the majority of its membership comprising large landlords, self-interest dictated that they did not toe a socialist line. The close affinities between the Communist Party and the Congress, however, meant that together they posed a political challenge to the Unionists. However, the surveillance and arrests of members meant that they remained an illegal challenge dealt with more by the brute force of the state than political debates with the Unionists.

The Khaksar Movement

Another significant political movement was the Khaksar movement, which was popular during the same period in the Punjab.[103] The movement started in 1931 and came into direct conflict with the Unionists. Its leader Inayatullah Khan said it was started to 'organise Muhammadans for the purpose of social service and in order to prove their unity and self-efficiency to attain *swaraj* in a shorter time than the methods employed by the Congress'.[104] The government, however, viewed it as a seditious movement whose

> ... ultimate object is far from innocuous....The objects of the society were described in a book named 'Ishaarat' published by Inayatullah Khan in 1931. This book belied the idea that the author was in any way sympathetic to, or had any respect for, the British Government. The first nine chapters dealt with the necessity for Muslim regeneration all over the world. The next four displayed sympathy for the Congress civil disobedience movement and hostility and hatred for the British Government, with the last part described his apparently innocuous movement.[105]

The Khaksar movement was a fascist organization whose aims included uniting the community, promoting mutual love and affection by persuading people to serve one another; exalting the vision of the people by turning them into servants of God;

establishing uniformity by making people wear clothes of one colour; providing the community with an Islamic symbol, the *belcha* (spade); training the community in drill; and disciplining the community under one Amir.[106]

What distinguished the Khaksar movement were the 'training camps' for members where they learnt martial skills. Despite Inayatullah's claims that there were branches of the movement all over the province, the police reports indicate that apart from Lahore, Amritsar, and Saloh, a village in the Jullundur district, no branches were in active existence. The report describes their activities as follows:

> The conduct of the Khaksars in the Punjab has hitherto been unexceptionable: they do nothing but drill with their khaki clothes and belchas, perform occasional social services, and appear in formation at Muhammadan festivals…. There is sufficient to cause suspicion that this apparently innocuous movement is in reality intended by its founder to be used eventually for subversive ends…. It is significant that the rules of the Anjuman call for unquestioning obedience of every Khaksar to the orders of his leader, and that the pan-Islamic atmosphere pervades the whole scheme. If it attains the proportions hoped for by Inayatullah, it will eventually provide him with a very large and disciplined body ready at a moment's notice to turn its activities in any direction ordered by the Amir.[107]

In their own way, the Khaksars had developed a political and economic vision for the Muslim community in the Punjab; however, their efforts remained largely urban and did not gain currency among the rural populace. Despite generating suspicion and anxiety among colonial officials, their influence remained limited.

Conclusion

The Punjab Alienation of Land Act and subsequent legislations put forth by the Unionist Party in the 1930s represented much more than an attempt at economic amelioration of the indebted peasantry. They provided the framework in which the Unionist Party formulated and refined its politics, in the face of ever-increasing political challenges from more ideologically grounded forces. The Congress, the Muslim League, the Khaksars, the communists, and the Ahrars – all had a conception of the political and economic that went beyond focusing on debt and demonizing the moneylender. However, the Unionists sheltered under the umbrella of indebtedness and remedial legislation, partly captive to their colonial loyalties and partly because it served their individual economic interests. By establishing themselves as loyalist landlords and friends of the British, Unionist politicians were able to dominate positions of political power and privilege throughout the interwar period, running one of the most stable governments after the passage of the Montagu–Chelmsford reforms. However, with the increasing tide of nationalism and communalism, the edifice on which their power rested began to crumble. During his ministry (1937–42), Sikandar Hayat had negotiated ably with the leaders of different parties and movements and maintained the Unionist position. But after his sudden death in 1942, his successor Khizr Tiwana overestimated the power and popularity of the Unionists, and in subsequent elections the party was almost completely routed.

The language of indebtedness and the popular appeal of demonizing moneylenders were eclipsed by the demand for Pakistan and a rejection of colonial rule. The very categories and context that had given rise to the Unionists became irrelevant, a situation that was exacerbated when many members of the party switched over to the Muslim League. Fazl-i-Husain, the force behind the secular, agriculturist party, died in 1936, followed by Sikandar Hayat in 1942, and Chhotu Ram in 1945. The succeeding leadership was unable to further the Unionist agenda, and after 1947 the party ceased to exist – most of its leadership had joined the Muslim League; the remainder had opposed the demand for Pakistan and found no place in the politics of the post-colonial state. Khizr Tiwana, who succeeded Sikandar Hayat as the prime minister of the Punjab in 1942, resigned from his post in March 1947 and, after August 1947, left the Indian subcontinent, returning to Pakistan only in 1949 on a private visit. He took no further part in the active politics of the independent state. However, understanding the centrality and use of peasant indebtedness in Unionist politics allows an appreciation of the ways in which they assumed and retained power during the colonial period. This gives an added significance to the issue of indebtedness, as it served the political interests of the elite and allowed them to remain popular in a period when other parties and social movements were also vying for popular support. The eventual demise of the party was also driven by the changing political scenario in which it was more expedient for the elite to align with nationalist parties to retain influence in the post-colonial era.

The legal changes introduced by the Unionists represented an important instance of institutional reform that served elite interests and also set a precedent for them to use legislation to further their agenda. In the post-colonial state of Pakistan, many former Unionists would remain members of the Parliament and block any effective attempt at land reforms or redistribution. It is therefore questionable how 'colonial' the institutions and laws governing property rights truly are, as even under imperial control local politicians were able to dominate the assembly agenda for their own ends.

Notes

1 Frantz Fanon, *The Wretched of the Earth* (London: Penguin UK, 2001 [1961]), p. 79.

2 Hernando de Soto, *The Mystery of Capital: Why Capitalism Triumphs in the West and Fails Everywhere Else* (New York: Bantam Press, 2000).

3 See Douglass North, *Institutions, Institutional Change and Economic Performance* (Cambridge: Cambridge University Press, 1990).

4 For a discussion of colonialism and effects on growth in colonial India, see Peter Robb, 'British Rule and Indian Improvement', *Economic History Review* 34, no. 4 (1981): 507–23. On the role of institutions and rent-seeking in the underdevelopment of South Asia, see Burton Stein and Sanjay Subrahmanyam (eds.), *Institutions and Economic Change in South Asia* (Oxford: Oxford University Press, 1996); and Gunnar Myrdal, *Asian Drama: An Inquiry into the Poverty of Nations* (Harmondsworth: Penguin Books, 1968). For an excellent summary of these issues, see B. R. Tomlinson, *The Economy of Modern India 1860–1970* (Cambridge: Cambridge University Press, 1993), pp. 1–29.

5 See, for instance, Dani Rodrik, 'Institutions for High-Quality Growth: What They Are and How to Acquire Them', *Studies in Comparative International Development* 35, no. 3 (2000): 3–31.

6 Sebastian Galiani and Itai Sened, 'Introduction', in Sebastian Galiani and Itai Sened (eds.), *Institutions, Property Rights and Economic Growth: The Legacy of Douglass North* (New York: Cambridge University Press, 2014), p. 2.

7 Galiani and Sened, 'Introduction', p. 3.

8 Kenneth A. Shepsle, 'Institutional Equilibrium and Equilibrium Institutions', in Herbert Weisberg (ed.), *Political Science: The Science of Politics* (New York: Agathon Press, 1986), pp. 51–55.

9 Galiani and Sened, 'Introduction', p. 6.

10 Galiani and Sened, 'Introduction', p. 6.

11 See, for instance, O. Galor and O. Moav. 'From Physical to Human Capital Accumulation: Inequality and the Process of Development', *Review of Economic Studies* 71, no. 4 (2004): 1001–26.

12 See Soto, *The Mystery of Capital.*

13 See, for instance, Elinor Ostrom, *Governing the Commons: The Evolution of Institutions for Collective Action* (Cambridge: Cambridge University Press, 1990).

14 Abhijit Banerjee and Lakshmi Iyer, 'History, Institutions and Economic Performance: The Legacy of Colonial Land Tenure Systems in India', *American Economic Review* 95, no. 4 (2005): 1190–1213.

15 D. Acemoglu, J. Robinson, and S. Johnson, 'The Colonial Origins of Comparative Development: An Empirical Investigation', *American Economic Review* 102, no. 6 (2012): 3077–3110.

16 See Daron Acemoglu and Simon Johnson, 'Unbundling Institutions', *Journal of Political Economy* 113, no. 5 (2005): 949–95.

17   Timothy Besley and Torsten Persson, 'The Origins of State Capacity: Property Rights, Taxation and Politics', *American Economic Review* 99, no. 4 (2009): 1218–44.

18   See, for instance, Ayesha Jalal, *Democracy and Authoritarianism in South Asia: A Comparative and Historical Perspective* (Cambridge: Cambridge University Press, 1995).

19   This is discussed in detail in Chapter 3.

20   C. F. Strickland, 'Cooperation and the Rural Problem of India', *Quarterly Journal of Economics* 43, no. 3 (1929): 500–31.

21   S. S. Thorburn, *Mussalmans and the Moneylenders in the Punjab* (Edinburgh: William Blackwood & Sons, 1884).

22   Rivaz was the first Finance Commissioner of the Punjab and a Member of the Legislative Council of Punjab province. He was also a permanent Member of the Council of the Viceroy of India from 1898, and he later served as the Lieutenant-Governor of the Punjab (1902–07).

23   Indian Legislative Council debates, 27 September 1899, Lahore, Punjab Archives, p. 237.

24   By 1940, the Act had been amended 10 times: by Act I of 1907; Act XVIII of 1920; Act I of 1931; Act VII of 1936; Government of India Adoption of Indian Laws Order, 1937; Act II of 1938; Act X of 1938; Act V of 1938; Act VIII of 1938; and Act VIII of 1940.

25   Hubert Calvert, *The Wealth and Welfare of the Punjab: Being Some Studies in Punjab Rural Economics* (Lahore: Civil and Military Gazette Press, 1922), p. 8.

26   Calvert, *The Wealth and Welfare of the Punjab*, p. 130.

27   Calvert, *The Wealth and Welfare of the Punjab*, p. 130.

28   Annual report of the working of the Punjab Alienation of Land Act 13 of 1900 for the year ending 30ᵗʰ September 1901 (Lahore, 1902), Cambridge, Cambridge University Library, p. 1.

29   Annual report of the working of the Punjab Alienation of Land Act 13 of 1900 for the year ending 30th September 1901 (Lahore, 1902), Cambridge, Cambridge University Library, p. 1.

30   Annual report of the working of the Punjab Alienation of Land Act 13 of 1900 for the year ending 30th September 1901 (Lahore, 1902), Cambridge, Cambridge University Library, p. 7.

31   The issue of indebtedness was a central one in Unionist economic policy and a key means through which it maintained popularity in rural areas. Almost 90 per cent of government revenue came from agriculture. In 1925–26, the peasants of Punjab paid 13.5 crore rupees as interest.

32   Prem Chowdhry, *Punjab Politics and the Role of Chhotu Ram* (Delhi: Vikas, 1984), p. 278.

33   Raghuvendra Tanwar, *Politics of Sharing Power: The Punjab Unionist Party 1923-1947* (New Delhi: Manohar, 1999), p. 63.

34   Azim Husain, *Fazl-i-Hussain: A Political Biography* (New York: Longmans, Green & Co., 1946), p. 146.

35 Punjab Legislative Council Debates, vol. 11, 22 February 1928, Lahore, Punjab Archives, pp. 96–97.

36 Tanwar, *Politics of Sharing Power*, p. 70.

37 Chhotu Ram was also instrumental in providing relief through other legislative measures. On 11 May 1931, Ram made a memorable speech in the council while moving a resolution to grant a special remission of land revenue and *abiana* for the year 1931, leading to the passage of the motion. On the persistent pleas of Ram, in particular in the years 1930–33, the government allowed the remission of 265 lakh rupees in land revenue and irrigation tax in addition to the 200 lakh rupees remitted under existing rules of damage to crops.

38 The new Act, however, had provided that if creditors failed to appear before these Boards or prove by documents their claims, the case of the creditors against the debtors was to be discharged. Besides a provision in the Act added that if a creditor refused to accept the settlement decision of these Boards, he would not be able to claim any interest on the amount after the date of the decision of the Board.

39 Report on the working of Debt Conciliation Boards in the Punjab from the dates of their inception up to the 31st December, 1939, Cambridge, Cambridge University Library, p. 1.

40 Report on the working of Debt Conciliation Boards in the Punjab from the dates of their inception up to the 31st December, 1939, Cambridge, Cambridge University Library, p. 3.

41 Report on the working of Debt Conciliation Boards in the Punjab from the dates of their inception up to the 31st December, 1939, Cambridge, Cambridge University Library, p. 3.

42 This Act provided that an ancestral property owned by the successor of a debtor could be liable for execution of a decree for a debt of the owner's predecessor. The Act also stated that sufficient property was to be left in the ownership of the debtor so that his family could subsist, and in no case was alienation of land a result of the execution of a debt decree to exceed 20 years. The most thoughtful provision in the new Act was its provision that crops, cattle, and trees were exempted from the execution of a decree.

43 Raja Narendar Nath, 'The Punjab Agrarian Laws and their Economic and Constitutional Bearings', *Modern Review* 65 (January 1939): 29–36.

44 Tanwar, *Politics of Sharing Power*, p. 113.

45 'Punjab Provincial Banking Enquiry Committee, 1929–30', vol. 1, Cambridge, Cambridge University Library, pp. 219–20.

46 Waheed Ahmed, *Diary and Notes of Fazl-I-Husain* (Lahore: Research Society of Pakistan, 1977), entry of 17 July 1935.

47 Tanwar, *Politics of Sharing Power*, p. 126.

48 *Economic and Political Weekly*, 23 April 1977.

49 Raja Najendra Nath, 'Address to the Non-Agriculturist Conference at Dera Baba Nanak', *The Tribune*, 28 April 1936.

50 See N. G. Barrier, *The Punjab Alienation of Land Bill of 1900* (Durham, NC: Duke University Press, 1966); and P. H. M. van den Dungen, *The Punjab Tradition: Influence and Authority in Nineteenth-Century India* (London: Allen & Unwin Ltd, 1972) for a detailed discussion of the debates in officialdom preceding the passage of the Act.

51 This echoed the 'Janus-faced' description of the colonial system given in David A. Washbrook, 'Law, State and Agrarian Society in Colonial India', *Modern Asian Studies* 15, no. 3 (1981): 649–721.

52 See David Gilmartin, *Empire and Islam: Punjab and the Making of Pakistan* (Berkeley: University of California Press, 1988), pp. 12–15.

53 For a discussion of the debates on agricultural tribes and the passage of the act, see Gilmartin, *Empire and Islam*, pp. 34–38.

54 Ian Talbot, *Khizr Tiwana: The Punjab Unionist Party and the Partition of India* (Richmond: Taylor & Francis Ltd, 1996), p. 57.

55 Memorandum to Lord Minto from Punjab Hindu Sabha, 24 June 1909, Lahore, Punjab Archives, Board of Revenue file 441/212 A.

56 Punjab Legislative Council Debates, Lahore, Punjab Archives, vol. 12 (1928–29), p. 709.

57 Statement of Pandit Nanak Chand, Legislative Council Debates, Lahore, Punjab Archives, vol. 9 A (1926), p. 842.

58 For a detailed discussion, see Nina Puri, *Political Elite and Society in the Punjab* (New Delhi: Vikas, 1985).

59 Quoted in Puri, *Political Elite*, p. 65, from *The Tribune*, 14 April 1900.

60 For a detailed discussion of the establishment of the party, see Husain, *Fazl-i-Husain*; Talbot, *Khizr Tiwana*; and Iftikhar Haider Malik, *Sikandar Hayat Khan (1892–1942): A Political Biography* (Islamabad: National Institute of Historical and Cultural Research, 1985). For a discussion of the relations between the Unionists and other parties, especially the Muslim League, see Ayesha Jalal, *The Sole Spokesman: Jinnah, the Muslim League and the Demand for Pakistan* (Cambridge: Cambridge University Press, 1985).

61 Gilmartin, *Empire and Islam*, p. 118.

62 Husain, *Fazl-i-Husain*, p. 91.

63 See a detailed discussion in Gilmartin, *Empire and Islam*, pp. 121–23.

64 Gilmartin, *Empire and Islam*, p. 125.

65 Gilmartin, *Empire and Islam*, p. 118.

66 For a detailed biography, see Madan Gopal, *Sir Chhotu Ram: A Political Biography* (New Delhi: B.R. Publishing Corporation, 1977). Also see Ian Talbot, *Khizr Tiwana*, pp. 58–62.

67 Gopal, *Sir Chhotu Ram*, p. 26.

68 See a detailed discussion in Gopal, *Sir Chhotu Ram*, pp. 58–62.

69 Chowdhry, *Punjab Politics*, p. 1.

70 Quoted in Chowdhry, *Punjab Politics*, pp. 206–07.

71 Chhotu Ram, 'Bechara Zamindar', *Jat Gazette*, 19 July 1933.

72 Chowdhry, *Punjab Politics*, p. 209.

73 Chhotu Ram, 'Bechara Zamindar', *Jat Gazette*, 28 May 1933.

74 See Chowdhry, *Punjab Politics*, p. 225, for a summary.

75 Another leader who advocated the exemption of tax for small farmers was Muhammad Iqbal, the poet-philosopher. See a discussion in Imdad Ali Khan, 'Allama Iqbal and National Development: An Analysis of His Socio-Political Thoughts', *Journal of Rural Development and Administration* 28, no. 3 (1996): 45–57.

76 See Chowdhry, *Punjab Politics*, pp. 220–21, for an account.

77 See Husain, *Fazl-i-Husain*, pp. 160–01 and pp. 274–75, for a description of official opposition to the Unionist party. See also Chowdhry, *Punjab Politics*, pp. 177–78; and Gopal, *Sir Chhotu Ram*, pp. 68–71.

78 See Gilmartin, *Empire and Islam*, p. 128.

79 See Hussain, *Fazl-i-Hussain*, pp. 318–20, for an account of Iqbal's criticism; and Talbot, *Khizr Tiwana*, p. 92, for a discussion on Mian Nurullah's politics.

80 Talbot, *Khizr Tiwana*, pp. 111–24; and Gilmartin, *Empire and Islam*, pp. 150–51. See also Jalal, *The Sole Spokesman*, pp. 35–125.

81 Another force was the Hindu extremist group Arya Samaj, but their activities were considered seditious and policed directly by the government.

82 See, for instance, Gilmartin, *Empire and Islam*; Jalal, *The Sole Spokesman*; Husain, *Fazl-i-Husain*; Malik, *Sikandar Hayat Khan*; and Talbot, *Khizr Tiwana*.

83 Prem Chowdhry, 'Social Support Base and Electoral Politics: The Congress in Colonial Southeast Punjab', *Modern Asian Studies* 25, no. 4 (1991): 811–31.

84 See Ian Talbot, *A History of Modern South Asia: Politics, States, Diasporas* (Yale: Yale University Press, 2016), p. 186.

85 See Iqbal Singh Sevea, *The Political Philosophy of Muhammad Iqbal: Islam and Nationalism in Late Colonial India* (Cambridge: Cambridge University Press, 2012), p. 185.

86 See, for instance, Ian Talbot, 'Planning for Pakistan: The Planning Committee of the All-India Muslim League 1943–46', *Modern Asian Studies* 28, no. 4 (1994): 875–89.

87 'The Ahrar Movement in the Punjab, 1931–38', Government of Punjab Secret Document (Lahore, 1939), Islamabad, National Documentation Centre, S-358.

88 See Malik, *Sikandar Hayat*, pp. 55–56, on the origins of the party.

89 'The Ahmadiyya Sect: Notes on the Origin, Development and History of the Movement up to the Year 1938', Government of Punjab Secret Document (Lahore, 1938), Islamabad, National Documentaion Centre, S-359.

90 'The Ahmadiyya Sect: Notes on the Origin, Development and History of the Movement up to the Year 1938', Government of Punjab Secret Document (Lahore, 1938), Islamabad, National Documentaion Centre, S-359.

91 Malik, *Sikandar Hayat*, p. 57.

92   Malik, *Sikandar Hayat*, p. 57.

93   See Malik, *Sikandar Hayat*, p. 61, for a full account.

94   For a general discussion of the communist movement in the Punjab see Shalini Sharma, '"Communism and 'democracy": Punjab radicals and representative politics in the 1930s', *South Asian History and Culture* 4, no. 4 (2013): 443–64.

95   'Communism (General Aspects)', Government of Punjab Secret Pamphlet, 25 April 1934, Islamabad, National Documentation Centre, S-358, p. 10.

96   'Communism (General Aspects)', Government of Punjab Secret Pamphlet, 25 April 1934, Islamabad, National Documentation Centre, S-358, p. 11.

97   Other communist organizations were also active in the province. For example, the Workers and Peasants Party was established in the Punjab in April 1928. See Dushka H. Saiyid, *Exporting Communism to India: Why Moscow Failed* (Islamabad: National Institute of Historical and Cultural Research, 1995), pp. 91–127, for a discussion of the various peasant movements all over India in the interwar period.

98   Secret cover letter from J. T. M. Bennett, Esquire, C.B.E. M.C. I.P. Deputy Inspector General of Police, C.I.D., Punjab, attached to 'Communism (General Aspects)', Government of Punjab Secret Pamphlet, 25 April 1934, Islamabad, National Documentation Centre, S-358.

99   Alan Mitchell, Esquire, I.C.S., Commissioner, Lahore Division, Simla to Deputy Commissioner's Office, Gujranwala, 7 August 1934, Islamabad, National Documentation Centre, File no. 83/C.

100 C. C. Garbett, Chief Secretary to Government, Punjab, to All Deputy Commissioners in the Punjab, 5 November 1934, Islamabad, National Documentation Centre, Secret file No. 12467-34-9-S.B.

101 Cuthbert King, Commissioner Lahore Division to Deputy Commissioner Lahore, 5 May 1943, Secret file, Islamabad, National Documentation Centre, S-361.

102 Chhotu Ram to Fazl-i-Hussain, 30 June 1936, London, British Library, Fazl-i-Husain Papers, MSS Eur. E 352/10-11.

103 For a detailed discussion of the Khaksar movement, see S. Chander, 'Congress-Raj Conflict and the Rise of the Muslim League in the Ministry Period, 1937–39', *Modern Asian Studies* 21, no. 2 (1987): 303–28; and Iftikhar H. Malik, 'Identity Formation and Muslim Party Politics in the Punjab, 1897–1936: A Retrospective Analysis', *Modern Asian Studies* 29, no. 2 (1985); 293–323.

104 'Notes on the Khaksar Movement 1940 (with Addendum 1940–4)', Punjab Government Secret Document, Islamabad, National Documentation Centre, S-360.

105 'Notes on the Khaksar Movement 1940 (with Addendum 1940–4)', Punjab Government Secret Document, Islamabad, National Documentation Centre, S-360, p. 1.

106 'Notes on the Khaksar Movement 1940 (with Addendum 1940–4)', Punjab Government Secret Document, Islamabad, National Documentation Centre, S-360, p. 1.

107 'Notes on the Khaksar Movement 1940 (with Addendum 1940–4)', Punjab Government Secret Document, Islamabad, National Documentation Centre, S-360, pp. 3–4.

4 | COMBATING INDEBTEDNESS II
Community Development in Colonial Punjab

I would like, then, to end by putting in a good word for the non-industrious poor. At least they aren't hurting anyone. Insofar as the time they are taking time off from work is being spent with friends and family, enjoying and caring for those they love, they're probably improving the world more than we acknowledge.

—David Graeber, *Debt: The First 5000 Years*[1]

Building on the legal architecture of reform, colonial officers championed a wide-ranging grassroots response to indebtedness. This centred around the establishment of credit cooperatives of various kinds, whose main purpose was to 'reform' the peasant and relieve him from the shackles of debt. The initiative tapped into many of the urges of the colonial state, including the shifting of emphasis from colonial policies as a potential cause of indebtedness (such as the onerous revenue demand), and also utilized the youthful aspirations of 'missionary' officers who found a painstaking purpose in reforming the habits of indolent and habitually indebted peasants. Credit cooperatives remained varied in form and definition throughout the Punjab, and this chapter unveils the different manifestations and articulations of the idea. Overall, the cooperative movement became the major policy response on the ground to indebtedness. It evaluates how the provision of credit from cooperatives had limited success and uses this 'policy intervention' to understand institutional failure and the nature and scope of development policy in the Punjab. It also draws close parallels with more contemporary solutions to underdevelopment, including community development programmes and the popularization of microfinance.

The Cooperative Movement in the Punjab

Large-scale peasant indebtedness was not unique to the Punjab, and the worst peasant riots and disturbances in this regard were arguably seen in the south of India in the late nineteenth and early twentieth centuries. Cooperation as a tool of economic reform was also first used in the south. In 1892, the Government of Madras appointed a senior officer, Sir Frederick Nicholson, to study agricultural banks in Europe and the possibilities of adapting them in India. Nicholson's report recommended the establishment of cooperative credit societies in India similar to German Raiffeisen societies. His report was circulated among other Indian states and in the United Provinces. H. Dupernex also wrote a book, *Peoples' Banks for Northern India*, during the same period. In the wake of famines at the end of the nineteenth century, the viceroy Lord Curzon appointed a committee in 1901, which included both Nicholson and Dupernex as members. This committee recommended the establishment of cooperative credit societies throughout India, and in 1904 the Cooperative Credit Societies Act was passed.

The inspiration for the project came from England itself where modern cooperation started with the experiments of Robert Owen in 1844 when a group of 28 flannel weavers opened a small cooperative shop in Rochdale. In Germany, similar efforts by F. W. Raiffeisen and Hermann Schulze were made, and in Italy, Luigi Luzzatti set up the People's Bank of Italy. It was the Raiffeisen model that took root in India with the basic principles of a Raiffeisen society being a limited area of operation, small shares, and a permanent and indivisible reserve fund. By 1910–11, there were 5,262 cooperative societies all over India with 299,376 members and a working capital of 15,331,702 rupees.[2] In 1912, the Act was modified to expand the scope of the credit societies. Cooperative societies could now be formed for distribution, marketing, production, insurance, and so on. Two years later, in 1914, a committee was established to evaluate the progress made, and it concluded that no one could fail 'to be struck by the magnitude which the growth had already attained or to be convinced that the movement had taken firm root'.[3]

In the Punjab, some colonial officers, including Malcolm Darling, C. F. Strickland, Henry Calvert, and F. Brayne, had supported the movement passionately. At the time, the Punjab was divided into five divisions, each administered by a commissioner, and these divisions were further divided into 29 districts, under the control of a district commissioner. By the 1920s and 1930s, cooperation was also spreading fast in Ireland, and some experts at the time drew comparisons between Ireland and the Punjab. The popular narratives for the initiative were similar in the two cases: in Ireland the gombeen man was demonized in a similar way as the moneylender in the Punjab, the populations of both territories were deemed lazy and responsible for their ills, and rural development was seen as the palliative rather than any policy of industrialization.

In the Punjab, the interest in the establishment of credit societies dates back to the debates prior to the passage of the Punjab Alienation of Land Act. Nicholson's report was discussed and various proposals for establishing credit societies in the Punjab put forward.[4] The various deputy commissioners reported whether any indigenous credit societies existed in their districts and some also voiced their opposition to the setting up of cooperative societies by the government. In April 1901, the deputy commissioner for Gurdaspur stated: 'I do not consider the formation of cooperative societies feasible in the Gurdaspur district with or without the encouragement of Government officers within a measurable period.'[5]

The opening of the first cooperative societies in the Punjab (one in each of the five administrative divisions) drew mixed responses from British officials. The first report of the Cooperative Credit Societies in the Punjab published in 1905 documented the initial six months of operation. It is clear that district officers in some cases were vehemently opposed to the setting up of these societies. Gordon Walker, Financial Commissioner of the Punjab, wrote in his remarks prefacing the report that he deplored the lack of support shown in particular by the deputy commissioners in Montgomery and Rawalpindi districts for the opening of societies in their districts.

> They may have their own private opinions about the probability of success and no one can feel sure of the result. But the intent of Government is that this experiment shall have a fair trial with all the advantages which the cooperation of its officers can give it, and the latter must regulate their conduct accordingly. If, as appears from the Registrar's report, there is hope for success in Jhelum, there appears no good reason for not making the experiment in the adjacent district of Rawalpindi, which is similarly in respect of population and other circumstances.[6]

The lack of enthusiasm included the half-hearted efforts of those appointed to lead the movement. For example, the first registrar of the Cooperative Societies was S. D. Butler, Indian Civil Servant (ICS), who assumed charge of the office on 19 September 1904 but almost immediately relinquished it, and William Wilberforce was then appointed and assumed charge on 21 October 1904. The five districts selected for opening the first societies were Karnal, Hoshiarpur, Montgomery, Mianwali, and Rawalpindi. In Karnal and Hoshiarpur, the officers were supportive and societies were established, whereas in the case of Mianwali, societies had already been started informally in the late nineteenth century. The deputy commissioners in Montgomery and Rawalpindi, however, opposed the opening of societies there, as mentioned previously. Initial assessments were also discouraging, drawing the ire of senior officials. The Financial Commissioner observed: 'So far the initiative has been left to the Registrar, which is wrong and the experiment has been strictly confined to five districts, of which three are altogether unpromising. No general instructions have been issued and outside of these five districts no Deputy Commissioner considers himself concerned in the matter.'[7] Most crucially, no financial assistance from the government was given to any society and it was expected that the societies be self-financed from the beginning. This would greatly undermine any efforts to make the movement successful.

Despite these humble and unpromising beginnings, by 1906 the number of registered societies in the Punjab had increased to 151 and five new districts (Ludhiana, Multan, Shahpur, Ambala, and Gurdaspur) were added. Interestingly, out of the 151 societies, 108 were in two districts alone: Gurdaspur (65) and Jullundur (43). Even more surprising was the fact that all the societies in Gurdaspur were registered in February and March 1906, while 40 of the ones in Jullundur were also registered in the last two months before the report for 1906 was published. This questions the reliability of the data and the possibility that many of these societies existed on paper alone or were hurriedly opened so they could be mentioned in the statistics. Nevertheless, by 1907, the number of societies doubled and 328 societies were declared to be in full working order. Officials continued to lament the societies that failed to take off and enjoyed a brief existence. For example, the Junior Secretary remarked in 1908: 'The most unsatisfactory feature in the history of the movement so far has been the large number of societies that have died at birth or been wound up after a brief and inglorious existence. In most cases misguided official zeal has been the cause of the fiasco.'[8] In the following year, while 88 new societies were set up, 34 of the existing ones wound up their operations.

District officials were generally ambivalent in their attitude towards the societies, promoting the effort in promising districts and letting others languish. Coupled with the limited staff and concern with administrative efficiency discussed later, this may have undercut the movement from the very beginning. This attitude reflected policy directives issued from the higher levels with the financial commissioner stating 'the general policy will therefore be to concentrate efforts on a limited number of promising districts and while not refusing applications from outside, not to encourage them.'[9]

However, despite a difficult inception, the tentacles of the movement spread, in large part through the boundless enthusiasm of the junior officers posted in the field to popularize the cause. Figures 4.1a and 4.1b show the large increase in the number of cooperative societies and their members during the first 31 years of their operation. By 1913, some of the native states, including Bhawalpur, Poonch, and Kashmir, showed interest in starting cooperative societies there.

The increase in numbers was accompanied by a diversification in the objectives of the cooperatives that soon expanded from being purely financial institutions giving loans to the peasants, to cultivating a more holistic vision of 'economic development' in the province. As early as 1910, the cooperatives had started trading goods like agricultural machinery, wood, cattle, and other merchandise. At Panjawar in Hoshiarpur district, the societies were used to prevent land erosion, and in Jullundur,

Figure 4.1a   Growth in the number of cooperative societies in the Punjab, 1906–38

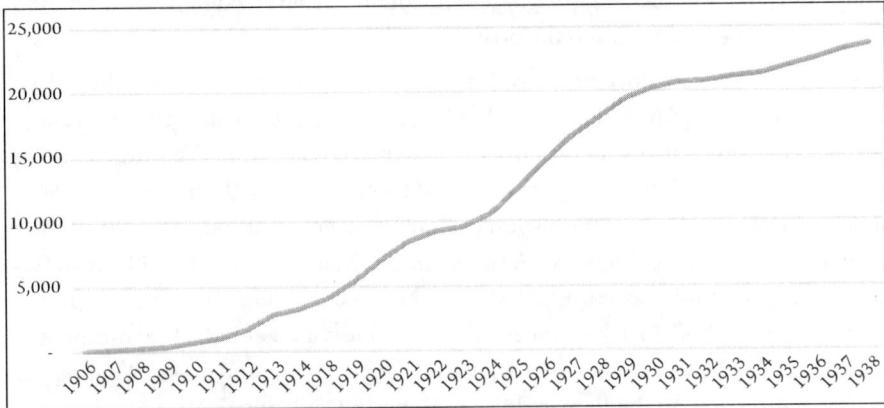

Source: Annual reports on the working of cooperative credit societies in the Punjab for the relevant years, National Documentation Centre, Islamabad.

Figure 4.1b   Growth in the number of members of cooperative societies in the Punjab, 1906–38

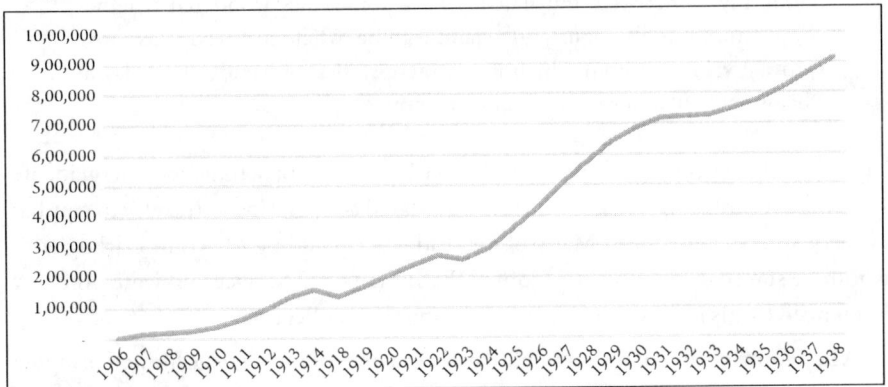

Source: Annual reports on the working of cooperative credit societies in the Punjab for the relevant years, National Documentation Centre, Islamabad.

they served to start a scholarship for a secondary school. In some districts, they became the panchayats, informal village institutions for settling petty disputes.[10] By 1919, many commodities were being sold through cooperatives specifically designated supply and distribution societies. The goods sold included salt, cloth, oil, seed, and foodstuffs. In Gurdaspur, a poultry society was started in the same year, which was deemed a success after it sent 1,000 eggs in a month to a supply society 'and though they have had to travel 52 miles ... only two have arrived broken and not more than six were bad'.[11] Two years later, in 1921, societies had been established for diverse groups and purposes, including *tongawallas*, cattle and sheep breeding, mare insurance, day school, ladies knitting, and the post office.[12]

Proponents of the movement saw it is a key means of revolutionizing the village economy and pointed towards the productive uses of the debt incurred by proprietors through the cooperatives. Between 1919 and 1929, cultivators used the loans for constructing over 27,000 masonry wells and bringing 750,000 acres of virgin land under cultivation.[13] Perhaps the biggest testimonial in favour of cooperatives was their impact on reducing indebtedness. A survey in 1919 on the working of 140 societies in 14 districts found that out of 6,740 members, 28 per cent were entirely free of debt, having paid off 17 lakh rupees of debt and leaving behind 11 lakh rupees.[14] C. R. Fay, a British economic historian based at Cambridge and a valiant supporter of cooperation, toured the Punjab during this period and remarked:

> The red letter day of my visit to India was that which I spent as the guest of Sir Jogendra Singh, the Minister of Agriculture, inspecting the consolidation at Phillaur – compact holdings, good roads, improved wells, and real men. I talked with the village elders and they seemed to understand me even before my words were translated. I have sometimes wondered whether cooperation was all I constantly claim it to be, whether it really has those spiritual values without which it is a mere statistical parade. That day at Philaur will not allow me to doubt any more.[15]

Fay was teaching a course called the 'Economic Development of India' to undergraduate students at Cambridge at this point and advocated cooperation as the way to combat poverty and backwardness. Many of his students (including Malcolm Darling with whom he stayed during this trip) joined the Indian Civil Service and were probably influenced by his ideas on cooperation during their college years.

A key contribution of the cooperatives was in invigorating village life and bringing diverse groups together in the pursuit of certain shared objectives. Annual conferences were held in the districts with representatives from 100–200 villages discussing common problems and devising solutions to them.[16] The role of cooperatives in fostering a sense of community was paramount, especially among groups that enjoyed strained or hostile relations. Since cooperative societies were started both in the villages and the urban areas, annual conferences also provided an opportunity for urban and rural members to engage with each other. Such interaction, however, was not always congenial, though the report for 1924 mentions the tensions between rural and urban members were declining and goes on to say that 'the tendency of the urban members to look down upon their rural brethren is still present, but the rural brethren are coming into their own. The gap between those who are provided with chairs (urban members) and those who are expected to be content with the floor is disappearing'.[17] Similarly, hostility towards the poor, menial castes, and the depressed classes was said to be decreasing, with a lowly *chamar* (leather worker) becoming the president of a society of the superior Sikh Jats in Ludhiana in 1925 and a weaver becoming the president of of a Rajput society in Ambala. In Sialkot and Gujranwala, 18 per cent of the members of all rural credit societies belonged to castes considered menial.[18]

The membership of the societies included representatives from all castes, including the higher castes like Brahmans and Rajputs as well as Criminal Tribes. In 1920, the first society for Criminal Tribes was established among the criminal Baurias in the Samundri tehsil 'after a careful selection of members', each one swearing to be honest and 'anxious to remove the stigma attached to them'.[19] The movement also extended to women with a woman inspectress appointed in 1926 to set up societies exclusively for women. By 1928, Miss Ahmad Shah, the inspectress in question, had succeeded in establishing 112 such societies.[20] Not even children were excluded, with societies for them set up inspired by the cooperative movement in Bulgaria. In 1938, there were 11 societies for children in the Punjab with officials believing it was never too early for the habits of thrift and careful spending to be inculcated among the population.[21]

In order to attract as many groups in society towards the movement as possible, the ways of popularizing it included the distribution of pamphlets and books as well as teaching by song. By 1926, 'rugged bards' had 'sprung up in several districts who express themselves with a pungency that pricks the guilty mind. It is impossible to suppose that twenty years of shaking have not awakened the drowsy'.[22] The native press, particularly the newspaper *Zamindar*, championed the cause of cooperation in the Punjab, carrying promotional materials and articles relating to the benefits of the schemes.[23] The newspaper *Watan* also carried information about the movement. The annual report for 1908 mentions these efforts cautiously as follows:

> The Editor of *Watan* who has written a broadminded book (sale price annas 10) on the morality of Mohammedans taking interest presented me with

40 copies for distribution. They have had an excellent effect. The editor of the Zamindar prints periodical pamphlets on agricultural improvements which, he suggested, might be circulated to Cooperative Credit Societies. Though these pamphlets are full of useful information, I am doubtful whether the ordinary village would derive much benefit from them.[24]

Other newspapers also reported on the activities of the cooperative societies. For example, in 1916, the eighth cooperative conference was held in the United Provinces which was widely attended by ICS bureaucracy.[25]

In some ways, the narrative built on an earlier colonial understanding: Sir Henry Maine's 'Village Communities in the East and West', published in 1871, had first floated the idea that Indian society was best understood not through its literature or its laws but through village customs, and he wrote in great detail about Indian village life.[26] Clive Dewey has demonstrated how the popularization of historical anthropology among Oxbridge students in the late nineteenth century fed into this approach of understanding India from below, by developing an intimate understanding of village life.[26] Cooperatives were merely another colonial initiative that glorified the rural and sought to cure indebtedness by reforming the peasant's financial habits.

With the increase in members, societies, and working capital, district officers did not view cooperative societies merely as means for alleviating indebtedness. Instead, they were seen as key levers for promoting 'moral and material progress' in the province. This term itself was not an innovation but had been understood differently before. A memorandum on Moral and Material Progress in the Punjab in 1902–12 printed by the Government of the Punjab discussed 'Moral Progress' by detailing the activities of Christian missionaries in the Punjab. Officials in charge of cooperative societies began to have a very different interpretation of moral progress – that is, actions falling under the heading of moral progress now involved leaving unhealthy habits and customs. In the report from 1919, the registrar waxes eloquent on the moral impact of the movement on the character and habits of the population with litigation and wastefulness declining. In the Gujar *panchayat* of the Gurdaspur district, 263 petty disputes were decided outside the courts, saving expense on legal fees. As early as 1913, the Gujar and Dogar societies in Hoshiarpur also agreed to reduce marriage expenses.[27] The Arain community in Lahore passed a bye-law prohibiting extravagance in 1919 and imposed fines if it was violated: 'Thrice in seven years has a penalty of Rs 100 been exacted for breach of the bye-law and this year three fines of ten or fifteen rupees have been imposed. More business-like habits are also slowly being formed.'[28] Similar bye-laws banning dancing girls at marriages and the use of fireworks, as well as resolutions checking indolence, are cited in the report for the following year. The most poignant example of this is when 'the committee considered that a member spent too much time in the mosque and so put his maximum credit at the low figure of Rs. 30 until he bestirred himself over his fields. He took the hint.'[29]

These 'moral' injunctions were soon categorized under the more secular term 'Better Living' in English and *Dehat Sudhar* in the vernacular (literally, 'Reforming the Rural'), and societies were set up under these names fully devoted to the task of 'moral reform.' There was also a section titled 'Better Living' in the annual reports of the cooperative societies, which detailed the achievements and constraints and signalled the widening conception of the aims of cooperation. Reducing extravagance was a recurrent theme – for example, in 1927, in Montgomery villages the cost of weddings was said to have reduced from 2,000 rupees to 300 rupees. But no less salient was the giving up of unsavoury practices – for example, a backward community was said to have left the practice of eating corpses (though perhaps dead animals were intended). A dramatic example of this thrift was quoted in a report thus: 'A sensation was locally caused by an Assistant Registrar who at the marriage of his two brothers gave spiritual food to the company in the form of 3 hours lectures on better living and then fed them on a simple diet. The district association of his tribe including many of the guests has been converted to support of the movement.'[30] Tribes passed resolutions against the giving of false evidence and forbidden sweetmeats as well as to enjoin temperance.[31] Better Living Societies grew in number steadily and, by 1935, it was estimated that 4.5 per cent of the 34,000 villages in the province had at least one such society. By 1946, it was estimated that there were 2,097 Better Living Societies in the Punjab and 106 Health and Medical Cooperative Societies in the province. The connections between Better Living with missionary activity are discussed in the next chapter.

As the aims and spheres of influence of the cooperative societies grew, the government utilized them in diverse ways. After the outbreak of the First World War, the cooperatives were used to gather contribution towards the Imperial Relief Fund for the aid of Indian troops fighting in the British Army.[32] At the same time, the interest and passion of the colonial officers in charge increased. Two officers who spearheaded the efforts, Malcolm Darling and C. F. Strickland, were sent on deputation to Europe in 1920 to study the working of cooperative societies there. C. F. Strickland later studied cooperation in Scandinavia, agricultural banking in Egypt, and central banking in Belgium and Holland to devise a plan for expanding the cooperative effort in the Punjab. Malcolm Darling studied cooperation in Eastern Europe and the Middle East and became a world-renowned authority on the subject, authoring books and delivering lectures in several countries on the topic.[33] It is difficult to overstate the contribution of this group of local officers in the mushrooming of cooperative societies and their increasing belief in the metamorphic role it could play. At the same time, this became the Achilles' heel as when the same officers were replaced by less motivated officials, growth in the movement stagnated. The following sections describe this phenomenon, among other factors, leading to the gradual unravelling of the societies.

The Undoing of the Movement: Institutional Practices

Despite the salutary effect of many efforts undertaken in the name of cooperation in the Punjab, even its most ardent supporters would not call the experiment a success. In 1947 when the British left India, the movement reached less than a tenth of the population of the Punjab and seemed to have had little impact on reducing indebtedness. The year 1947 also marked the partition of the Punjab with the eastern declared part of India and the western half of Pakistan. The two countries embarked on divergent policies in their respective halves. Indian Punjab quickly underwent large-scale land reforms and was divided into several smaller provinces, whereas in Pakistan the Punjab emerged as the preponderant province, home to the feudal, military, and bureaucratic elites that would dominate Pakistani politics. In both cases, the cooperative effort slowly petered out, but the rot had started even in the colonial era. This section explores some of the everyday practices and institutional distortions evident in the operations of the movement, while the next section explores some deeper political and ideological causes underlying the failure.

One of the most important reasons for the limited impact of cooperation was the paucity of staff and resources. In 1907, the regular staff of the registrar included a personal assistant and a clerk only, though it was 'suggested' that three inspectors should be recruited from *naib-tehsildars* and clerks. By 1909, the staff had increased to three trained inspectors and two experienced clerks. However, the annual reports of the cooperative societies continuously lament the shortage of staff and declare this to be the limiting factor in the spread of the movement. At the same time, the financial commissioner and other senior officials seemed reluctant to divert more resources towards recruitment. Especially in the early years when there was stiff resistance to the experiment, the government was reluctant to devote any staff or resources towards the effort in the avowed belief that it should be self-financed. This concern for its financial viability formed a consistent theme in the recommendations of senior officers to the registrar of the cooperative societies. At its heart was a colonial narrative that blamed the peasant for his indebtedness and transferred the responsibility for emerging out of it on to his shoulders. Cooperation was thus an elaborate exercise in self-help and was not meant to be championed financially by the colonial state in a substantial way. The staff were given low salaries even though this meant that it would be impossible to find qualified people to provide assistance, forcing the registrar to look for volunteers who might be willing to help the government.[34]

By 1913, the obsession with reducing operational costs was showing results, and the annual cost to government of running a society had declined from a paltry 51 rupees per year in 1905 to a miniscule 11–12 rupees, most of the reduction achieved by charging the costs of administration to the members. Even this cost seemed onerous, however, as the financial commissioner in his remarks on the report noted: 'Though it is satisfactory to find the societies beginning to undertake some part of the burden, still I think they ought to contribute considerably more than they do.'[35] During this period, there was a small increase in staff but one that did not keep pace with the growth of the movement.

These economies were won at the cost of foregoing regular inspections and many societies existed without having been examined by an official even once. By 1916, the impact of this was felt in the rising liquidation of societies with 104 societies ceasing operations in 1915–16. The primary reason cited was the lack of staff, some societies having persisted for three to four years without a single visit by an inspector; others had never been inspected at all. In the Jullundur and Hoshiarpur districts, there were only two inspectors for 900 societies in 1916.[36] By 1917, only eight of the original 30 societies were functioning, and those that had survived owed their existence to the interest and enthusiasm of the 'leadership of influential landowners.'[37] The lack of finances also constrained expansion, as it was not possible to start additional societies without the necessary support on the ground.

It was perhaps as a result of this stringent and insufficient official patronage that the more formal financial institutions also remained reluctant to promote the movement or to lend money for its expansion. In 1908, societies failed to obtain assistance from national banks, even as they attracted savings from farmers to a far greater extent than in any other province (the contributions of the Punjabi farmers nearly equalled those of all other provinces combined).[38]

By 1921, when the cooperative societies were being managed by the passionate Henry Calvert, matters had reached a point where Calvert openly pleaded for more funds from the provincial government. E. R. Abbott, the Financial Commissioner (Development), Punjab, at the time curtly noted that the 'Ministry of Agriculture cannot but regret that the financial condition of the Province make it impossible to put at Mr Calvert's disposal increased funds for further developments.'[39]

A persistent Calvert continued to battle against budget cuts and strongly protested the reduction in funds that had prevented the publication of the Urdu edition of the annual report, which was the chief tool for dissemination among the population. He lamented that only 400 rupees were required for the purpose and it was the principal means of apprising the literate about the progress of the movement. In his account, he regretted that while he had been asked to prepare a simple book in Urdu on cooperation, it was futile to do so when funds were then not provided for printing and publication.[40] If Calvert was expecting an opening up of the provincial coffers or a more sympathetic attitude from his superiors, he was mistaken as he was instead chastened for writing a lengthy report by H. P. Tollinton, Financial Commissioner, Punjab, thus: 'Mr Calvert has submitted a report more than three times the prescribed length. Future reports should present a more condensed account of the year's work.'[41] This reflected a general disinterestedness among senior officers to be apprised of the detailed functioning of societies. For example, the Lieutenant Governor remarked on the report for 1911 that he 'does not think it necessary to review it year by year in quite the same detail.'[42]

Another cause for concern was the attitude of the judiciary towards the movement. In 1912, the Lieutenant Governor remarked that some subordinate civil courts were harassing members of the societies.[43] More crucial was the opposition of certain landlords and members of the local elite to the movement. For example, in 1916, when the leader of a tribe in Western Punjab was urged to join the local society to help eradicate poverty from his area, he replied: 'If all these people become well-to-do, from whom shall I buy land?'[44] By 1938, the extent to which the local elite in villages were undercutting cooperation had increased with officials lamenting that they (the village notables) take 'in their own name or those of their dupes large loans from societies, obstruct all efforts to make them repay and if pressure is brought to bear upon them, retaliate by active and malicious propaganda against the movement and against local officials who have presumed to take action against them.'[45] Such attitudes were by no means uncommon and the local *patwari*s (officials in charge of property documents) also joined hands to oppose the movement. *Patwari*s were opposed to the consolidation of land holdings being advocated by the societies, quickly realizing that the fewer the plots of land, the fewer were the number of *patwari*s required to maintain land records.[46]

These various voices of disgruntlement soon translated into the routine occurrence of corruption within the societies, as the more unscrupulous saw opportunities for rent-seeking. As early as 1916, the case of a retired *tehsildar* was reported who founded a society and proceeded to lend to himself all the assets of the society to purchase land in his name. At the same time, a growing tendency among some society heads to give loans to their family members and friends emerged, with the infrequent inspections allowing such practices to go largely unreported.[47] In 1917, a particularly severe case of a man in the Jullundur district emerged who had been a passionate advocate of the movement in its early years. He was the president of a large society as well as an honorary sub-inspector but was reported to have cheated a depositor out of 800 rupees. When this was discovered, he attempted to doctor the books and was ultimately convicted of fraud and sentenced to seven years' imprisonment each on three charges of breach of trust and forgery.[48] These instances rose over the years – for example, in 1936, 359 cases of dishonesty were reported[49] and, in the following year, a liquidator in Multan was accused of 19 different cases of embezzlement.[50] Other groups in society also took advantage of opportunities for corrupt dealings. Dishonest traders who were using cooperative societies to buy and sell goods would sell an item – for example, a cow – to a peasant in yearly installments that exaggerated the total value of the item. Since these transactions were not classified as usurious loans, such fraudulent practices continued unabated.[51] Infrequent inspections and limited support also resulted in default, and, in 1932, 1,071 people defaulted in the Lyallpur district alone.[52]

Deeper Causes of Failure: Conceptual and Systemic Weaknesses

The Many Meanings of Cooperation

While the scarcity of funds and infrequent inspections provided opportunities for corruption and limited the scope of the cooperative effort, there were certain more crucial weaknesses underpinning the exercise. These ranged from an ambiguity surrounding the very purpose and meaning of cooperation to the divergent ideological opinions shared by officials manning the various tiers of the bureaucratic structure in the Punjab. It is these fundamental failings that may be tasked with the overall failure of the movement to take root in the Punjab. The various inefficiencies detailed in the last section may also be seen as the superficial symptoms of an underlying diseased structure.

Perhaps the most crucial failing was that surrounding the definition and aims of the cooperative movement. Officers seemed to have varying conceptions of what cooperation meant and what its role should be in the province. For example, Henry Calvert saw it as 'a form of organisation wherein persons voluntarily associate together as human beings on a basis of equality for the promotion of the economic interests of themselves'. In the official pamphlets and literature distributed among the officers and villages, cooperation was defined merely as an association of individuals for the promotion of some common economic objective. However, over and above these basic definitions were various other layers of meaning that may or may not have formed part of an individual colonial officer's understanding of the term. For example,

Ata Ullah, an Indian recruited to help popularize the movement, was trained to believe that 'members join the movement not as capitalists but as human beings whose chief asset is their character, hence on terms of perfect equality'.[53] One colonial officer defined cooperation as 'the act of persons, voluntarily united, of utilizing reciprocally their own forces, resources, or both, under their mutual management to their common profit or loss', whereas Horace Plunkett, a British champion of the movement, defined it as 'self-help made effective by organisation'. W. R. S. Sattianadhan and J. C. Ryan described it as 'a special mode of doing business. It does not aim at enriching its votaries at the expense of others; nor does it endeavor to benefit others by doling out charity to them'. They added that its object 'is to promote the economic welfare of its constituents through self-help and mutual help ... the cooperative movement is a vast and growing one and it provides a perfect medium between capitalism and state socialism'.[54]

In the early years, the major impetus had been that cooperation would be a tool to reduce indebtedness in the Punjab and reduce the power of the moneylenders. Later, the committee on cooperation in the Punjab saw it as a more general movement for social uplift and economic prosperity, declaring:

> ... the theory of cooperation is, very briefly, that an isolated and powerless individual can, by association with others and by moral development and mutual support, obtain in his own degree the material advantages available to wealthy or powerful persons and thereby develop himself to the fullest extent of his natural abilities. By the union of forces material advancement is secured, and by united action self-reliance is fostered, and it is from the interaction of these influences that it is hoped to attain the effective realisation of the higher and more prosperous standard of life which has been characterised as better business, better farming and better living ... we have in our report been compelled to deal mainly with the cooperative organisation from a business standpoint. But we wish clearly to express our opinion that is to true cooperation alone that is to a cooperation which recognizes the moral aspects of the question, that Government must look for the amelioration of the masses, and not a pseudo-cooperative edifice, however imposing, which is built in ignorance of cooperative principles.

It was perhaps this variable and grandiose understanding of cooperation that ultimately undermined the movement.

These varying understandings of the term affected the nature and conduct of operations of the societies on a daily basis. They also led to policy wars between the various tiers of administration. Was it meant to be a profitable financial enterprise or a philanthropic one? In the initial years, the idea that cooperative societies were charitable entities was used to explain the failure of the movement to take off. For example, in 1907, the financial commissioner remarked that 'based as they are more on philanthropic than on business principle, they do not appeal to the interest-loving Hindu, while the Muhammadan refusing as he often fails to take any interest on his deposits, prefers private to public charity'.[55] However, the British were clearly opposed to the idea of using these societies for welfare purposes and severely criticized the indigenous societies that were operating along philanthropic lines. In the report for the year 1906, an incident is related, which illustrates this impulse well:

> In Shahpur an old Society founded by Malik Umar Hayat of Kalra also exists. It has made little progress and has not brilliant prospects. The liberal founder of the Society is it worst enemy as he never refuses a loan to his tenants and takes no interest therefrom. There is little incentive, therefore, for the agriculturist to borrow from the Society and pay interest on loans obtained therefrom.[56]

In the report for the following year, the aims of the movement are sketchily defined, and it is no wonder that the performance on the ground remained sluggish and unimpressive given these fundamental uncertainties regarding the nature, scope, and meaning that the movement was meant to have.

There was also significant official opposition to the very idea of cooperation in the Punjab, as some officers deemed it an unnecessary fad that would interfere in the way of the government. The annual reports of the department therefore make mention of the extent of official opposition in a particular year. For example, in the report for 1909, it was said: 'Opposition on the part of officials seems to be decreasing. No instances have been reported to the Financial Commissioner during the year, and it is encouraging to see that the Registrar acknowledges assistance from officials and non-officials alike.'[57] By 1920, the financial commissioner felt the tide had turned, and the growth in members allowed him to be more sanguine, commending the officials at the forefront of the effort thus:

> It is not always that the seed of ideas falls upon favourable ground; but those who initiated and who still carry on the propaganda of Cooperation have a satisfaction which can only be compared with the satisfaction of the pioneer who has introduced a new crop into a new country and has seen it flourish far and wide, until its permanence is assured by the universal conviction that it has added to the well-being of man.[58]

However, the debate over whether cooperation was intended merely to reduce indebtedness or to contribute to a holistic vision of economic development continued. In 1922, the financial commissioner remarked that while other features of the movement were of interest, the registrar should focus on how cooperation was contributing towards the reduction in indebtedness. This drew a lengthy response from the then registrar, Henry Calvert, in 1923, in which he dwelt on what he understood cooperation to mean. (This is the same report in which Calvert was then reprimanded for exceeding the prescribed length for the report.) In his remarks on the meaning and purpose of cooperation, Calvert wrote:

> In my first report written in 1916 great stress was laid upon the need for proper teaching, it was pointed out that our object was to educate the people of the province in elementary economics and business methods, cooperation was originally introduced into India in order to provide capital for agriculture but it soon became clear that what was wanted was not so much capital as lessons in the wise use of it. Since then, my colleagues and myself have steadily pursued the policy of treating this department as one of adult education, of which the primary object was to instil into the people the need for organising themselves on economic lines if they were ever to escape from the burden of poverty and debt. In the review of last year's report it was stated that the 'aim of the society is to afford cheap credit and by so doing to reduce the total indebtedness of the members.' With great deference I would remark that I should be very sorry indeed if any of my staff held that view, and would be surprised if any of the members gave expression to it. Our object as we understand it is to examine the whole economic structure of the province, to study the defects which retard economic progress, and to discover the factors which contribute to the comparatively low standard of prosperity and then to devise schemes whereby the people can remedy these deficiencies and remove these factors by organising for self-help and mutual help ... the mere reduction of indebtedness and the provision of cheap credit are not our objects; what we do aim at is the provision of sound, well-controlled credit for productive purposes and the replacement of unproductive debt by productive borrowing. We would gladly see the debt of every co-operator doubled if the capital were invested in a source of profit and benefit to the borrower.[59]

These ideas regarding a holistic conception of welfare, which questioned whether or not debt was such a central problem, were not widely shared. While such an expansive and meaningful understanding of cooperation contributed to its growth under the supervision of Calvert and other equally passionate officers, these ideas were not part of the official policy. Senior officials retained their emphasis on making the societies self-sufficient and were content to let officials like Calvert experiment with their ideas as long as they did not burden the provincial treasury. However, without a real investment by the state in the movement, it allowed individual officers to support or ignore the movement, and cooperation never became a truly state-led or state-sponsored exercise. Instead, it remained the canvas on which individual officers painted their vision of a prosperous Punjabi peasantry with no assured afterlife for these visions.

Cooperation and Land Revenue

The colonial narrative on indebtedness in the Punjab squarely blamed the extravagant and illiterate peasant for his inability to stay afloat in a monetized economy. Even Malcolm Darling, who established himself as a great champion of the Punjabi peasant, blamed the peasant's lack of thrift and his expenditure on 'unproductive social occasions' as the cause for his financial misery. Darling famously defended the imperial government's large-scale development agenda in the Punjab in terms of developing canal colonies and irrigation systems and said that the peasant's poverty was a result of the *prosperity* of the province, as progress had provided him with many avenues from which to borrow.[60] Neither Darling nor the official commentaries on indebtedness in the Punjab take serious notice of how colonial land revenue policies may have been contributing towards the peasant's indebtedness.

This denial was in the face of statistical evidence that contradicted the official position. Cooperative societies, for instance, were tasked with noting the purpose for which a borrower was taking a loan. For most of the period between 1905 and 1938, payment of land revenue is cited as the reason in 20–25 per cent of the cases, while marriages funerals and other ceremonies account for no more than 6–8 per cent of the loans. About 25–30 per cent of the loans were for repayment of existing debt, while cattle and agricultural implements form the remainder. Officials went so far as to discount the reported statistics with the financial commissioner remarking in 1914 that what was cited as a loan for the payment of land revenue (21 per cent in the previous year) was 'in rural parlance an expression used to cover many other purposes which the borrower does not care to define more precisely'.[61]

Colonial officers remained reluctant to admit that the land revenue demand was onerous and excessive for the peasants or that the colonial economy had disrupted the traditional economy of the area without providing new safeguards or methods of insurance and welfare. Instead, a narrative of the peasant as wasteful, lazy, and simple-minded dominated official documents and debates.[62] Other factors that contributed to peasant indebtedness included crop failure from drought or seasonal calamities, purchase of new seeds, cattle, and implements, expenses relating to social events and debt litigation, the ease with which peasants could borrow from moneylenders, uneconomic land holdings, and a withering away of village industries to make way for agriculture as the primarily rural economic activity. However, reports and letters of officers in the period often ridicule the peasant and demonize the moneylender, avoiding discussion of the larger structural and economic changes the peasants were living through. There is no attempt to link grain prices, changing trade balances, or currency devaluation with the real incomes of farmers and their borrowing habits. It is hardly surprising therefore that agricultural debt continued to grow in the period, rising to 90 crore rupees in 1921, of which 75 crore rupees were from proprietors. By 1929, the debt had increased to 135 crore rupees.

Cooperation and the Fear of Political Agitation

Aside from the conceptual confusion or disagreement, there was an anxiety that successful cooperation might lead to a burgeoning support for socialism or, in the years leading up to the First World War, to support for the Caliphate in Turkey. Members of the movement were predominantly Muslim in the initial years, a fact that fuelled these fears. Equally important was the concern that cooperation might breed forms of collective action that may challenge the status quo. These reservations were articulated both in the published reports and the private memos circulated between officers. In 1913, for instance, the financial commissioner explicitly cautioned against this as follows:

> The striking preponderance of the Mussulman element in the membership of rural cooperative societies is noteworthy. It is to be sincerely hoped that attempts will not be made by unscrupulous agitators to capture the movement and divert it to so-called political ends. Such folly would of course cause irretrievable injury and would go far to dissipate the beneficial results of the movement. All attempts of the kind should be resisted by every available means.[63]

Similar concerns were voiced during the Akali movement of the 1920s, a rural movement organized by the Sikhs in the Punjab. Fearing that one society was helping the agitators, officials cancelled the society, sending five of its 11 members to jail.[64] These actions indicated that political concerns and a phobia of peasant revolt led the British government to be even more cautious in its support for cooperation. While this may have stunted the growth of the movement, it also meant that there was greater support for monitoring of the societies in the 1920s and 1930s compared to the initial years, even if the official motive was less a concern for efficiency and more a need for surveillance.

Cooperation and Racial Stereotypes

Officers in the Punjab were given to using sweeping generalizations and racial tropes in their descriptions of Punjabi society from the settlement reports of the nineteenth century. Sir Denzil Ibbetson, the most famous of such officers, ended up authoring a timeless book, *Punjab Castes*,[65] which categorized the population of the province under various tribal affiliations, each tribe believed to have certain distinct character traits that explained its socio-economic status. Later scholarship and critique would expose the tenuous relationship between tribal affiliation and personal characteristics, but, with publications like Ibbetson's made mandatory reading for the district officers, it was natural for the colonial administration to use such stereotypes in their discourse on the Punjab.

These stereotypes were also used in colonial accounts that explained the limited success of cooperation. Some categorizations extended to the population in general, which was deemed lazy and wasteful, and, in one report, an officer seems to regard defective drainage as particularly important:

> The obstacle in this district (Karnal) is not ignorance of the benefits of cooperation but the enervated character of the people caused by centuries of oppression and defective drainage. The result is that both public spirit and private enterprise are wanting and the people are either content with the present or hopeless of the future. They view any scheme for their improvement with languid indifference or suspicion. Few of their leading men are trusted or possess any influence. With such material, any form of progress is out of the question.[66]

Some castes were also privileged in relation to others. For example, the Jats were regarded favourably by the British: 'In many districts of the central Punjab the Jat is exceedingly well-off in most years – no agriculturist is more thrifty, for purchase of seed and of cattle he has ample funds.'[67] At the same time, Muslims were regarded as lacking enterprise and unlikely to succeed: 'In the western Punjab the agriculturists are mainly backward in education, rigid Muhammadans and without much business instinct.'[68] Muslims were also regarded as more likely to borrow. 'The Muhammadan is as a general rule less thrifty and more indebted,' states the report for 1913.[69] The racial stereotyping extended to other castes and groups as well. For example, in the annual report for 1906, the Balochis settled in the Punjab were described as 'children in money matters.… They enjoy nothing more than making a fine and extravagant display of their wealth in their native homes. One of the chief reasons for their reckless extravagance is that they cannot find any profitable employment of their money in the colony. After a good harvest all are lenders, after a failure most are borrowers'.[70] It is not merely a matter of description, as these stereotypes affected the attitude of the officers on the ground. In the same report, for instance, the registrar writes: 'No one recognises more thoroughly than I do what a tedious and laborious task it is to explain thoroughly the merits of the scheme day after day to slow-witted rustics and it would be absurd to expect most Deputy Commissioners to devote much of their time to the subject.'[71] Not all registrars saw the villagers as 'slow-witted rustics', however, with Calvert firmly asserting in 1923: 'The basic assumption on which we work is that the rural masses can be lifted on to a higher plane of wealth and culture, that "the poor illiterate peasant" need be neither poor nor illiterate; that "the stupid cultivator" will respond to efforts to make him intelligent.'[72]

These categorizations must be termed as futile analytical categories for they only encouraged the unhealthy practice of restricting societies to one caste or religion. By the late 1920s, this was said to contribute towards increasing communalism and there were at least 220 societies that openly restricted membership by religion or caste.[73] More importantly, this designation of certain castes or religious groups as inherently lazy, unenterprising, or backward blinded the officer to the potential of an individual, irrespective of caste or religion, and built in an accepted bias into the decision of who obtained loans and under what conditions. As such, it allowed rank prejudice to run through the movement, from the selection of districts and localities in which to start more societies, to the terms and conditions of the loans.

Social Groups and the Cooperative Movement

The Moneylenders

Finally, it is pertinent to examine two groups in Punjabi society affected most by the cooperative movement in closer detail: the moneylenders and the peasants. The moneylender, or *sahukar* as he was generally known in the Punjab, was the chief scapegoat for colonial accounts of indebtedness, criticized for his usurious dealings with the peasants. This echoed the British narrative in Ireland and England itself with the character of the moneylender demonized in official accounts and popular culture. It also served the colonial state's political interests to target the moneylender, rather than inequalities in land and privilege.

Data on the number and operations of moneylenders in the Punjab is available though unreliable, as, in many cases, the money was lent informally or through social networks and went unreported. Nevertheless, the income tax returns from the period can provide a rough estimate of the number of people engaged in moneylending. In 1918, for instance, 40,000 individuals reported moneylending as their primary source of income, but crucially, this did not include the number of agriculturist moneylenders or female moneylenders. Henry Calvert estimated the number of agriculturist moneylenders to be 19,000 in the province. By 1931, the data is more informative, and 30,293 males and 1,191 females reported themselves to be primarily bank managers, moneylenders, or moneychangers, and an additional 4,661 males and 86 females classified themselves as working dependants, bringing the total number of people engaged in moneylending to 36,863. In addition, 11,513 males and 86 females reported moneylending was a subsidiary economic activity for them and mostly classified themselves as agriculturalist moneylenders. Data for the year immediately after the passage of the Punjab Alienation of Land Act is considered suspect, as people may not have reported their occupation correctly due to unpopularity and fear of hostile policies. The point remains, however, that moneylending was a large-scale and highly important economic activity in the province. For example, in 1928–29, it accounted for 36 per cent of the total income tax paid by business and industry in the Punjab.

It is useful to distinguish between urban and rural moneylending in the Punjab. In urban areas, credit was obtained either from banks (that required collateral and financed trade and industry) or urban moneylenders (who usually financed consumption). While the banks charged interest rates of 6–9 per cent, moneylenders often charged between 9–12 per cent and sometimes as much as 18 per cent. In cases where no material security was provided, interest rates could be very high, giving rise to the phenomenon of the 'loan shark', who charged interest between 12 and 48 per cent. In accounts from the period, the Pathan is usually considered to be the loan shark, charging as much as 75 per cent interest. For recovery, Pathans depended mainly upon personal intimidation and force. In 1928–29, 2,292 moneylenders were taxed on an income of 79 lakh rupees, representing 8 per cent upon 9.25 crore rupees of capital invested in moneylending. In the same year, rural moneylenders (*sahukars*) made up almost 20 per cent of the income tax of the province with 5,998 moneylenders taxed upon an income of 170 lakh rupees driven by a capital of 13 crore rupees. In three districts (Karnal, Rothak, and Gurgaon), moneylenders made up 60 per cent of those taxed.[74]

Apart from the professional moneylenders in the rural areas (the *sahukars* alluded to above), the passage of the Punjab Alienation of Land Act provided an incentive to landlords to start engaging in moneylending: in the case of default by the debtor, the landlord's holdings would increase. In a survey carried out in 1928, 19,000 people reported themselves to be agriculturist moneylenders. One thousand of these were Muslims, but the large majority were Sikh Jats. In the military recruitment districts of northern Punjab, the large proportion were again Muslim. The Banking Committee recognized in its report from the year that the agriculturist moneylender posed the greatest danger to the spread of cooperation, as he was 'strongly impelled to oppose it, and being a Jat among Jats can oppose it more effectively'. On the part of the peasant, there were certain advantages to dealing with moneylenders as opposed to cooperatives, including ease of borrowing, no limit on the amount of the loan, secrecy in dealings, negotiable terms of repayment, no investigation into the object of the loan, and more bargaining power available to the peasant while negotiating interest rates.

An important aspect of the cooperative movement was the attitude of the British government towards the moneylenders. Initially, the government was hesitant in allowing them membership in cooperative societies, and in 1905 it was felt that 'the danger that their object may be to crush a society which they may regard as a dangerous rival, must be carefully guarded against. The professional moneylender should, His Honour thinks, in no case be allowed entrance into a society, or any voice in its management'.[75] It was noted that moneylenders were opposing the movement in some districts. For example, in Karnal, moneylenders spread the rumour that whoever joined a society would be sued at once on either a real or fictitious claim and treated with the greatest severity allowed by law.[76] On the other hand, some moneylenders complained that after the passage of the Punjab Alienation of Land Act, the status of the agriculturist moneylenders (who were mostly Jat landlords) had improved, while the professional moneylenders were suffering. For example, in Hoshiarpur, the Khatri and Brahman professional moneylenders' lot worsened and the agriculturist Jat moneylenders enjoyed a privileged position.[77]

By 1907, however, it was noted that there was a general tendency not to allow moneylenders admission into cooperative societies, even when the societies were not restrictive otherwise, admitting people from various castes and religions. The report for the year mentions how:

> The *zamindar* is aware of the superior cunning and intelligence of the moneylender, suspects his motives in joining and fears that he would soon wreck or control the society. Village *kamins* are sometimes admitted.... In some instances however if Hindus found a cooperative in a mixed village, only Muhammadans join. This is especially the case where a Hindu Jat *zaildar* founds a society in his village. He is rarely a prophet among his own brethren but for all that may be trusted by his Muhammadan neighbours.[78]

However, by the following year, 1908, the tune had changed again, and officials were advised to involve the moneylenders in the movement. The report for the year mentions how:

> ... there can be no question as to the advantage of enlisting the sympathies of the village moneylender. That he should show a certain amount of hostility to the movement is inevitable though the Registrar perhaps takes an exaggerated view of its intensity. But the *sahukar* is an excellent businessman and knows that the courts cannot recover for him anything like the amount found to be his due, and if he is convinced that financing a cooperative bank at a moderate rate of interest is an absolutely safe investment he will probably be willing to seek through its agency a suitable means of employing his capital.[79]

Perhaps this was partially because moneylenders were seen to misrepresent the movement and turn people away from it. However, despite this wavering attitude and misgivings in the reports, there was no attempt to pass any legislation or take concrete measures to check the power of the professional or agriculturist moneylenders, or their practice of refusing to accept repayment in order to keep the peasant in debt and compound the overall amount owed. In the report for 1909, the case of some professional *sahukar*s and 'Muhammadan Shylocks' of the landowning class was mentioned who refused to 'take payment of old debts just as they often refuse to accept redemption of mortgaged land. Legislation is required to meet such refusal: for it is quite inequitable to compel a man to remain in debt when he is able and willing to pay. Otherwise, one cannot object to the *sahukars'* not unnatural hostility'.[80]

In some cases, the moneylenders were undermining the movement very concretely. For example, the report for 1911 mentions such a case:

> ... when a *zamindar* owing money to a moneylender joins a society and gets a loan, his creditor puts him into court and gets a decree against him, not payable in installments as is usually the case, but in a lump sum, the idea of course being that the society will have to find the money. This idea is more often than not fallacious but the principle underlying the order is unfair to the societies and should I think be discountenanced.[81]

Yet in the same breath it is also said that 'the moneylender of course still resents the existence of societies, but so long as he keeps within bounds one cannot object to this and he too is coming to recognize the value of the societies as deposits by his class are becoming more frequent'.

In short, there was little effort to combat the power or influence of the moneylender, and the officers were content to act as observers. There is a passing anxiety at the continued grip of the moneylender and especially on the growth of the agriculturist moneylender, but the cooperative movement is never positioned to displace the moneylenders. This calls into question the aims of the movement itself and whether it was indeed meant to be an effective bulwark against usurious loans and indebtedness. Without a frontal attack on the moneylending classes, it was unclear how cooperation was intended to combat the scourge of indebtedness, except by providing credit for debt servicing. It also gives credence to the cynical belief that the Punjab Alienation of Land Act was passed to facilitate the agricultural elite of the province to allow them to occupy the land of poorer peasants by becoming their source of credit before the peasant's default.[82]

Local Responses

It is simplistic to refer to the Punjabi peasantry as one category, given the very different types of cultivators, tenants, and landlords who were involved in agriculture in the province. The generic term *zamindar* (landowner) may be used to make some general observations, however. The *zamindar*s were initially suspicious of the cooperative movement, thinking it might be a ploy by the government to take hold of their money, but over time, the criticism and reservations changed. A chief complaint was the long process involved in obtaining a loan from the cooperative bank, compared to the moneylender where no such obligation was present. The peasants also disliked the rigid payment deadlines and the requirement that the payments be in cash: the moneylender was generally more flexible, frequently altering repayment schedules or accepting things in kind. Peasants also disliked the visits by the officials of the cooperative department to their homes, which caused their debts to become public and a matter of embarrassment. (The moneylender usually kept dealings private.) Another objection was the leading role influential men in the village took in the committees, which shook the confidence of poorer peasants and weakened the avowed aims of social equality under the movement. The key advantage from the point of view of the peasant was the assurance of fair dealings and a fixed interest rate, but the attendant obligations and procedures made the option less favourable. The strictures on how the loan money was to be spent were also often excessive. For example, borrowers were not allowed to spend the loan money on any charitable activity.[83]

Part of the criticism of the cooperative banks arose from the fact that there were indigenous modes of cooperation already prevalent in the Punjab but which operated along very different lines. A few indigenous societies were fairly prosperous, generating enough revenue for constructing public works in their area of operation. For example, five societies founded in the Mianwali district in 1900 were flourishing, while in Hoshiarpur a society had existed since 1892. The latter was founded by a Sikh named Hira Singh and was regarded as the most prosperous cooperative society in the Punjab, though it never received any official support or patronage.[84] All the landlords of the Una Tehsil in Hoshiarpur (numbering 55 in total) joined the society and farmed common land, using it to relieve mortgages. Through a monopoly of moneylending by the committee and the influence of the members, it was able to handle domestic expenses, including wedding expenses, of its members, and also advised them on financial matters. In a conversation with the surveyor Ata Ullah, Hira Singh said:

> ... that the interference in the domestic affairs of his village is the society's most popular feature. His opinion is that there is no one more pleased than the borrower who gets an advance of only Rs 150 when he asks for an advance of Rs 1000. He satisfies his pride by asking for a larger advance and by abusing the Committee for their want of generosity and has the genuine satisfaction of having saved a considerable amount of money.[85]

Another indigenous effort was the Dhandla Fund in Mianwali. It was the most prosperous and well-managed fund in the district with a membership of 130 and funds amounting to 1,200 rupees.

There were also several Indians who joined the official efforts to spread cooperation, and, in the report for 1907, the registrar extols the contributions of

> ... Munshi Nabi Bakhsh Arain of Jullundur. Instinctively interested in the success of the movement he has worked tiringly and incessantly to explain the merits of cooperation at all times and places. Even on the railway where he has spent many weeks, he has gained several disciples. Since the new year his work has been most onerous. In February and March he was often compelled to work from early in the morning till late at night in thoroughly explaining all details and assisting people to form the bye-laws of their societies, which is no easy task in the Central Punjab, where people want to know the object of every bye-law and make many suggestions for their improvement.[86]

These examples of some responses to the idea of cooperation point towards the different ways in which cooperative ideas percolated through to the imagination of the peasantry. Whether it was through the independent setting up of indigenous societies or the voluntary support of the official societies, cooperation found its share of supporters in the hinterland and the major districts. Frustration with bureaucratic procedures and paperwork were responsible for undermining the movement as well as definitional issues.

Conclusion

Indebtedness in the Punjab led to a dual response: a legal and institutional response that was primarily championed by local politicians, and a grassroots cooperative movement encouraged by the state. Neither succeeded in making much headway against the problem of rural indebtedness, but both efforts demonstrated certain facts: first, the legal–institutional system was malleable and was being altered at the same time as a grassroots, community-based movement was taking hold – that is, it buttresses a central claim of this book regarding the simultaneity of institutional change and economic development. At this point in time, the failure of the cooperative movement was not due to an inherited colonial 'system' blocking socio-economic progress, but the underlying causes behind that convenient euphemism are detectable: a lack of resources, political will, commitment, and ideological biases. Unionist politicians were content with curbing moneylending and improving trading conditions instead of undertaking land reforms that would alter both the power dynamic and the distribution of resources in the rural economy. The colonial state was likewise comfortable blaming the peasant for a lack of thrift and discipline instead of initiating a robust programme for welfare and reducing the revenue demand.[87] Indebtedness provided a convenient social problem that allowed both the state and the landed elite to pass laws and set up credit societies that were palliative in nature and not too close to home to cause any fundamental change in power relations.

Second, the policy responses to indebtedness, whether the legal changes or the cooperatives, show the power of the 'individual' in achieving legislative reform or fostering a widespread rural programme. Chhotu Ram and Sikandar Hayat were able to woo over the landowners as well as the state to pass the laws against indebtedness, just as Darling and Calvert continued to spread the cooperative ideal throughout the Punjab. In both cases, the efforts proved insufficient, but they still depicted the heights and limits to which individual endeavour could have influence. Policy debates in the legislative council and among officials unveiled where opposition lay and how far reform would be tolerated.

A full understanding of economic reform must uncover the policy debates on which the reforms are predicated. The reservations and concerns expressed at this stage are relevant not only for understanding the meaning of policy change but also in appreciating how its implementation may be affected. The colonial case makes this extremely necessary, precisely because the debates are often not between elected representatives of the people but imperial bureaucrats viewing the world through the various ideological commitments.[88] From across the seas, John Maynard Keynes emerged as a strong advocate of cooperation despite the lack of evidence in its favour.[89] The backing of powerful intellectuals and enthusiastic bureaucrats allowed cooperation to be championed ahead of any other state-sponsored programmes of providing relief to the peasant. This humanizes the discourse on policy reform where individual agency, enthusiasm, and charisma are just as relevant as the letter of the law and official reports. During the implementation of reforms by bureaucrats, human agency is crucial, and this is also the stage where success or failure of reforms is determined.[90] The cooperative movement highlights these issues dramatically with the debates and anxieties of colonial officers, the landed elite in the Punjab, and security officials concerned with maintaining law and order, all impacting the work on the ground.

An important point about the cooperative movement is the close similarities it bears with more contemporary drives of community development. In the 1950s and 1960s, the notion of 'community' emerged as a source of inspiration for undertaking intensive programmes of rural development. Many of these were sponsored by the American government.[91] Interestingly enough, the two decades are now associated with theories of modernization, which advocated industrialization, large-scale development projects like dams, and the efforts at community development, much like the earlier colonial preoccupation with cooperation, lie forgotten. Modernization theory called for the replacement of small-scale traditional societies with mass, industrialized societies, but even while programmes supporting this were being initiated throughout the developing world, a strong movement for community development was also underway. By 1954, the United States had established a community development division within its foreign aid agency and, by 1956, this department was providing financial and personnel help to 47 community development programmes in 23 countries.[92] Interestingly enough, while colonial cooperation failed to eradicate indebtedness, the cooperative societies enjoyed an afterlife in Pakistan and retained a positive image in the poorer sections of society. In 1991, however, Prime Minister Nawaz Sharif was involved in the cooperative societies scandal where 700,000 poor Pakistanis lost their savings when these societies were declared bankrupt having given loans to Sharif's industrial group.

A final point can be made about the limited historical memory regarding the cooperative movement in the Punjab. It does not feature in any of the major economic or political histories of the region, and, indeed, when microfinance was introduced in the last two decades, it was seen as something new and unheard of. In many ways, microfinance replicated the earlier experiments with cooperation and met with the same, if not worse, consequences. Mass peasant suicides in India among borrowers of microfinance institutions shook the initial faith in the phenomenon, but no attempt was made to learn from earlier efforts at providing cheap credit. This may be true for development economics as a field in general which is forward-looking and ahistorical, presuming that the ultimate cure is yet to be found through theoretical innovation rather than a humble engagement with what has occurred and failed already.

Notes

1   David Graeber, *Debt: The First 5000 Years* (New York: Melville House Publishing, 2011).

2   W. R. S. Satthianadan and J. C. Ryan, *Cooperation: Oxford Pamphlets on Indian Affairs No. 39* (Oxford: Oxford University Press 1946), pp. 1–3.

3   Satthianadan and Ryan, *Cooperation*, p. 5.

4   See Department of Revenue and Agriculture Proceedings 1901, Punjab Government, Lahore, Punjab Archives, File No. 1.

5   Proposal to establish agricultural banks in the Punjab, Department of Revenue and Agriculture Proceedings 1901, Lahore, Punjab Archives, File No. 9. The reservations were shared by several other district officers as well and are described in the same file.

6   Annual report on the working of cooperative credit societies in the Punjab for the year ending 31st March 1905 (Lahore, 1905), Islamabad, National Documentation Centre, p. 1.

7   Annual report on the working of cooperative credit societies in the Punjab for the year ending 31st March 1905 (Lahore, 1905), Islamabad, National Documentation Centre, p. 2.

8   Letter no. 605 dated the 15th October 1908, from the Junior Secretary to the Financial Commissioner, Punjab, Lahore, Punjab Archives.

9   Annual report on the working of cooperative credit societies in the Punjab for the year ending 31st March 1909 (Lahore, 1910), Islamabad, National Documentation Centre, p. 1.

10   Annual report on the working of cooperative credit societies in the Punjab for the year ending 31st July 1910 (Lahore, 1911), Islamabad, National Documentation Centre, p. i.

11   Annual report on the working of cooperative credit societies in the Punjab for the year ending 31st March 1919 (Lahore, 1920), Islamabad, National Documentation Centre, p. 15.

12   Annual report on the working of cooperative credit societies in the Punjab for the year ending 31st March 1921 (Lahore, 1922), Islamabad, National Documentation Centre, p. 6.

13   Ata Ullah, *The Cooperative Movement in the Punjab* (London: George Allen & Unwin Ltd, 1937), p. 49.

14   Annual report on the working of cooperative credit societies in the Punjab for the year ending 31st March 1919 (Lahore, 1920), Islamabad, National Documentation Centre, p. 21.

15   C. R. Fay quoted in Ullah, *The Cooperative Movement in the Punjab*, p. 22.

16   Annual report on the working of cooperative credit societies in the Punjab for the year ending 31st July 1923 (Lahore, 1924), Islamabad, National Documentation Centre, p. 7.

17   Annual report on the working of cooperative credit societies in the Punjab for the year ending 31st July 1924 (Lahore, 1925), Islamabad, National Documentation Centre, p. 10.

18   Annual report on the working of cooperative credit societies in the Punjab for the year ending 31st July 1925 (Lahore, 1926), Islamabad, National Documentation Centre, p. 10.

19   Annual report on the working of cooperative credit societies in the Punjab for the year ending 31st July 1920 (Lahore, 1921), Islamabad, National Documentation Centre, p. 5.

20   Annual report on the working of cooperative credit societies in the Punjab for the year ending 31st July 1928 (Lahore, 1929), Islamabad, National Documentation Centre, p. 3.

21   Annual report on the working of cooperative credit societies in the Punjab for the year ending 31st July 1938 (Lahore, 1939), Islamabad, National Documentation Centre, p. 2.

22   Annual report on the working of cooperative credit societies in the Punjab for the year ending 31st July 1926 (Lahore, 1927), Islamabad, National Documentation Centre, p. 5.

23   Annual report on the working of cooperative credit societies in the Punjab for the year ending 31st March 1907 (Lahore, 1908), Islamabad, National Documentation Centre, p. 8.

24   Annual report on the working of cooperative credit societies in the Punjab for the year ending 31st July 1920 (Lahore, 1921), Islamabad, National Documentation Centre, p. 12.

25   See coverage in *The Pioneer*, 17 February 1916, Islamabad, National Archives.

26   Clive Dewey, 'The Official Mind and the Problem of Agrarian Indebtedness in India, 1870–1910' (unpublished Ph.D. dissertation, University of Cambridge, 1973).

27   Annual report on the working of cooperative credit societies in the Punjab for the year ending 31st July 1913 (Lahore, 1914), Islamabad, National Documentation Centre, p. 9.

28   Annual report on the working of cooperative credit societies in the Punjab for the year ending 31st July 1919 (Lahore, 1920), Islamabad, National Documentation Centre, p. 22.

29   Annual report on the working of cooperative credit societies in the Punjab for the year ending 31st July 1920 (Lahore, 1921), Islamabad, National Documentation Centre, p. 21.

30 Annual report on the working of cooperative credit societies in the Punjab for the year ending 31st July 1927 (Lahore, 1928), Islamabad, National Documentation Centre, pp. 39–40.

31 Annual report on the working of cooperative credit societies in the Punjab for the year ending 31st July 1926 (Lahore, 1927), Islamabad, National Documentation Centre, p. 30.

32 Annual report on the working of cooperative credit societies in the Punjab for the year ending 31st July 1915 (Lahore, 1916), Islamabad, National Documentation Centre, p. 1.

33 See details in the following chapter.

34 Annual report on the working of cooperative credit societies in the Punjab for the year ending 31st March 1909 (Lahore, 1910), Islamabad, National Documentation Centre, p. 11.

35 Annual report on the working of cooperative credit societies in the Punjab for the year ending 31st July 1913 (Lahore, 1914), Islamabad, National Documentation Centre, p. 1.

36 Annual report on the working of cooperative credit societies in the Punjab for the year ending 31st July 1916 (Lahore, 1917), Islamabad, National Documentation Centre, p. 3.

37 Annual report on the working of cooperative credit societies in the Punjab for the year ending 31st July 1917 (Lahore, 1918), Islamabad, National Documentation Centre, p. 11.

38 Annual report on the working of cooperative credit societies in the Punjab for the year ending 31st March 1908 (Lahore, 1909), Islamabad, National Documentation Centre, p. 11.

39 Annual report on the working of cooperative credit societies in the Punjab for the year ending 31st July 1921 (Lahore, 1922), Islamabad, National Documentation Centre, p. 6.

40 Annual report on the working of cooperative credit societies in the Punjab for the year ending 31st July 1923 (Lahore, 1924), Islamabad, National Documentation Centre, p. 4.

41 Annual report on the working of cooperative credit societies in the Punjab for the year ending 31st July 1923 (Lahore, 1924), Islamabad, National Documentation Centre, p. 5.

42 From the introductory remarks of H. P. Tollinton, Revenue secretary to government, Punjab, in Annual report on the working of cooperative credit societies in the Punjab for the year ending 30th June 1911 (Lahore, 1912), Islamabad, National Documentation Centre, p. 1.

43 Annual report on the working of cooperative credit societies in the Punjab for the year ending 31st July 1912 (Lahore, 1913), Islamabad, National Documentation Centre, p. 2.

44 Annual report on the working of cooperative credit societies in the Punjab for the year ending 31st July 1916 (Lahore, 1917), Islamabad, National Documentation Centre, p. 14.

45 Annual report on the working of cooperative credit societies in the Punjab for the year ending 31st July 1938 (Lahore, 1939), Islamabad, National Documentation Centre, p. 7.

46 Annual report on the working of cooperative credit societies in the Punjab for the year ending 31st July 1920 (Lahore, 1921), Islamabad, National Documentation Centre, p. 26.

47 Annual report on the working of cooperative credit societies in the Punjab for the year ending 31st July 1916 (Lahore, 1917), Islamabad, National Documentation Centre, p. 3.

48 Annual report on the working of cooperative credit societies in the Punjab for the year ending 31st July 1917 (Lahore, 1918), Islamabad, National Documentation Centre, p. 17.

49 Annual report on the working of cooperative credit societies in the Punjab for the year ending 31st July 1936 (Lahore, 1937), Islamabad, National Documentation Centre, p. 47.

50 Annual report on the working of cooperative credit societies in the Punjab for the year ending 31st July 1937 (Lahore, 1938), Islamabad, National Documentation Centre, p. 51.

51 Annual report on the working of cooperative credit societies in the Punjab for the year ending 31st July 1925 (Lahore, 1926), Islamabad, National Documentation Centre, p. 5.

52 Annual report on the working of cooperative credit societies in the Punjab for the year ending 31st July 1932 (Lahore, 1933), Islamabad, National Documentation Centre, p. 48.

53 Ullah, *The Cooperative Movement in the Punjab*, p. 48.

54 Ryan and Satthianadan, *Cooperation*, p. 1.

55 Annual report on the working of cooperative credit societies in the Punjab for the year ending 31st March 1907 (Lahore, 1908), Islamabad, National Documentation Centre, p. 2.

56 Annual Report on the working of cooperative credit societies in the Punjab for the year ending 31st March 1906 (Lahore, 1907), Islamabad, National Documentation Centre, p. 8.

57 Annual Report on the working of cooperative credit societies in the Punjab for the year ending 31st March 1909 (Lahore, 1910), Islamabad, National Documentation Centre, p. 2.

58 Annual Report on the working of cooperative credit societies in the Punjab for the year ending 31st July 1920 (Lahore, 1921), Islamabad, National Documentation Centre, p. 6.

59 Annual Report on the working of cooperative credit societies in the Punjab for the year ending 31st July 1923 (Lahore, 1924), Islamabad, National Documentation Centre, p. 5.

60 Malcolm Darling wrote numerous books and authored many other publications, including journal articles, essays in newspapers, and so on, on the predicament of the Punjab peasant. These are discussed in Chapter 3. His most famous book is *The Punjab Peasant in Prosperity and Debt*, first published in 1925, which ran through several editions and remains a classic. The central thesis is that the peasant lacks financial discipline, borrowing according to his opportunities, not needs.

61   Annual Report on the working of cooperative credit societies in the Punjab for the year ending 31st July 1914 (Lahore, 1915), Islamabad, National Documentation Centre, p. 2.

62   See details in the following chapter.

63   Annual report on the working of cooperative credit societies in the Punjab for the year ending 31st July 1913 (Lahore, 1914), Islamabad, National Documentation Centre, p. 1.

64   Annual report on the working of cooperative credit societies in the Punjab for the year ending 31st July 1924 (Lahore, 1925), Islamabad, National Documentation Centre, p. 4.

65   Denzil Ibbetson, *Punjab Castes* (Lahore: Superintendent, Government Printing, Punjab, 1916).

66   Quoted in Ullah, *Cooperative Movement in the Punjab*, p. 3.

67   Ullah, *Cooperative Movement in the Punjab*, p. 9.

68   Ullah, *Cooperative Movement in the Punjab*, p. 10.

69   Annual report on the working of cooperative credit societies in the Punjab for the year ending 31st July 1913 (Lahore, 1914), Islamabad, National Documentation Centre, p. 3.

70   Annual report on the working of cooperative credit societies in the Punjab for the year ending 31st March 1906 (Lahore, 1907), Islamabad, National Documentation Centre, p. 6.

71   Annual report on the working of cooperative credit societies in the Punjab for the year ending 31st March 1906 (Lahore, 1907), Islamabad, National Documentation Centre, p. 8.

72   Annual report on the working of cooperative credit societies in the Punjab for the year ending 31st July 1923 (Lahore, 1924), Islamabad, National Documentation Centre, p. 6.

73   Annual report on the working of cooperative credit societies in the Punjab for the year ending 31st July 1929 (Lahore, 1930), Islamabad, National Documentation Centre, p. 4.

74   Ullah, *Cooperative Movement in the Punjab*, p. 55.

75   Annual report on the working of cooperative credit societies in the Punjab for the year ending 31st March 1905 (Lahore, 1906), Islamabad, National Documentation Centre, p. 2.

76   Annual report on the working of cooperative credit societies in the Punjab for the year ending 31st March 1905 (Lahore, 1906), Islamabad, National Documentation Centre, p. 3.

77   Annual report on the working of cooperative credit societies in the Punjab for the year ending 31st March 1905 (Lahore, 1906), Islamabad, National Documentation Centre, p. 5.

78   Annual report on the working of cooperative credit societies in the Punjab for the year ending 31st March 1907 (Lahore, 1908), Islamabad, National Documentation Centre, p. 4.

79   Annual report on the working of cooperative credit societies in the Punjab for the year ending 31st March 1908 (Lahore, 1909), Islamabad, National Documentation Centre, p. 2.

80 Annual report on the working of cooperative credit societies in the Punjab for the year ending 31st March 1909 (Lahore, 1910), Islamabad, National Documentation Centre, p. 8.

81 Annual report on the working of cooperative credit societies in the Punjab for the year ending 31st July 1911 (Lahore, 1912), Islamabad, National Documentation Centre, p. 14.

82 This view of the Act was advanced by Norman Barrier who points towards the timing of the legislation. It was more than 15 years after the publication of Thorburn's findings in 1884 and also roughly 10 years after peasant revolts protesting indebtedness in the Punjab had subsided. The aftermath showed how it helped to aggrandize gains by the Punjabi landlords and it was suggested that they may have pushed for this legislation in the first instance.

83 Ullah, *Cooperative Movement in the Punjab*, p. 65.

84 Ullah, *Cooperative Movement in the Punjab*, pp. 1–2.

85 Ullah, *Cooperative Movement in the Punjab*, p. 6.

86 Annual report on the working of cooperative credit societies in the Punjab for the year ending 31st March 1907 (Lahore, 1908), Islamabad, National Documentation Centre, p. 11.

87 For a discussion of colonial perceptions of rural development, see Peter Robb, 'Bihar, the Colonial State and Agricultural Development in India, 1880–1920', *Indian Economic and Social History Review* 25, no. 2 (1988): 205–35.

88 See Clive Dewey, *Anglo-Indian Attitudes: Mind of the Indian Civil Service* (London: Hambledon Press, 1993), which details how Cambridge graduates taught at different points in the nineteenth century ended up having divergent views on *laissez faire* economics and capitalism, and how this training later impacted their performance as officers in the Indian Civil Service.

89 Anand Chandavarkar, *Keynes and India: A Study in Economics and Biography* (London: Macmillan, 1989), p. 41.

90 See C. A. Bayly, *Rulers, Townsmen and Bazaars* (Cambridge: Cambridge University Press, 1983) and the more recent Bhavani Raman, *Document Raj: Writing and Scribes in Early Colonial South India* (Chicago: Chicago University Press, 2012) for an account of how bureaucratic reforms are translated into everyday life.

91 See a detailed discussion of these programmes in the Postscript.

92 Daniel Immerwahr, *Thinking Small: The United States and the Lure of Community Development* (Cambridge, MA: Harvard University Press, 2014), p. 3.

5 | THE BUREAUCRAT'S BURDEN
Tales of Reform and Development

Take up the White Man's burden–
Send forth the best ye breed–
Go bind your sons to exile,
To serve your captives' need;
To wait in heavy harness,
On fluttered folk and wild–
Your new-caught sullen peoples,
Half devil and half child

—Rudyard Kipling, *The White Man's Burden*[1]

In February 1940, Sir Malcolm Darling, former Financial Commissioner of the Punjab and an expert on rural indebtedness in the province, delivered the presidential address at the first conference of the Indian Society of Agricultural Economics. Instead of a self-congratulatory speech on the many macro-level achievements of the imperial state in the Punjab (including the establishment of canal colonies, the construction of a vast railway network, and a phenomenal increase in agricultural output), Darling discussed the Punjabi peasant and the primacy that must be accorded to the *individual* in any sustained strategy of development:

> I have always been more interested in men than in things, in values than in value, in welfare than in wealth. Nor have I so much concerned myself with the way men should live as with the way they do live. Life is infinitely complex and even for oneself it is not always easy to say what is good and what is bad. I therefore feel a certain diffidence in prescribing for others, and in dealing with the peasant, my chief study, my object has been less to apply a spur than to hold up a mirror in which he might perhaps see his life as it is and judge for himself how far it should be changed. Finally I have

always sought contact with the individual rather than with the mass; the individual is more human and understandable, and ultimately the problem of human life is the problem of the individual.[2]

Darling's views on the Punjab peasant emerged from over 40 years of close study of rural life in the province, including numerous tours on horseback during which he had interlocutors from all walks of life. His book *The Punjab Peasant in Prosperity and Debt*, first published in 1925, remains a seminal account of indebtedness, replete with statistical data and ethnography of village life. He also wrote several other books and published numerous papers while being a career civil servant and continued to tour the Punjab even after his retirement. What emerged was a body of scholarship rich in insights even if it retains a crucial academic blindspot: an inability to critique the colonial state or policies systematically. Instead, Darling developed an understanding of rural poverty by focusing on the peasant and the improvement of his habits, thereby placing the blame of poverty and the burden of redemption on the peasant himself. Little wonder, then, that Darling was one of the foremost proponents of the cooperative movement in the Punjab, as it promoted an official agenda to cure rural impoverishment through self-help on the part of the peasant.

This chapter discusses some writings and private papers of Malcolm Darling, while interrogating reductive depictions of colonial officials as either blind proponents of economic liberalism or impotent executors of generally extractive colonial policies or both. In the context of peasant indebtedness in the Punjab, it refers to the experiences and efforts of a small but significant group of officers who sought to provide the peasant with relief from financial hardship as part of a larger effort to 'reform' his habits, customs, and worldview in other ways. A key part of these efforts was the system of credit cooperatives in the Punjab, which were initially used to provide an alternative means of borrowing for the peasant to the often usurious moneylender. Later, these credit cooperative societies became focal points of community reform in terms of education, hygiene, and 'better living' in general. Within this group of officers, approaches differed, with some being more prescriptive about the kind of changes the peasant needed to incorporate; others were fired with missionary zeal like Frank Brayne, while Darling remained a more earnest observer and was less high-handed in his approach. An important ideological commitment shared by the varying strains, however, was the belief that the onus of both poverty and remedial measures lay with the peasant; the state or local power structures never became the object of critique in any substantive way.

Retrospectively, this historical experience may be dismissed as an ultimately ineffectual ripple in the general tide of regressive development in the Punjab. The attempted amelioration of the peasant through setting up alternative sources of finance, like cooperative banks, and devoting manpower and resources towards the collection of extensive statistical data on the finances of the peasant, had negligible lasting impact. However, it is significant in its ability to illuminate discussions of the effects of colonial institutions on human development in the long run. Furthermore, the intellectual and administrative journeys of figures like Malcolm Darling help identify formidable bottlenecks in the institutional apparatus of the Punjab, which even these powerful officials were unable to overcome. This rekindles debates on the role of knowledge and power in the imperial project, and the practical limitations imposed by the ideological training of colonial officials in the design and execution of policies. In this respect, the discussion of these experiences enables an understanding of the precise constraints that hinder institutional reform and the sites of contestation in the design of policies and projects.

This chapter advances the study of debt and institutional change in the Punjab by analysing the career and writings of Malcolm Darling, as well as prominent contemporaries including F. L. Brayne. Darling continued to be associated with the subcontinent in the post-colonial era, consulting for various governments in South Asia as well as international organizations. His private papers also reveal deep intellectual engagements and friendships with people as diverse as John Maynard Keynes, E. M. Forster, M. K. Gandhi, Jawaharlal Nehru, and Allama Muhammad Iqbal. Through a close examination of the life and times of this idiosyncratic officer, we glean a history that often escapes the broad strokes of the brush-pen: the history of a contrarian, thinking officer; the stories of peasants encountered in various rural contexts; a glimpse into everyday economic life; and attempts at socio-economic reform. The close perusal of Darling's papers also reveals a longer and more interesting narrative: the making of a 'technocrat', the expert on poverty who gathers 'data', diagnoses poverty, and prescribes authoritatively. While Darling may have been spurred by personal intellectual interests, he was a harbinger of a post-colonial ethos of dispatching 'experts' to developing countries and commissioning wide-ranging 'studies' that constructed the intellectual problem of underdevelopment and its modern, usually Western, solution. This represented the academization of social issues, creating a culture of information gathering and scholarly publication. By locating Darling in a larger intellectual context, we observe how the omnipotent colonial officer transitions into the globetrotting expert, much as the examination of his earlier career in the Indian Civil Service provides lived expression of colonial economic reform in the Punjab from the perspective of the executor.

The chapter is divided into four sections: the first provides a brief biographical sketch of Darling and discusses his intellectual life as well as his contemporaries in the Indian Civil Service. The next section focuses on the vision of economic development shared by various officers and the primacy accorded to the peasant's habits and worldview. The third section discusses the role of cooperation, and the final section analyses how officials engaged with some of the institutional problems associated with reform.

Malcolm Darling and 'The Land of Regrets'

We have not yet come across any European gentleman of your parts – the model of plain living and high thinking – who unmindful of his high erudition and official position could condescend (so) freely, in sweet social intercourse, with those not quite of his own rank and station in life- a thorough-going Indian among the Indians. Such men carry about them an atmosphere of peace and goodwill which always tells. By sheer force of their angelic nature, they help bridge the gap between East and West.[3]

Malcolm Lyall Darling was born in 1880 to an affluent family, schooled at Eton, and later King's College, Cambridge. He was well-connected (his guardian was Sir Alfred Lyall, the former Lieutenant Governor of the Punjab) and well-read (he grew up in Bloomsbury, was intimate friends with E. M. Forster, and was a cultured humanist). In 1903, he took the civil service exam and was offered places in the civil service, both in England and in India. He later wrote that this presented the most perplexing decision of his life, but eventually he made up his mind to go to India because he thought he would despise himself if he feared to take the plunge and felt he was guided by instinct.[4] This led to a career spanning over 30 years in active service in the Punjab from his initial posting in 1904. Among the various appointments he held were the Chair of the Punjab Banking Enquiry in 1930, the vice chancellorship of Punjab University (in 1931 and 1937), the Chair of the Punjab Land Revenue Committee (in 1938), and the Financial Commissioner of the Punjab (1936–39). He was awarded the Companion of the Order of the Indian Empire (CIE) in 1934 and the Knight Commander of the Order of the Indian Empire (KCIE) in 1939. He published numerous books on the Punjabi peasant, including *Some Aspects of Cooperation* (1922), *The Punjab Peasant in Prosperity and Debt* (1925), *Rusticus Loquitur* (1930), *Wisdom and Waste* (1934), *At Freedom's Door* (1949), and the autobiographical *Apprentice to Power* (1966).[5] He remained active even after his retirement and became the Indian Editor of the BBC in England from 1940–44. In 1946–47, he undertook a tour of India on horseback to examine rural conditions in the lead-up to the British exit, the findings of which were recorded in his book *At Freedom's Door*. In the 1950s and 1960s, he consulted for governments in Greece, Egypt, Yugoslavia, Pakistan, and India, and remained involved in various committees in England. He died in London on 1 January 1969, at the age of 88.

In his private papers and diaries, Darling refers to the intellectual figures he looked up to and the influence they had on his conduct and career. Alfred Lyall greatly influenced Darling with his free-thinking ideas, and the intellectual context of Bloomsbury ensured that he was no closeted conservative. Darling had all the advantages of an affluent background, privileged schooling, and influential family connections that may have led to the expectation that he would be a conservative, establishment man. Indeed, at the start of his career, he was predicted to be as successful as his guardian and was also appointed in 1907 as tutor to an Indian *maharaja*, the Raja of Dewas, a small Maratha state, no mean feat for a junior officer. However, Darling was viewed with suspicion by his colleagues for his congenial attitude and deep friendships with Indians. In his book *Apprentice to Power*, Darling bemoaned the vibrant and intellectually stimulating conversations he was used to having in Cambridge and reflected on Anglo-Indian society and his inability to wholly assimilate to the 'club culture' of the *sahibs*: 'I never felt completely at home with Anglo-Indians,' he wrote in his diary. This echoes the remarks of his Cambridge tutor, G. L. Dickinson, who stayed with Darling on his visit to India: 'Anglo-Indian society is the devil – it's the women worse than the men. There they are, with empty minds and hearts, trying to fill them by despising the natives.'[6]

Before forming deep friendships with Indians and discovering his interest in the rural, Darling had a difficult time adjusting to his new life as a colonial officer. His diaries from the early years testify to this, and in one entry he writes: 'There are a few compensations out here, of which the chief is that you are somebody instead of being nobody at home.' At another point he quotes and muses over the following verses written by his guardian, Alfred Lyall, on India, in a poem titled 'The Land of Regrets':

> What lured him to life in the tropic?
> Did he venture for fame or for pelf?
> Did he seek a career philanthropic?
> Or simply to better himself?[7]

In an early letter, he discusses the problems of adjustment in greater and almost flippant detail:

> This letter is rather a wail, but one cannot help a spasm before becoming absorbed into this society. In a sense I feel I can judge it better now for not being in it than a year or two later when I am become a complete Anglo-Indian fossil. As it is, I feel it stealing upon me: I treat the servants more peremptorily (though still without the suggestion of an impending kick); I am learning to do nothing for myself, and in my spare moments I devise

subtle methods of employing the two servants whose lord and giver of life I am. The servants were a *chapraasi* (orderly) and a bearer … the question was how to keep them occupied. With the bearer, the meekest of men, when everything else failed, "I make him take off my boots". But with the *chapraasi* "it takes me a whole day to think of something to give him to do" and one day in desperation I sent him to the station for a time-table, though there was one at the Club two minutes away.[8]

Eventually, he became interested in the problem of rural poverty. Perhaps this interest can be traced to 1919 when, after the Jallianwala Bagh massacre, Malcolm Darling was one of the few serving colonial officers to criticize the killing of Indians. It is probable that the ill-will thus generated among the imperial administration unwittingly derailed what may have been as illustrious a career as that of his guardian.

Darling's private papers, including his correspondence and diaries, detail his many and varied friendships and intellectual relationships. One finds letters from Gandhi, Keynes, Nehru, and G. B. Shaw, and a burgeoning correspondence with his contemporary in college E. M. Forster. He not only cherished these connections for their friendship but also regularly sought opinion and advice on matters relating to governance and economic reform in the Punjab. These interactions enabled him to develop a nuanced understanding of socio-economic issues in India and also shaped his outlook on reform. In an article he wrote on 'Ethics and Economics' in the *Indian Journal of Economics*, he discusses Keynes and his ideas of capitalism as follows:

> Of modern capitalism Keynes says that it is 'absolutely irreligious, without internal union, without much public spirit, often, though not always, a mere congeries of possessors and pursuers.' And adds: 'one begins to wonder whether the material advantages of keeping business and religion in different compartments are sufficient to balance the moral disadvantages.'[9]

Not only did Darling seek Keynes's opinion on how to alleviate indebtedness among the Punjabi peasantry but he also discussed private matters with the economist. Keynes wrote to him in 1932, discussing the export of gold from India and also updated him on the progress of his son's education at Cambridge.[10] In a later memo, dated 8 February 1934, Darling kept notes of a wide-ranging discussion with Keynes on borrowing, cooperation, Marxism, and rural reconstruction. Darling mentions Keynes thus:[11]

> He [Keynes] was not a Marxian – he found it impossible to read Marx. A friend had marked for him passages of importance, but they were so dull

and so turgidly involved in the economic doctrines of 1840 that he had
found it quite impossible to get through Das Capital. He doubted whether
many Communists had read him. When I said that it sounded as dull as the
Koran, he agreed that it was just that.

Darling was also closely associated with the local intelligentsia and political leaders. His
diaries contain accounts of his first meeting with Muhammad Ali Jinnah, discussions
with Dr Taseer and the Communist poet Faiz Ahmad Faiz in Lahore, as well as with
prominent personalities like Sir Zafrulla Khan. Another close friend was the poet
Muhammad Iqbal whom Darling first met at the Coronation Dinner in 1911 and
who became a steadfast friend till his demise in 1939.

While writing his books on the peasantry, Darling wrote to local connections asking
for information and clarification on various points. The ensuing correspondence
testifies to the colonial officer's ignorance of many facets of social life in the Punjab,
even for someone as relatively well-informed as Darling. There is also a palpable
orientalist slant to some of the questions. In 1933, eight years after the publication of
his famous book on the Punjab peasant, Darling wrote to a Sikh *sardar* and, among
other things, asked the following questions:

> Is it correct that the Sikh Jat is the only tribe amongst our zamindars that
> can be called in any way businesslike?
> Touring through the Manjha in 1931 I was told that, if wives were beaten
> it was usually done with a stick? Is this the case generally in the central and
> southern Punjab? In the salt range I was told it was usually done with a
> shoe.
> At one place (Manan near Tarn Taran) I found that Brahmins were
> members of a society that called itself the Kamins' Credit Society. When
> I expressed surprise the Jat Sikhs there said the Brahmins were village
> servants. Is this typical of the attitude of the Sikh Jat to the Brahmin?
> Do you find the peasant anywhere beginning to take an interest in
> politics? When I toured in 1931, I found almost no interest. Has Mr Gandhi
> any following amongst either Sikh or Hindu peasantry?'

The *sardar*'s response to these questions was non-committal mostly – for example,
in response to the first question, he wrote: 'The beating of wives is a question of the
dead past. The only remnant of it is browbeating. The sticks and shoes stand buried
and the slap is a rare practice if at all. It is the same all over central Punjab.[12]'

Darling's private papers also contain many letters written to other officers in the
civil service, sometimes to discuss official matters. Lord Linlithgow sought his opinion

on whether the Punjab Alienation of Land Act should be repealed, as it enacted an arbitrary distinction between castes. Darling's response was characteristically nuanced, and he discussed the differential impact of the legislation in various parts of the Punjab while also pointing towards rising communalism which he felt deserved more urgent attention.[13]

Evidence of how different Darling was from most of his service peers can be seen in how his efforts to study the peasantry were perceived by fellow officers. When he wanted to tour India in 1946–47 on horseback to study conditions before the British left, the government of India refused to give him two horses to conduct the village tour, despite his repeated pleas even to the viceroy's office.[14] Some of his policy recommendations were also ignored. In 1942, towards the end of the Second World War, Darling suggested Britain repay its debt to India, a suggestion unlikely to appeal to the government:

> I have one more suggestion to make. During the last war India offered Britain a gift of £100 millions towards the cost of the war and I understand that £70 millions were actually paid. It would be a graceful gesture if at the end of this war Britain were to give India 100 crores – that is £75 millions – as a thank you offering for her assistance to us during the war.... I suggest further that the gift should be separately funded, perhaps on the lines of the Indian Famine Fund, and that the annual interest, which be in the neighbourhood of three crores, should be handed over to the Provincial Governments in proportion to population for expenditure on schemes for improving the lot of the Indian peasant.[15]

In 1943, he became involved in a heated debate with other civil servants while discussing Roosevelt's Four Freedoms and their relevance for India. Darling disagreed with the others about the importance of political freedom alone and discussed economic and spiritual freedoms as equally important for India. His responses display a sensitivity and deep understanding of the non-material forces shaping the worldview of the Indian peasant. Some extracts from this discussion follow:

> I should doubt myself whether any purely Western notion will suit India without a good deal of modification. I have seen too many Western notions going wrong there, for example, our legal system. I sympathise strongly with what Pundit Moti Lall Nehru said nearly twenty years ago: 'What I want (he said) is a system which is native to India and of which we have no experience in Europe and America.' We should remember too that India was the cradle of spiritual freedom, and surely in the post-war world spiritual freedom will be as important as any other kind of freedom? ... if

the post war world is to be settled mainly on a materialistic basis, that won't suit India, or indeed many of us over here.

Steed: But can one safely mix up religion and politics?

Darling: Perhaps not religion and politics, but surely ethics and politics. In India religion and ethics are virtually identical, and they have always been mixed up with politics. No one there had so great a hold upon the popular imagination as the saint.

Steed: I suppose Mahatma Gandhi is an example of this?

Darling: This is the secret of his influence in the village, as has been the case with many others in the past. To the Indian peasant – and he numbers nearly 300 out of India's 400 millions – spiritual freedom has always been the thing that ultimately mattered, as remote from his daily life no doubt as the great Himalayan peaks but dominating the background of his mind. Of other kinds of freedom he has thought little – of political freedom not at all … in India, poverty is so great that for the ordinary man, whether in the fields or the bazaar, to fill the belly is the paramount consideration. Everyone who goes to India from England for the first time is horrified at the contrast. 'It burns like acid into the brain' is what one observer said recently….There has not been nearly enough reverence in the past for the common humanity of everyday people.[16]

Even after his retirement, Darling remained actively involved in various committees and commissions. He was invited to join a committee set up by the Colonial Office, Downing Street, on cooperation in the colonies in 1946 and served successive three-year terms till 1959. In 1952–54, he was invited to join a mission of the International Labour Organisation (ILO) to Pakistan to study agricultural conditions. He remained convinced that cooperation could play a vital and transformative role in rural uplift. In 1956, he was sought by B. H. Farmer of the Ceylon Commission on matters relating to proprietary rights in the Punjab. In 1960, he consulted for the Pakistan government. The Indian Planning Commission also sought his expertise for the technical cooperation scheme part of the Colombo Plan of 1956.[17]

These many official assignments and academic predilections also fed into Darling's scholarly output. Apart from the books mentioned earlier, he wrote numerous articles in academic journals and other magazines. These ranged from his experiences in Italy, Ireland, India, Turkey, Bulgaria, Yugoslavia, Austria, and so on,[18] to his ideas regarding cooperation and its uses. He also gave regular radio broadcasts (for example, one on *The Peasant and Politics* was given in 1951).[19] His books were widely reviewed in newspapers, magazines, and journals across Europe and India, from publications as varied as the *Manchester Guardian*, the *Statesman*, Royal Asiatic Society, and academic journals of economics. His private papers contain notes on his extensive travels in

Europe and Asia and also on his reading on other regions. One finds detailed notes on rural conditions in Denmark, Japan, Palestine, Persia, Burma, Hungary, Russia, Italy, England, China, Switzerland, and Ireland; and, in India, Orissa, Uttar Pradesh, Maharashtra, Bengal, and Oudh. Some of the most interesting are his detailed notes on his horseback tour of 1,400 miles in 1946–47. Darling spoke of this tour at a conference in Oxford in 1951 as follows:

> 'Why do you ride on horseback?' I was asked as I set out from Peshawar. A pertinent question, which some of you may ask again. To answer it I must go back 20 years to when, as Registrar of Cooperative societies, my chief concern was the welfare of the Punjab peasant. Twice in those days I rode 700 miles or more from village to village, learning all I could about the peasant's way of life – the first step I thought towards helping him to improve it. I soon learnt how little I knew and even when the rides were done I felt I had only touched the fringe of all there was to know for peasant life is as varied as nature's with roots as deep.... The tour was I think the most strenuous thing I ever did – I was almost 66 when we started but it was the most interesting.[20]

Possibly due to his generally humble and scholarly disposition, Darling never became a passionate social reformer as some other British officials of the time, such as F. L. Brayne. Fired by a religious Evangelical streak, Brayne was the architect of the Gurgaon experiment in the Punjab, which was intended to reform the 700,000 residents of the Gurgaon district near Delhi into industrious and frugal workers. Brayne designed pamphlets for sanitation and hygiene, devoted himself to long hours and ambitious projects, and single-mindedly blamed the poor for their condition: 'Mr Brayne told the agriculturists in the plainest of language, without any beating about the bush, where their defects lay. He told them they were poor because they were extravagant and wasteful.'[21] While referring to him, Gandhi wrote to Mahadev Desai in November 1929: 'That man's zeal amazes me.' And in Brayne's own writings, the solutions were clear: 'What has uplifted rural England? The lamp of culture was kept alight, the example set to others, and the work started by the selfless work of the country parson.'[22]

However, even an individual like Brayne, who was self-motivated, energetic, and enjoyed a moderate degree of influence, felt the implacable character of the imperial state. Even in the short run, Brayne's efforts proved worthless and were criticized generally: 'The Gurgaon Experiment must be pronounced virtually a failure. The reform was superimposed from without. Mr Brayne put as much pressure as he could upon his subordinates and upon the people themselves, but the conviction so essential to success was lacking.'[23]

F. L. Brayne was a front runner in the cooperative movement in the Punjab as well as a pioneer of what became generally known as 'rural reconstruction'. The term Brayne preferred to use was 'village uplift'. Like Darling, Brayne wrote a series of books and pamphlets popularizing his ideas, though his work was more missionary in approach and less intellectual in its treatment of rural problems.[24] Towards the end of his 40 years' service, he joined the Indian Army and attempted to implement his ideas among the sepoys on how to improve their homes and villages. He is most known for the Gurgaon experiment, which became a landmark attempt at community development, though it ultimately achieved little. In a note on the development of Gurgaon, Brayne summarized his thoughts as follows:

> Development therefore means first and foremost uplift. Teaching the people how to spend their money, how to clean their homes and villages, how to make their homes healthy and comfortable, how to avoid ill health and epidemics, how to bring up their girls and boys in health and cleanliness, how to educate them and how to lead happy, healthy and rational lives.[25]

Brayne's many publications elaborate on his ideas of the kind of life the peasant should lead. Like most of officialdom at the time, he agreed that it was the peasant's own habits and lifestyle that were the cause of his poverty. Brayne emphasized the importance of change from below, beginning with a peasant's home: 'Instead of planning from above downwards – and perhaps never reaching the home – we must start from the home and plan from below upwards.'[26] He went on to say:

> In spite of the introduction of railways, metaled roads, telegraphs, canals, schools, colleges and hospitals, of agricultural, veterinary and health departments and all the machinery of modern administration, village people in many countries still refuse to change their ways.... The new money produced by canals and other improvements either brings idleness or is spent not on libraries, flower gardens, education or maternity homes, but on gold and silver ornaments, litigation or bursts of extravagance at weddings and other occasions which leave generations of debt in their wake.[27]

He continued: 'One is tempted to say "Happy people! Why disturb them?" Their happiness however is only superficial and is too often the listlessness of malnutrition, malaria, hookworm or debt. At best it can only be short-lived.'[28]

While Darling shied away from prescribing for the peasant, Brayne was very clear on where the problems lay and what needed to be done: 'The task is to make not merely a few pioneers but the whole population change its age-old ways. The villager's conservatism has been proof against all the efforts so far made to induce him to change his ways and to try new things and improved methods.'[29] He bemoans the negative use made of the prosperity in the canal colonies:

> The canals that brought life-giving water to the Punjab Colonies should also have brought civilizing missions to teach the people how to use their new wealth to raise their standards of living. As it was the new money was spent in the old way. Gold ornaments replaced silver, the law suit was carried to the High Court instead of stopping in the District Court, weddings and other social ceremonies were celebrated with incredible extravagance and debts were multiplied.[30]

In another publication, Brayne stated his aim as follows: 'Our object is not to make rich but to make happy. We only try to remove poverty as poverty brings disease, misery, suffering and unhappiness.'[31] He went on to discuss the many defects of the peasant and the vision of rural development he had:

> The increasing of the wealth, however, without the radical changing of the ideals and habits of the people is utterly useless. The Gurgaon people have no idea how to spend the money they have now so what is the use of giving them any more until we have taught them not to waste their money on useless ornaments, useless display on marriages, funerals and other ceremonies, useless litigation and so on! Development therefore means first and foremost UPLIFT, teaching the people how to spend their money, how to clean their homes and villages, how to make their homes healthy and comfortable, how to avoid ill health and epidemics, how to bring up their girls and boys in health and cleanliness, how to educate them and how to lead happy, healthy and rational lives.[32]

Brayne criticized the peasant's habits and also pointed out defects in government policy:

> Not only does Government omit to attack the standard of living itself but it never attempts to describe the standard which its beneficent plans are aimed to produce.... The usual method for drawing up plans is to call upon the departments of Government to produce 'schemes.' These are listed and sent to a Committee which is dominated by 'finance.' Those schemes which least embarrass future budgets are chosen for execution and the rest are pigeonholed.[33]

Brayne was a passionate advocate of national planning and believed it should rest on rural foundations. He was also motivated by his religious beliefs in the design of such plans:

> The reformer's task is to put to the people a picture of a new manner of living which is so obviously better, not merely in his eyes, but in their eyes also, than their present way of life that they will gradually consent to do all the extra work, the saving and scraping, the breaking of the chains of harmful custom, and the laying aside of besetting sins, which will be necessary for the achievement of the new standard of desire.[34]

He goes on to write:

> Christianity, by linking home with the kingdom of Heaven, exploits the most powerful incentive of all to the intensification of human effort and endeavor. Not only does it teach the dignity of labour and encourage hard work and good craftsmanship but it teaches mankind to work to the glory of God.[35]

He was also in constant communication with church representatives in India, encouraging them to open schools and supported the design of a village education course that sought to cure the peasant's bad habits (from litigation to lack of friendly spirit) through Biblical stories.[36]

In an appendix to the work *The Peasant's Home*, Brayne describes his village utopia in great detail and sees his mission as necessary and divine. In another publication, *The Neglected Partner*,[37] he focuses on the role of women and their place in rural reconstruction. Two of his leading books were *Better Villages*[38] and *Village Uplift in India*,[39] which discussed the Gurgaon experiment in detail. Brayne also published several other books and pamphlets, including *New Weapons for Old Enemies: How Malaria Can Be Defeated by Paludrine, DDT and Gammexane*[40] and *Cooperation, Waste and Craftsmanship*. Brayne focused more on popularizing his remedy for rural reconstruction and had no ambiguity about what needed to be done: his approach was motivated by a religious zeal and a sense of authority which focused less on producing academic monographs and more on practical actions and endeavours to improve rural conditions. Brayne would emerge as a pioneer of community development, and in a discussion in *Vilayatpur*, a book focusing on a Punjabi village by Tom Kessinger, the author writes:

> A deputy commissioner in several districts in Punjab, Brayne used the power of his office to implement schemes for rural uplift including the

construction of manure pits, latrines, chimneys on fireplaces, and the like. Brayne considered villagers lazy and unenlightened and sought to motivate them to self-improvement through propaganda and strict supervision. Malcolm Darling, another British civil servant familiar with rural conditions, was critical of Brayne's characterization of villagers and his methods because he did not involve local residents in his schemes.[41]

However, Brayne gained a wide following in the 1930s, and probationers in the Indian Civil Service attended a course on 'Rural Reconstruction in India' before setting sail for India. Bill Cowley, an Indian Civil Service (ICS) officer, recounts in his memoirs how he was taught economics at Cambridge by Pigou and Keynes, as well as a special subject for part two of the Tripos on the 'Economic Development of India' by C. R. Fay. A few years later, Cowley joined the ICS and attended the seminar on 'Rural Reconstruction for Probationers'. After being posted in India, he met Brayne in Gurgaon and prefaces the meeting thus:

> There were only two people from the Punjab whose names I had heard of before ever coming to India. One was F. L. Brayne, an ICS man who had spent many years in Gurgaon as Deputy Commissioner, and devoted himself to the improvement of village life and farming. His enthusiasm for manure pits and latrine was a source of some amusement to many of his colleagues and he never received in the Punjab the recognition he deserved. But his work became known in many other countries and his influence lasted longer than that of many more orthodox and more highly decorated contemporaries.[42]

Malcolm Darling's approach to the problem of rural poverty was quite different from Brayne's. Driven by an academic interest in the problem and a natural reticence to prescribe and impose, he encouraged the growth of the cooperative movement in the province as the way to provide peasants with cheap credit and provide an alternate source of finance to them, freeing them from oppressive contracts with local moneylenders. Like Brayne, Darling was convinced that it was not merely an economic problem that had to be solved but a moral or spiritual one – one which necessitated sustained, long-term commitment from the state. And so, the cooperatives set up in the Punjab were more than economic entities. C. F. Strickland referred to the peculiar nature of these cooperatives as follows: 'Cooperative societies for economical purposes are familiar throughout the world; the peculiarity of the Punjab movement is the formation of moral societies.'[43]

The Punjab Peasant

Malcolm Darling's lasting contribution remains his lifelike studies of the Punjabi peasant, and his notes, diaries, and publications reveal the underlying attitude towards the peasant's situation. This section builds on the earlier engagement in this book with cooperation as the preferred official response to peasant indebtedness and its similarities with more contemporary attempts at 'community development'. It explores the centrality given to this vein of reform and the underpinning commitment it rested on: blaming the peasant for his lot. It also looks at differing reactions within the colonial bureaucracy to cooperation: some viewed it as a vessel for imposing their vision of the 'good life' on the peasant. For example, Brayne approached the problem of rural backwardness with a missionary impulse to civilize the peasant. Darling treated it as an intellectual problem, admitting no simple solution, even as he promoted the cause of cooperation.

Darling's approach differed from the dogmatic or paternalist policy of officers like Brayne, and even as he advocated the adoption of cooperation on a wide scale, he remained cautious and willing to reconsider his opinions. At a speech delivered at the 21st session of the UP Cooperative Conference in 1937, he said: 'We must feel for the peasant, for without feeling there can be no understanding, and if we do not understand him, we shall certainly mislead him, and also ourselves.'[44] He was also aware of the slow pace and rigidity of rural life in India and fully conscious of the long period of sustained effort needed to dismantle some of the entrenched exploitative relationships in the countryside. In the same speech, he said: 'Great patience is needed and patience is at present an unfashionable virtue. Five year plans are popular enough but who is prepared to support a 25-year plan? Yet this is the very least that is needed to build up the habits of mind and character which are the only sure foundation for a system of cheap and abundant credit.'[45] Statements such as these not only indicated that the root cause, according to Darling, was the peasant's own faulty habits but also that no structural or bureaucratic change was deemed necessary to improve rural conditions.

In a later article on the Indian peasant, Darling discussed the essentials of village life in India:

> The motto of the modern world might be – God proposes, man disposes. With the Indian peasant man hardly even proposes.... All this illustrates some of the most characteristic traits of village life in India: its essential kindness, its great hospitality, its quarrels, its absence of privacy, its interest in religion, its superstitions, its readiness to follow good examples, its naivety and finally – what trick must I play? So many tricks have been played upon the peasant since Joseph made the Egyptian peasant give up

his land and cattle for bread that no wonder the peasant has been forced to resort to tricks in return. But the chief moral is his response to selfless devotion.[46]

So while retaining a friendly and sympathetic attitude towards the peasantry, the official position also remained one of calculated observation: to ensure that matters did not worsen to the point of rebellion or unrest, while at the same time peddling the dogma of cooperation and self-help as the solutions to poverty.

Darling felt that the Indian peasant was essentially apolitical and strongly influenced by his religious worldview. In an article titled 'The Peasant Strength of India', he wrote:

> Man, said Aristotle, is a political animal. This may be true of urban man, perhaps even of western man, but it certainly is not true of the Indian peasant. On the contrary, he is essentially a non-political animal. He has always "let the legions thunder past" and plunged into work again – the work of wrestling for daily bread with a despotic and capricious nature. But great changes are taking place. His life is no longer bounded by the distance that a horse or a bullock-cart or a small donkey will take him in a day.[47]

During his presidential address at a conference of agricultural economics in 1940, he echoed these sentiments and further let slip a sense of superiority expected from a colonial officer, however sympathetic: 'If however the Indian peasant is illiterate he is certainly not deaf and not always dumb.'[48]

In a letter written to a relative in 1933, Darling mentioned his conversations with junior officers as well as some observations on the peasant. He wrote:

> When we approach the village, if we have been brought up in the town or in the school of commercial and industrial economics, we must divest ourselves of our urban notions and realise that, in India at least, the village is of greater importance than the town and far more acceptable to the bulk of its people.[49]

While colonial officers varied in their views on how the peasant's lifestyle could be changed, most of them shared the idea that such change was necessary. Henry Calvert, another officer at the forefront of the cooperative movement, wrote:

> No substantial improvement in agriculture can be effected unless the cultivator has the will to achieve a better standard of living and the capacity in terms of mental equipment and of physical health, to take advantage of

the opportunities which science, wise laws and good administration may place at his disposal. Of all the factors making for prosperous agriculture, by far the most important is the outlook of the peasant himself.[50]

He goes on to describe various aspects of the peasant's life that need reform, including religion: 'The Punjab is poor because it is not organised on the lines that lead to wealth. Such organisation as has existed has been more or less military, designed to preserve in power the dynasty of the day or religious.'[51]

In one of his books, *Rusticus Loquitur*, Darling discusses the necessity to reform the habits of the peasant while framing it in the colonial belief that some castes were superior to others:

> The very word credit implies character and where it does not exist, it is as demoralizing to borrow as it is dangerous to lend. This is the difficulty in depressed districts like Muzaffargarh and Gurgaon. On the one hand, the peasant cannot shake off the yoke of the moneylender without money; on the other, he cannot be trusted voluntarily to repay the smallest sums. Even small sums, therefore, can only be advanced when close supervision is possible. It is safe to say that had the Punjab peasant everywhere the character and intelligence of the peasant in Jullundur, he could be advanced twice as much as can safely be given at present. The money is there, or could probably be found, but character and intelligence in sufficient degree are lacking.... To build up the character of the peasant and develop his intelligence is therefore indispensable to the cure of his financial ills, and once this is done money will flow freely enough into the village.[52]

These examples indicate the firm belief of the officers engaged in rural reconstruction that it was the peasant's worldview and habits that was the root cause for his financial ills. Such an approach automatically dropped the state and political elites from the equation, which fulfilled the overarching imperial need to maintain stability in the province.

Cooperation in the Punjab

Darling was one of the strongest proponents of introducing cooperation in the Punjab as a means of social and economic uplift and made a thorough study of cooperation in other parts of the world to devise mechanisms most suited to the local context. He was closely associated with the cooperative movement in the Punjab, which started in 1905 with the setting up of the first cooperative credit society. In 1947, when the British exited India, there were 170,000 societies with nine million members. However, this amounted to less than 15 per cent of the population of the country. The movement was most entrenched in Bombay, Madras, and the Punjab. Darling's private papers contain a wealth of information on the movement in the province and all over the world. His own interest in the subject started at Cambridge under the influence of Alfred Marshall, the economist, who viewed cooperation as the only means of reducing inequality. Darling was well acquainted with Marshall's pupils as well, including Pigou, Keynes, and Fay;[53] the latter also visited him in the Punjab to examine cooperation there. Over the years, Darling became a global authority on cooperation, touring and consulting in various countries in Africa, the Middle East, Europe, and South Asia. He met other experts and intellectuals, including the Italian Prime Minister Luigi Luzzatti who had started the first cooperative bank in Italy, the Banca Popolare, or People's Bank of Milan.[54]

The cooperative movement in the Punjab started with the Village Thrift and Credit Society based on the German Raiffesian model that Darling championed – that is, there was unlimited liability, no immediate disbursement of profits, and operations were restricted to one village. His connection with the movement in the Punjab began in 1915 when he started a central cooperative bank in a district. Darling believed the Raiffesian model was essential to break the power of the moneylender and he discussed how:

> Our first object was to free the peasant from the stranglehold of the moneylender – to give him economic freedom rather than raise his standard of living. The moneylender had existed in India from time immemorial, *but until the British came he had been the servant, and not the master of the village.* With the introduction of the rule of law, the positions were reversed and bonds signed in their ignorance by an illiterate peasantry became a millstone round their necks. By 1900 it could be truly said that the vast majority of peasants were born in debt, lived in debt and died in debt. An enquiry made 18 years later showed that nearly 80% of the peasant proprietors of the Punjab were in debt.... Compound interest was particularly insidious in its effects. At 25%, a very general rate, a debt will double in less than 3.5 years and at 60%, a not impossible rate, a debt of £1, as Professor Marshall once pointed out, will become £100 in 8 years.[55]

Initially the cooperative societies were viewed with suspicion by the villagers, and Darling recounted how they felt that this was a device by the government to take away their money. He mentioned a particular instance of this in a 'remote upland village':

There was no hospital, school or post office within ten miles, but many moneylenders. No one had the least idea what was meant by a village bank – some dodge the thought of government's to take hold of their land and cash. What would government's share of the profits be? I was asked. They looked at me incredulously when I said – none.[56]

Darling also discussed how it was difficult to spread cooperation among an illiterate peasantry. But he chose to take an optimistic view of the situation, considering that cooperation would lead to better financial management and later autonomy: 'It was not the least advantage of a thrift and credit society, or village bank as we called it, that it did something to educate its members in the use of money and in the management of their own affairs. In this way it was capable of becoming the foundation of self-government in the country as a whole.'[57]

There is exuberant mention of societies that were doing well. This gives an insight into the day-to-day working of these societies and how they impacted the borrowers. Darling discussed one successful society in the following terms:

Where all these difficulties were overcome, the results justified our highest hopes. Take for example the village of Madar in the Punjab. A society was started there in 1908 with 19 members. 20 years later over 100 of the 150 families in the village had joined it. The majority were small peasant proprietors who owned on the average no more than 8 or 9 acres each. But the society was open to all who lived in the village and amongst its members were potters, carpenters, dyers, oilmen, watermen and sweepers. In these 20 years, it had accumulated over £2000 in shares and reserve and had distributed £2500 in dividends. It had also contributed to the paving of the village lanes, till then often a quagmire of mud and water, and it had even led to a thrift society for women.

It seemed the entire brunt of welfare policy in the Punjab would be soaked by the idea of cooperation. Yet it can be wondered why an experienced officer like Darling felt it would be so transformative without any structural change in the truly exploitative relationships otherwise continuing in the villages – for example, between landlord and serf, *patwari* and cultivator, judge and petitioner, and so on. And not all cooperative societies were performing well as Darling acknowledged:

There were bad societies as well as good. Take for instance this society formed of only 10 members, some rich, some poor. On paper everything smiled: in 10 years a capital of over £2000 has been accumulated. The rich president and his family had invested £900 in shares. But they had borrowed £1350, what was worse they had encouraged the poorer members to borrow too, and when they didn't repay, they bought in their lands.[58]

The failure of the movement, however, was in part blamed to nature and the temperament of the peasant, in a manner characteristic of the colonial officer using caste stereotypes to understand the locals. Darling wrote:

> For the peasant it must be admitted that his difficulties were often overwhelming. A hot climate does not make for energy, and generations of despotic government do not make for self-reliance. These two factors alone are sufficient to account for the fatalism of the East; but there is a third which makes fatalism almost inevitable – a devastating nature, very different from the capricious goddess who rules over us here, destroying crops wholesale by drought or flood and man and beast by disease. In addition there is caste with all its restrictive taboos. Let me take the 10 defaulters in a society I saw many years ago. The first had lost all its cattle and was working as a coolie, the second had taken a lease at too high a rent, the third had repaid his moneylender and had nothing left for the bank; the fourth was a minor, the fifth had too large a family; the sixth was down with fever; the seventh was the victim of a cheating contractor, the eighth went mad and was in an asylum; the ninth lost half a dozen members of his family from plague and cheered himself by spending £75 on marrying two of the survivors. Finally the tenth admittedly frankly that he had been idle for two years.[59]

At another point, while musing over the limited success of the movement, he noted:

Our two great mistakes were

1. Not to link credit more closely with thrift – greater effort should have been made to get local deposits.
2. Not to give our staff more training. The importance of the second was early recognised in the Punjab, but the first was an almost universal defect.

But somewhere in between the misplaced enthusiasm and glorified hopes associated with cooperation were buried stories of individual endeavour, and it is to Darling's credit that he sought to engage with many different peasants, society managers, inspectors, and landlords to gain a real sense of the impact of the movement. He mentioned the difficulties of finding worthy leadership among the peasants and then wrote:

It is rare to find a good society in the Indian village without a good leader.... What good leadership can do is shown by another Punjabi. Allah Rakha as he was called, inherited only 3.5 acres from his father but by dint of hard work and thrift, he was able in time to buy another 12 acres. He then became headman of his village and it was at the very moment when the cooperative movement started and he became interested in it. He got together nine of his neighbours who all agreed to form a society but when the time came to pay their shares, they all ratted. Undeterred, he got together nine more on a promise that he would pay up their shares for them; he also offered to deposit with the society a mortgage loan of £23 which he had just been repaid. And so the bank was launched. But this was only the beginning. The mornings he spent on his land, but after the midday meal when others took their rest, he went about preaching the gospel of cooperation. 'Cooperation has cast a spell on him' was his neighbours' comment. The result was the birth of societies grouped together in a banking union, with deposits when I saw it, of over £7000, and within a 5 mile radius of his village, 85% of the householders had become cooperators. But, alas, such men are rare anywhere.[60]

Such descriptions and details are reminiscent of accounts of projects of community development in South Asia in the 1950s and 1960s, where the struggles of individuals and households were deified as success stories. Just as community development projects transitioned into a nationwide movement in the 1960s, the cooperative movement also spread to urban areas with the establishment of urban credit societies. There was tremendous opportunity for this, as rapid urbanization had meant many towns did not have any banks at all. Darling mentioned how, in India by the 1930s, such urban societies numbered 650 with nearly two million members 'and a working capital of £30 million as against £18 million in agricultural credit societies. There were over 4,000 industrial societies for weavers, carpenters, potters tanners and suchlike. All these societies deal primarily in short term credit. For long-term credit there are 260 cooperative land mortgage banks.'[61]

Perhaps most interesting are the notes from his tours around various villages and his conversations with peasants. Often these presented a different picture than the official account and statistic. For example, in 1930–31, while touring the Shahpur district, Darling had the following exchange:

The president of the thrift society thought that the Rural Community council was doing some good, and said that the number of improved implements in the village had increased owing to its propaganda; but when

I asked one of the best type of zamindars who had attended a meeting at Bhalwal what he had heard at it, he said he remembered nothing.[62]

Darling continued to support the cooperative movement in his retirement and in his account of a conference on agricultural cooperation remarked: 'What was most impressive was the conviction of all present, repeatedly expressed, that for the farmer, whether in Europe, Asia, Africa or America there could be no improvement in welfare without cooperation.'[63]

The transition from a purely financial entity, meant to alleviate the peasant's lot by providing an alternative to borrowing from a moneylender, to a tool of welfare had occurred to Darling while serving in the Punjab. Indeed, he dwelt less on the financial impact of the movement and more on the changes in the social practices and relationships brought about through cooperation. In an article on 'Ethics and Economics' published in 1928, he described cooperation in a Punjabi village as follows:

> A year ago enquiry in a Rajput village showed that a population of 824 spent something like Rs 1200 a year upon tobacco; and it was estimated that if smoking were stopped for 25 years, enough would be saved to give the village a small dispensary, a veterinary hospital and a middle school, and even to pave the village lanes. When this was brought home to the people, they decided to form a co-operative Better Living Society to wean themselves from the habit of smoking. This case may not be altogether typical but a good judge estimates that a Sikh with an average holding saves in tobacco enough to pay his land revenue, and what is even more important, he saves a great deal of time.[64]

Non-credit societies were established on a large scale in the Punjab in the 1930s, and Darling mentioned societies set up to achieve various aims while addressing the UP Cooperative Conference in 1937:

> Two years ago, the Punjab and Bengal were the only two provinces where non-credit societies exceeded a thousand. Twenty years ago the moneylender was so powerful that we all felt that our first object must be to free the cultivator from his domination, and that this was the best way of increasing the cultivator's income and raising his standard of living, since it would mean less borrowing and far lower rates of interest. But we did not realise sufficiently the cultivator's voracious capacity for borrowing and his persistent tendency to default. The fall in prices, which also we could not

anticipate, has laid these two weaknesses painfully bare and compels us, I think, to view the problem of raising his standard of living from a somewhat different angle. Even before the fall in prices we had started Marketing Societies to procure him better prices for his produce, Arbitration societies to protect him from the ruinous cost of litigation, Better Living Societies to reduce extravagant expenditure on social ceremonies, Cattle Breeding Societies to increase his income from cattle, and Consolidation Societies to consolidate his small and greatly scattered holdings. [65]

Darling charted the evolution of cooperative credit societies from financial entities designed to 'free the peasant from the stranglehold of the moneylender' to Better Living societies to free him from the stranglehold of custom. He wrote:

> We began to realise this when we saw how often loans were being made in our societies for marriage and other social ceremonies, loans that could only be classed as unproductive.... By 1947 over 2000 Better Living societies had been formed in the Punjab, primarily to reduce expenditure on social ceremonial to reasonable limits but ultimately to provide villages with better conditions of life. Extremely varied were their activities, touching education, sanitation, ventilation, the improvement of drinking wells, the deepening of village tanks, and the repair of temple and mosque, occasionally even the provision of a small library. One society, which consisted solely of untouchables, had only two rules – one that members should brush their teeth once a day, and the other that they should wash themselves once a week. Before they formed their society they were unapproachable to anyone with a nose, but when I inspected them we sat almost cheek by jowl without the slightest inconvenience on my side.[66]

Interestingly, despite his close observance of rural conditions, Darling bought into the prevalent colonial discourse of the peasant suffering from debt due to his indebtedness. An obsession with cooperation as the tool to reform the peasant's habits and financial dealings aided this perception. Nowhere does Darling question the land revenue demand or taxation, or the role of privileging the military, the landlords, and the bureaucracy in the Punjab. The monetization of the economy and the sudden vulnerability of the peasant to international grain prices also do not figure into his analyses, and he is instead content with an increasingly specialized treatment of cooperation as it sprouted into many societies with multifarious aims. The only real anxiety that keeps surfacing is the thought that increased cooperation may fan communist sentiment in the province, and Darling is noticeably perturbed by the thought. In an account of the development of cooperation in his notes, he writes: 'One must remember too that without cooperation all along the line the Indian peasant cannot hope to obtain any large measure of economic freedom. The only alternative is Communism, but at what a price!'[67]

It is interesting to note that Darling's faith in cooperation was shared not only among others in the civil service but also by local activists and thinkers. Darling's ideas were not dissimilar to initiatives promoted later by the Gokhale Institute, for instance, or Rabindranath Tagore in the Bengal.[68] The micro approach, focusing on individual households and villages, would also later become the hallmark of the community development movement.

Institutional Backwardness and Economic Reform

Darling's notes and diaries contain vivid descriptions of life in the countryside and the power wielded by landlords over their tenants. These allow an appreciation of how power was distributed in the rural areas and how, despite awareness of the inequalities and corruption, the colonial state did not attempt to address it through its agenda of economic reform. In a diary from the 1930s, Darling discusses the power of the big feudal families of the Noons and Tiwanas while on a tour of the Shahpur district:

> At Bhalwal the Tahsildar who knows the tehsil well says that most of the Tiwanas and Noons will advance grain or money free of interest to their tenants and settle their disputes – they are mostly Honorary Magistrates … few do much for their lands. Umar Hayat is liked because he helps the poor as well as the rich but his son, Khizar Hayat is hated because he is hard, and miserly and wenches with the womenfolk of his tenants. He is the only one who does this badly. The Noons are much better than the Tiwanas but even they hold a bit aloof from the people: the Tiwanas are very bad in this way, give themselves great airs and think scorn of the mean estate. They mostly show favour too in the courts.[69]

Such observations are made without any criticism or need for reform. Darling also recorded his observations of landlords and moneylenders in other diaries. This allows a further lens through which to view indebtedness in the Punjab in this period. Not only does he recount the situation in specific villages and tribes but he also covers the issue from various angles. In his notes on his tour on the Hajipur subdivision, he mentioned how all the affluent *zamindars* were without debt and had assumed the role of moneylender after the passage of the Punjab Alienation of Land Act. He mentioned how the *zamindar* extracted both interest and unpaid labour from the indebted peasant while 'his ultimate aim is to get their land'.[70] In the Gurdaspur district, he noticed a similar trend among the agriculturist moneylenders who charged high interest rates and took little interest in cultivation. He also noted that the Lyallpur district, the richest in India, was also heavily indebted with an average debt of 4,000 rupees to 5,000 rupees per head.[71] The same entry also mentions the reform being championed by the zealous colonial officer F. Brayne in unflattering terms:

> The Tahsildar here, a Wahraich Jat from Jalalpur Jattan (Gujrat) was till a few months ago Tehsildar of Jhelum. He spoke at length about Brayne's methods there ... most of the people used by Brayne are Khatris and Hindus who are not in sympathy with the zamindars. All around him work simply to curry favour with him, not from real love of the work.[72]

A crucial aspect of studying debt relations during this period was the violence usually perpetrated against a moneylender by a village community. Court records from the period are replete with cases in which moneylenders were attacked, killed, or their property destroyed. Darling also recounts a murder case which shows the social position of the moneylenders vis-à-vis other members of rural society in the district:

> The bank had been severely shaken by a murder case and sitting on the ground in front of me were the two alleged murderers ... the story they told was this: a moneylender in the next village lent the stripling's father a sum of money which was still unpaid when the father died. A suit for Rs 1800 followed but on a plea of minority was rejected. Undaunted the moneylender got the young man's cousin into his clutches and obtained a decree against him for Rs 1500. One day he came with a large party to execute the decree and arrest the cousin. This led to a fight, and his death. A savage fight it must have been, for the High Court judgment shows that he received 23 injuries, two of which fractured his skull. Both sides complained to the police but as the moneylender was clearly dead, the complaint from his side was taken up and the other filed.... The sessions Judge found them all guilty and sentenced the two first to be hung and the two blue beards to twenty years' imprisonment ... and yet they were hardly criminals in the western sense of the word, for in India a moneylender who presses a false or an extortionate claim to extremes places himself outside the pale of village law, and this is one reason why 34 moneylenders have been made away with this year in the Punjab.[73]

The account shows the precarious position of the moneylender despite the exploitative power that he may exercise by taking peasants to court. In a close rural community, he was still the outsider whose life and property were at risk from a close-knit group.

The Darling papers illuminate various other social issues in the Punjab, such as the prevalence of corruption, the religious beliefs of peasants, the colonial obsession with inculcating 'thrift' and how the populace reacted to it, political consciousness among the Punjabi peasants, and so on. The following section explores some of these themes and excavates the diaries and notes for developing an understanding of these.

Religion, Ethics, and Finance

For Darling, the indebtedness of the peasant was not just a question of financial ruin but a moral one. He notes: 'It is now not so much a case of achieving material progress as of arresting a manifest spiritual decline.'[74] He was deeply interested in the role of religion in the life of the Punjabi peasant and sought to study the religious traditions of the region and how they were practised. His notes contain extensive quotations from the Quran, the Bible, the Hindu scriptures, and so on. He made extensive notes on the concept of usury and how it was perceived in the local religions. For Hinduism, he notes: 'The universal belief of Hindus is that men who die without discharging their proper debts become sons of their creditors in their next birth and extract their dues in the shape of parental obligations.' Of Islam, he wrote: 'Islam impresses me after reading a substantial part of the Koran as essentially an ethical code, designed moreover for a people of simple habits, who lived mainly by pasture, a little by trade and hardly at all by agriculture and who were in constant danger of attack from their enemies.'[75] He goes on to say:

> [The Muslim] must neither pay nor accept *riba*.... This is typified by the reply of a Maulvi to a member of the cooperative department who offered him alms that he would accept nothing from one who served an organisation which allowed the taking of interest. The other party is in favour of distinguishing between interest and usury and of allowing the one and forbidding the other. The question whether a Muslim may lawfully become a member of a cooperative society which charges but does not pay interest had already been decided by the highest Muslim authority in favour of the cooperative society [See Annual Report on the Working of the Cooperative Societies of the Federated Malay States 1925–26, p. 12–13].... In the Punjabi Muhammadan is beginning to take interest like any ordinary moneylender. The Khojas of Chiniot and Sharakpur have long been known for this and are said to be even more exacting than the Hindu Sahukar. In excuse for the Khoja it may be said that he was once a Hindu and has always been a trader. But it is not the Khoja only who takes interest. The Pathan moneylender has penetrated as far as Ceylon, and all over the

Punjab the Muhammadan peasant with spare cash is beginning to advance loans at interest.[76]

He noted how despite the religious stipulations, Muslim moneylenders in the Punjab also charged interest, especially the Pathans who operated all over India and the Khojas from Chiniot who were regarded as 'even more exacting than the Hindu Sahukar'.[77]

Darling also observed the impact of economic change on ethical considerations:

> In India too the boundaries between ethics and economics are shifting but in the contrary direction, that is to say, in favour of economics ... the word morality however it would regard as almost synonymous with custom one example of which I may give you, as it illustrates the tendency when economic conditions become fixed for religion, ethics and custom to be fused into one. In a part of the Punjab, where a certain religious body had made some way amongst the cultivators I asked the village headman whether the effect had been good or bad, he replied at once that it had been bad. And when I asked him, in what respect, expecting to hear of some deterioration of character, he added solemnly that the funeral feast on the thirty-ninth day after death was no longer observed.[78]

In other places, he had made notes on usury, polygamy, extravagance, and alms in the local religions, including Hindu proverbs like 'agriculture is the best life and service the worst'.[79] The pervading concern was to see how a better understanding of religious precepts would help improve the financial behavior of the peasant. While addressing the UP Cooperative Conference in 1937, Darling remarked:

> The problem of agricultural credit is, indeed, not to find more money for the peasant but to teach him to use it economically and productively ... in the Punjab I have again and again found peasants of the most modest means able to borrow at 12 percent on their mere personal security, and the reason invariably given me for this by their creditors was that they could be trusted to repay punctually.[80]

In other notes, he writes:

> Cheap credit is a blessing to a rural population only where the average cultivator is possessed of the knowledge and strength of character required, to induce him on the one hand to limit his borrowing within the range of his capacity to repay, and on the other to apply the greater part of the borrowed money to sound productive purpose ... the solution of the problem of

indebtedness is only to be found in the cumulative effect of the spread of literacy and in the cooperative movement.... Any permanent cure must touch the 'root problem' which is that the peasant doesn't understand the use of credit.[81]

Based on the European experience, Darling also lamented that 'perhaps the most serious of all the difficulties confronting Indian agriculture is the lack of an agricultural aristocracy and of an educated agricultural middle class. Many of the great advances in western agriculture are due to men of this type'.[82] However, he did not reflect on this further to suggest how the inequalities in society may be reduced or how this middle class would emerge from economic transformation.

Corruption and Official Resistance

When we poor blacks take bribes, we perform what we are bribed to perform, and the Law discovers us in consequence. The English take and do nothing. I admire them.

—E. M. Forster, *A Passage to India*[83]

Darling also provides material on corruption in colonial Punjab, both among the locals and the British. In a letter written in 1934, F. Brayne wrote to Darling, describing the situation with great concern:

I have rather strong views on the question of corruption in Government Services. It is certainly difficulty to exempt the public of their share of the blame, but I think, and most others think, that Government has not done a fraction of what is should or could possibly do in the matter. I know that it is an up-hill task but like every big thing done or attempted in India during the course of the last century it has to be done by Government. I think the position admits of no further pause it is time to act and act strongly.[84]

This and similar correspondence help dispel certain notions about corruption in colonial India, for instance, that it was a problem of the lower ranks only. Darling's papers contain correspondence that discusses the prevalence of corruption at all ranks of the service. The letter is typical of Brayne's style, in its zeal and enthusiasm for improving the situation. He begins by detailing how horrendous an occurrence it is:

Corruption in the government departments is one of the saddest subjects a man has to think, speak or write about. The very contemplation of it makes one's heart sick and the prevalence of it constitutes the worst weakness of the British rule in India – its very shame. The cup is full and indeed stinking.... I do not quite agree nor is it the opinion of the most who get canal waters that corruption is confined to "more or less petty officials." Though the hand that receives the money is mostly the hand of the Patwari, the pocket that holds it ultimately is of the man behind the chicks. The money percolates as does water in the channel and sometimes regular accounts are kept and rendered. It is not possible to find out or say exactly how many are dishonest. But the general opinion is that majority of them in the Canal are not above board. The Patwari – small man though he is—is the golden key that opens most locks. In himself he is too weak to refuse remissions where due. He is strong in the strength of his patron and the patron is safe behind the special circumstances of the situation.

This extract questions the prevalent discourse around corruption which saw it as a problem of petty native functionaries, absolving more senior officers. Brayne openly acknowledged that the precedent for corruption arose from the habits of the more senior officers and it lay well within their power to do more about it. He then lapsed into religious metaphor to discuss the situation further:

The corrupt officials are quite a big class now. They have developed a system and a science of their own and nothing but a drastic action and a bold policy will avail. And, for a Christian Government the remedy is not far to seek – "if thy right hand offend thee, cut it off and cast it from thee." To make this possible the first necessary step as suggested by you is the simplification of procedure to bring the offenders to book. Without this no roughing on a large scale is possible and the sword laid bare half the battle will be won.

Such a discussion of moral decrepitude testifies to Brayne's religious motivations for reform in the Punjab. However, he also realized the nature of power and how sometimes the lower rungs of bureaucracy act against peasant interests, not due to corruption but out of a fear of government, which did not always champion rural interests:

Speaking of the 'difficulties of the struggling cultivator', I should say that corruption in services though an important factor is not the only factor that deprives him of legitimate relief in matters of payment of land and water rates when crops fail. The most honest official even is apt to think that relief to agriculturists means so much loss to the Government.

A loss to Government means a discredit to himself. Obsessed with this prejudice in favour of – shall I say fear of – Government, he is unable in 9 cases out of 10 to do justice to the helpless farmer. This weakness always present is more pronounced now when the budgets are becoming more difficult to balance.... Only a few months back I happened to by a Canal Rest house. The S. D. O. was also there and there was a big gathering of the people wanting to see him. The hail-storm having done a very bad damage to the standing rice, he was required to inspect the crop. The S. D. O. (an honest man on all accounts) was a bit shy to go out and see. I felt necessary to approach him on behalf of the Zamindars and was shown a telegram pulling him up and warning him against exaggerated stories of losses. The wordings were somewhat ominous but the official read more into them than the apparent. I told him this but the reply was "You are not in the Line." I thanked God I was not in the line. The budget considerations obsessed all sense of honour and fair play and there was weighing with false weights and false measures. The same happens frequently on the revenue side. Touring in one of the Ambala tehsils last year I was informed of the high arrears of land revenue and found the staff unusually active in its collections. There was no money with the people and some of them had little to live on. Why was the demand fixed when the crops fared so bad? The position was thus explained by the R.A. with whom I was staying – "At the time of Girdwari we counted on the sale of Gold. We find it now that most of it had left already." It was not the grain in the field but the gold on the wife's ears that dictated the entries in the Girdwari. This happens very often and I am not sure whether it is the corruption or such psychology of the official mind that deprives more the cultivator of his just share of the relief.[85]

This demonstrates how the autocratic nature of governance in the Punjab prompted even the local bureaucracy to be harsh and unhelpful, tendencies which undermined progress and made conditions oppressive for the peasant. Unfortunately, while this discussion could take place in personal letters being exchanged between officials, it did not impact the path of economic reform, which continued to castigate the wasteful and lazy peasant, expecting him to better his lot without any structural change in the surrounding political and economic structure. There was occasional criticism in newspapers about corruption in government.[86]

Darling recounts other instances of corruption in his diaries. In October 1945, he wrote:

We stood at his gate for some time talking. He had been negotiating a large purchase of land in Sind. Everything had been arranged when there was a sudden change of Minister and all had to be begun again. 'It cost me 10,000 rupees,' he said significantly, this led him to talk about the widespread corruption, of which everyone speaks. There is a flood of money flowing through the country, and the Europeans, especially the army, (he said) are as bad as anyone. He told Linlithgow that the British are getting as much loot as possible before they clear out of the country – 'the last phase', he described it.[87]

His daughter, April Darling, who accompanied him on the horseback tour in 1946–47 presents a more sanguine picture of British rule in her account of a conversation with a *sirdar*:

> Father asked him about a problem which has been worrying him during the last few days, as he has been reproached sorrowfully and indignantly again and again when he has told people like Zaildars, safedposhs, etc of our intention to quit India. He quoted Muzaffar's remark and also the plea made by a number of peasants that we who had given them insaf (justice) could not now leave them to the wolves. The sirdar questioned the fact of our having given them Insaf and was entirely critical of our legal system. He did however admit that Englishmen tended to be more impartial and fairer than Indians, also that the people who had spoken to Father of 'insaf' were sincere although he did not think that by 'insaf' they meant justice but rather security.[88]

Such a discussion captures the extent to which the people could discern the entrenchment of local elites within the colonial structure. It also points to the room for discretionary authority, which could make the judicial system fair or unfair depending on the person in charge. Even with detailed laws and penal codes, the governing structures admitted such arbitrary exercises of power and made institutional change in the Punjab personal, even as it had a modern and bureaucratic façade.

The Brayne papers catalogue the bureaucratic obstacles and steady official opposition to his schemes of rural uplift. While giving evidence before the Royal Commission of Agriculture in 1927, Brayne said:

> First I would insist with all my power that no improvement of agriculture is of any use whatever without uplift.... Government is so entangled and obsessed with paper work that the percentage of gazette officers able to visit the villages themselves and gain any first hand knowledge and experience of actual rural conditions is infinitesimally small. To show the immense difficulties in the way of rural uplift and development I may give the case of Gurgaon district. For six years I have been struggling by every

means in my power, by official, demi-official and private correspondence, by interviews, with officials and ministers, by the front door and by the back door, by the good officers of members of council and with the help of the press, and I may say that as far as getting official recognition of the necessity for developing the district and for getting Government help for uplifting the people I have cut extremely little ice in return for many years of overwork. I sent up a development scheme in 1922 and again in 1926 and yet again in 1926 I asked for instruction to submit a scheme for a party of the district rapidly becoming depopulated from continued neglect. The first and the last Government refused to contemplate and the second has, I believe, been pigeonholed. Six years is an exceptional period for any official to stay in a district and if so little can be done with Government in six years you can imagine how little those with local knowledge can ever hope to effect.[89]

He further said:

The attitude of Government towards the proposals of local officers is not always that of sympathy and support. The work is all centralized, the central offices are overworked, local schemes increase work and are, therefore, likely to be unpopular.... A great obstacle to progress is the rapid transfers of the Deputy Commissioner's assistants, often with complete disregard of the Deputy Commissioner's wishes and the work in hand. As soon as the Deputy Commissioner has trained an assistant for his uplift campaign he may be immediately moved elsewhere and the result is the Deputy Commissioner's work is continually being spoilt in a most disheartening manner.[90]

The difficulties were not just at superior levels of administration but also among local officers who did not want to be burdened with additional work in connection with rural reconstruction. Commenting on the situation, Brayne wrote that deputy commissioners were 'squealing before they are pinched' and 'they would be the first to resent any action taken in their districts independently of them and yet they strongly object to being asked to do anything themselves. We therefore reach a deadlock: rural reconstruction must stop and rather must never start'.[91]

A most graphic illustration of the opposition from fellow officers can be seen in Brayne's correspondence with F. Wace, Registrar of Cooperative Societies in the Punjab, in 1935. On a note from Brayne on hygienic defecation as part of a village uplift scheme, Wace pencilled in the comment: 'Need one have so much on defecation?' Brayne wrote a passionate three-page letter in response, describing why he considered the matter important from the point of view of hygiene and self-dignity. He concluded the letter by saying: 'I have answered your question. In return will you now have the gist of it tactfully put into Urdu and published in your cooperation magazine?' Wace replied: 'My dear Brayne, I call this too sweet. But if you want to exhibit the national bottom to cooperators I don't see why I should have the task of wiping it first. Personally I should sent it to the poetry review and call it "A Rhapsody on Shit".'[92]

The difficulties were financial as well as attitudinal. In December 1939, Brayne's request for a development loan was turned down with the comment that 'a development loan during the war is an impossibility'.[93] In 1943, Brayne wrote to a fellow officer about the provincial demands for development expenditure. He wrote:

> I have been feeling for some time very much in the same way as you have and I had become very hopeless of ever getting even an acceptance by the provinces of what we were prepared to give them. Not a single scheme has been put forward by them.... The only step in that direction has been the undifferentiated demand for Rs 150 crores by the Punjab. That of course is utterly useless. No one is going to give them 150 crores or even one crore unless they know what they are going to expend it on. And the Punjab government certainly did not know and do not know now.[94]

Communalism and Political Consciousness

The extensive notes, diaries, letters, and other papers also allow one to trace the exacerbation of communal violence and the popularity of nationalist leaders among the Punjabi peasantry. In a letter to Lord Linlithgow in 1928, Darling discussed the Alienation of Land Act and its impact on communalism. The letter was written in response to Linlithgow's query to Darling regarding what the latter felt about the repeal of the Act.

> I agree with you entirely in looking upon the Act [Land Alienation Act] as 'a crutch'; but perhaps its greatest disadvantage is that it tends to accentuate divisions which are out of place in a modern state. When the Act was passed, the problem was to protect the peasant from wholesale expropriation. Now thanks to cooperation and the awakening that is taking place throughout the province, the risk of this, even without the Act, though still by no means negligible, is much less serious than it was. A more serious problem is to find a cure for communalism and get people to act together for good ends irrespective of religion and caste: in fact to weld the heterogeneous elements of the province into a harmonious whole. From this point of view, the Act is open to obvious objection, and I look forward therefore to a time when it will no longer be required.[95]

In the cooperative societies, Darling had already observed the increasing tendency for separate societies based on religious denomination being set up. While touring Sangla, he wrote in his diary:

> Separate cooperative societies exist here for Moslem and Hindu shopkeepers, and they are a sign of the rivalry which too often divides Hindu and Moslem in the town. It had been arranged that I should see both societies together but unwisely in the courtyard of a Moslem and the Hindus sent the inevitable message that they would not come here.[96]

At the same time, he was also curious about the popularity of nationalist leaders in far-flung villages. While touring the Shahpur district in 1930–31, he wrote that while Gandhi's name was known, the peasants said that 'we have no certain knowledge of what he teaches – we have not seen him'.[97] In an even more interesting trip to Bhalwal, also in the Shahpur district, he describes a village where he spent three hours with 34 cultivators and a few schoolmasters who

> … had collected for the weekly meeting of their cooperative thrift society…. Five had heard of the Round Table Conference but all they knew about it was that leaders had gone to London to ask for power (hakumat) and that each community wanted power for itself. 'We have heard' said a Mohammadan 'that the Hindus want the land and would become King'. More was known about the administration, and the different rounds in the official hierarchy, executive and judicial, were correctly stated except for a slight to the Financial Commissioners, who were ignobly placed under the Sessions Judge. But – significant omission – in naming everyone from patwari to King, no one mentioned the Ministers. When I asked who they were they said 'they are made by our votes; we have no knowledge what they do, nor why they are made; everyone is for himself.' They mentioned two by name, and knew that one was for education and the other for revenue. 'The maliks (the big landlords of the district – one is a Minister) gain, not we. They exist for their advantage, not ours.[98]

Miscellaneous Glimpses

Darling's papers and diaries are also replete with evocative descriptions of village life in the Punjab. In terms of health and education, he mentions how there was one doctor per 10,000 of population as against one for 800–1,200 in European countries. He discussed the role of teaching in improving agricultural practices in an article published in 1927, and mentioned:

In the Punjab agriculture is taught as an optional subject in about 100 vernacular middle schools which have a garden attached to them for the purpose and in 1925–26 over 6,000 boys took it as a subject. But so far no attempt has been made to give any vocational training either to the grown-up peasant or to the boy whose education stops at the primary school. The immediate problem is to combat the almost universal illiteracy of the countryside hence the 3200 adult schools with their 100,000 pupils all learning the three Rs. And there is another problem even more urgent namely how to make rural education really rural.[99]

In a description of a village, he wrote:

The village had one of Fielden's radio sets but as in the other villages it got out of order. The *safedposh* present, a remarkable old *zemindar*, with a large beaked nose, said they liked hearing the prices but he shook his head over the songs. He had been only once to the cinema, ten years ago, and that was enough for him. The *lambardar* sitting at his side admitted having been twice, but a young B.A. present, who belonged to the village but worked in Delhi went frequently, and when asked he did not live in the village, said it must first become like the city! Yet he admitted that in Delhi one could not get pure milk or *ghi* or such good *ata* as in the village.[100]

In 1945, while touring the countryside, he wrote:

I got such a nice smile today – no, not from a lady but from a passing rustic. He was driving a bullock cart and I stopped to admire his pair of bullocks as they marched majestically past. He must have seen something in my eye, for his face broke into the broadest and most childlike of grins. You wouldn't get that in any London street I thought and indeed it was India from one end of the grin to the other, and an India that we English take too little account of ... my Sikh major talked freely of Punjab politics. He says that Firoz is called 'a seasonal quail' (fasali batera) for joining the Muslim league for the elections and he can get out of them.... I asked him and the two or three others standing by – all Muslims – whether they wanted Pakistan. Yes, they said, and when asked why, they added then there will be no more octroi and no more 'control' over prices![101]

He mentioned the following incident from his horseback tour of India in 1945–46 when he was accompanied by his daughter:

One communist was a large, well-fed Sikh, who came to one of our gatherings with a sickly looking infant in his arms. At one point he got very excited, and as he talked the infant was in peril of slipping off his lap. My daughter saw this with concern and when I pulled him up he looked down and exclaimed: 'It is true my thoughts had wandered a little bit away from it to you' and he rearranged the bundle in his arms. Touched at the sight of the skinny little thing my Daughter asked how it had got into this state. 'How can it be otherwise (he said) when the state of the people is so weak? Even the babies have nothing to eat.' 'Is the mother weak?' my Daughter asked. 'Yes, yes, she too has nothing to eat.' 'Well then,' said my daughter, 'you are a strong well-fed man, you should give her some of your food.' This unexpected attack turned the laugh against him but he took it well and with a disarming smile said – 'Acha Memsahib – I'll do it.' This tiny incident was typical of the way in which an unfriendly beginning – which indeed was rare – would turn to friendliness … the peasant is nothing if not hospitable, and however poor the village, it would almost invariably offer us milk for ourselves and grass for our horses.[102]

His descriptions of urban centres are also insightful, and of the Haus Khan in Delhi he wrote: 'Here there were colonnades and pavilions of squat stone pillars supporting low flat stone arches and large heavy black stone domes. As I looked at them and at the obscene looking vulture perched on top, I felt all the weight of a universe made to crush man.'[103]

Conclusion

On first arrival, if a (Civilian) is a man of generous disposition he feels indignant at the manner in which he finds the people of the country spoken of by some Europeans of longer standing in the country than himself. After a little, when he himself comes in close contact with the people, he is shocked by much of what he sees that he undergoes a revulsion of feeling, and if you meet him at that stage, you will probably find that he displays the very prejudices that so shocked him on his arrival. Meet him again a few years further on, and you will find that he has come at last to understand the actual position, to see that he is dealing with people of wholly different type from himself, who are better than him in some ways, worse than him in other ways, and (not) to be judged by the same standards.

—Sir Dennis Fitzpatrick, Governor of the Punjab[104]

The official approach to indebtedness in the Punjab remained one which held the peasant primarily responsible for his situation. In his diary for 1945, Malcolm Darling noted:

> Cheap credit is a blessing to a rural population only where the average
> cultivator is possessed of the knowledge and strength of character required,
> to induce him on the one hand to limit his borrowing within the range of his
> capacity to repay, and on the other to apply the greater part of the borrowed
> money to sound productive purpose ... the solution of the problem of
> indebtedness is only to be found in the cumulative effect of the spread of
> literacy and in the cooperative movement.... Any permanent cure must
> touch the "root problem" which is that the peasant doesn't understand the
> use of credit.[105]

Such a diagnosis is a convenient one for the colonial officer, as it absolves the state
or government of any responsibility for the situation. As discussed in the previous
chapter, local politicians saw the land revenue demand as a crucial factor in this
alongside various other policies and judicial processes that were exploitative of the
peasant. However, Darling retains this intellectual blind spot, which prevents any
searching look at official policy regarding land revenue.

In part, Darling shared the disappointment that F. L. Brayne had faced in his
dealings with the resistant nature of the state. Whereas for Brayne, it was official
opposition that frustrated him the most, for Darling it was the peasant's own habits
and decisions that continued to thwart attempts at sustained economic development.
Writing to a fellow officer in the Punjab administration, Brayne wrote:

> Whatever ambition I ever had, has long evaporated. My wife and I have
> some reason to be bitter. We both want to do what we can to help the
> Punjabi make his villages brighter, but we both feel that we are up against
> such a solid block of official opposition that we are only busting ourselves
> in going on trying. What guarantees have I that my schemes will be received
> with less contempt than those I have been sending up for the last ten years?
> I worked to the bone in Gurgaon, but that did not help.[106]

Darling instead stressed the need for a long-term and consistent attention to the
problem of rural poverty in a letter to Brayne in 1941: 'Twenty years ago, I believed
in five-year plans, ten years ago in twenty-five year plans; now I have sorrowfully
come to the conclusion that what we need is a fifty-year plan.'[107] The efforts were
not completely futile, retrospectively speaking, as the detailed statistical information
and interviews collected during these years of reform in Punjabi villages are an
invaluable resource for contemporary discussions on rural development in the
wake of their continued popularity. Darling's intellectual journey also captures the
freedom possessed by colonial officers in shaping policies and initiating projects in
the Punjab, while also showing the limited agency officers had due both to their own

intellectual commitments and stonewalling by superior officers. In some ways, he is a precursor to the consultant or technocrat called in to advise on socioeconomic problems, preferably not by recommending any fundamental reordering of state or social structures but by presenting a magic pill, for example, cooperation. The strategy protects all existing entrenched interests while blaming the poor for their own lack of industry and discipline. It is interesting to find this parallel in a time of colonial rule and to observe its striking similarity to piecemeal recommendations for problems of underdevelopment. By making development a problem of the poor, in its causes and solutions, the elite and the state are absolved of any responsibility or action.

A key insight which emerges from going through the Darling papers is the realization that despite being schooled in the prevailing ideologies of the day, officers retained some capacity of learning from their experiences in the field. While Brayne and Darling may have been exceptional in this case, their existence points towards the capacity for a colonial system to allow such officers to operate in the countryside. However, this also points towards the lack of any such revolutionary or reformist tendencies in the highest offices of administration itself, which remained preoccupied with serving elite and military interests in the Punjab and in ensuring that various strategic and economic imperatives of the colonial state were met. Perhaps then the enduring lesson from this historical episode is the cosmetic and transitory impact that micro-level reform strategies can have while retaining large-scale networks and relations of power, privilege, and extraction. Even with the best of intentions, dedicated officers, collection of data, and creativity of thought, the efforts of Malcolm Darling, F. L. Brayne, H. Calvert, and others remained marginal and ineffective for powerful landlords and military interests remained entrenched. It is noteworthy, however, that Darling's thought evolves over time and, instead of rigid prescriptions, he used the failures and partial successes in the Punjab to modify his ideas. Initially, he only conceived of credit cooperatives as a source of finance or a bank that would lend at lower interest rates to the peasant, but later he saw their pedagogic value in educating the peasant to lead a 'better life', and so the cooperative officer's role became more sophisticated. It also reflects Darling's realization that any sustained strategy of reform would require reforming the habits of the peasant and also needed continued and active state patronage of credit cooperatives.

Furthermore, it illustrates the limits to which officers were willing to go in their reformist zeal. Darling, for instance, never attached any blame to extractive policies imposed by the government, including high revenue demands and the subjugation of rural interests to those of the military. His political convictions ensured that he remained opposed to communism even as he admitted that cooperative efforts would have to be more large-scale to be effective. In this vein, the careers and memoirs of officers like Darling tell us of the limits to knowledge and the limits of power in the governance of colonial territories: in the first instance, the ideological convictions of officers constrain the diagnosis and interpretation of socio-economic problems and even with the commissioning of more information or knowledge, the impact of the most well-intentioned and well-planned reforms are limited by the degree of power vested in these officers. Often the very officers seeking to expand their understanding of the society were those divested of accomplishing any real change in the prevailing institutional arrangements – including Darling, who never became Lieutenant Governor and whose alma mater King's College, Cambridge, refused to host his funeral, saying he was not important enough to merit the consideration.

Images

Figure 5.1   First conference of the Indian Society of Agricultural Economics, Delhi, 1940. Malcolm Darling is seated in the first row in the centre.

Source: Malcolm Darling papers, Centre of South Asian Studies, University of Cambridge, UK.

Figure 5.2   Speech in honour of Malcolm Darling, Round Table Club, Lahore

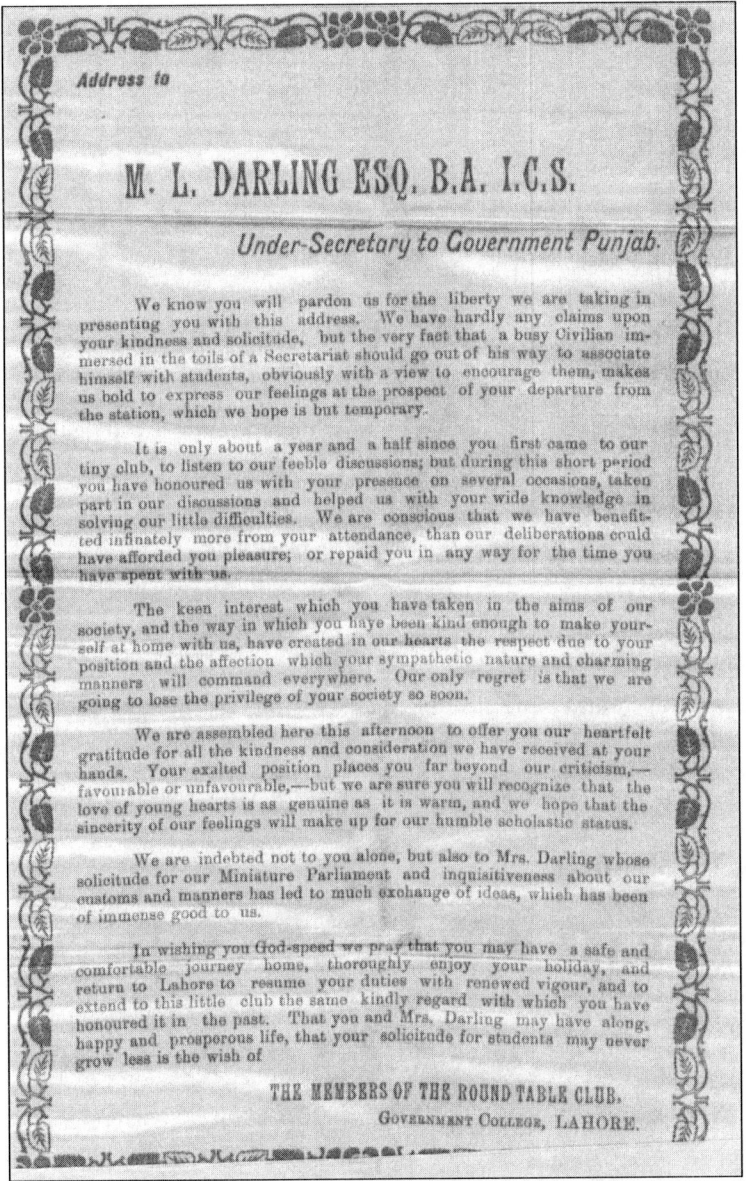

Address to

M. L. DARLING ESQ. B.A. I.C.S.

Under-Secretary to Government Punjab.

We know you will pardon us for the liberty we are taking in presenting you with this address. We have hardly any claims upon your kindness and solicitude, but the very fact that a busy Civilian immersed in the toils of a Secretariat should go out of his way to associate himself with students, obviously with a view to encourage them, makes us bold to express our feelings at the prospect of your departure from the station, which we hope is but temporary.

It is only about a year and a half since you first came to our tiny club, to listen to our feeble discussions; but during this short period you have honoured us with your presence on several occasions, taken part in our discussions and helped us with your wide knowledge in solving our little difficulties. We are conscious that we have benefitted infinately more from your attendance, than our deliberations could have afforded you pleasure; or repaid you in any way for the time you have spent with us.

The keen interest which you have taken in the aims of our society, and the way in which you have been kind enough to make yourself at home with us, have created in our hearts the respect due to your position and the affection which your sympathetic nature and charming manners will command everywhere. Our only regret is that we are going to lose the privilege of your society so soon.

We are assembled here this afternoon to offer you our heartfelt gratitude for all the kindness and consideration we have received at your hands. Your exalted position places you far beyond our criticism,— favourable or unfavourable,—but we are sure you will recognize that the love of young hearts is as genuine as it is warm, and we hope that the sincerity of our feelings will make up for our humble scholastic status.

We are indebted not to you alone, but also to Mrs. Darling whose solicitude for our Miniature Parliament and inquisitiveness about our customs and manners has led to much exchange of ideas, which has been of immense good to us.

In wishing you God-speed we pray that you may have a safe and comfortable journey home, thoroughly enjoy your holiday, and return to Lahore to resume your duties with renewed vigour, and to extend to this little club the same kindly regard with which you have honoured it in the past. That you and Mrs. Darling may have along, happy and prosperous life, that your solicitude for students may never grow less is the wish of

THE MEMBERS OF THE ROUND TABLE CLUB.
GOVERNMENT COLLEGE, LAHORE.

Source: Malcolm Darling papers, Centre of South Asian Studies, University of Cambridge, UK.

Figure 5.3 Cartoon relating to Malcolm Darling's appointment in an ILO mission to Pakistan in 1953

Source: Malcolm Darling papers, Centre of South Asian Studies, University of Cambridge, UK.

Figure 5.4 Malcolm Darling meeting Ayub Khan, in Rawalpindi, Pakistan, 1960

Source: Malcolm Darling papers, Centre of South Asian Studies, University of Cambridge, UK.

Figure 5.5 Images from F. L. Brayne's pamphlet *Cooperation, Waste and Craftmanship*. The captions read 'Waste of Money: Load your children with good health and education, not with silver and gold. Put your money in the Savings Bank' and 'Waste of Time: This is waste of time and fuel. The best time for hard work is the early morning. Get warm by working'.

Source: Malcolm Darling papers, Centre of South Asian Studies, University of Cambridge, UK.

Figure 5.6   Images from F. L. Brayne's book *Better Villages*. The captions read 'They are happy but bricks should be carried in wheelbarrows' and 'A welfare worker and her class'.

Source: F. L. Brayne, *Better Villages* (London: Oxford University Press, 1937).

Figure 5.7 'The village radio' from F. L. Brayne's book *Better Villages*

THE VILLAGE RADIO

Source: Malcolm Darling papers, Centre of South Asian Studies, University of Cambridge, UK.

Notes

1 Rudyard Kipling, 'The White Man's Burden', *The Collected Poems of Rudyard Kipling* (Ware: Wordsworth Editions Ltd, 1994), p. 334.

2 Text of speech, February 1940, Cambridge, Centre of South Asian Studies, University of Cambridge, Malcolm Darling Papers, Box 1.

3 Farewell address to M. L. Darling, The Tukojirao Club, 14 May 1908, Cambridge, Centre of South Asian Studies, University of Cambridge, Malcolm Darling Papers, Box 1.

4 Papers relating to Darling's obituary, Cambridge, Centre of South Asian Studies, University of Cambridge, Malcolm Darling Papers, Box 12.

5 The complete titles are *Some Aspects of Co-operation in Germany, Italy and Ireland* (Lahore: Superintendent, Government Printing, Punjab, 1922), *The Punjab Peasant in Prosperity and Debt* (Bombay: Oxford University Press, 1925), *Rusticus Loquitur: The Old Light and the New in the Punjab Village* (London: Oxford University Press,

1930), *Wisdom and Waste in the Punjab Village* (Oxford: Oxford University Press, 1934), *At Freedom's Door* (Oxford: Oxford University Press, 1949) and *Apprentice to Power* (London: Hogarth Press, 1966).

6   G. L. Dickinson to H. O. Meredith, 29 January 1913, Cambridge, Centre of South Asian Studies, University of Cambridge, Malcolm Darling Papers, Box I.

7   Miscellaneous notes, Cambridge, Centre of South Asian Studies, University of Cambridge, Malcolm Darling Papers, Box 8:3.

8   Miscellaneous notes, Cambridge, Centre of South Asian Studies, University of Cambridge, Malcolm Darling Papers, Box 8:3.

9   Malcolm Darling, 'Ethics and Economics', *Indian Journal of Economics* 8, no. 3 (1928): 492–95.

10   J. M. Keynes to Malcolm Darling, 6 June 1932, Cambridge, Centre of South Asian Studies, University of Cambridge, Malcolm Darling Papers, Box 6.

11   Miscellaneous correspondence, Cambridge, Centre of South Asian Studies, University of Cambridge, Malcolm Darling Papers, Box 4:1.

12   Darling to Sardar Sahib, 18 October 1933, Cambridge, Centre of South Asian Studies, University of Cambridge, Malcolm Darling Papers, Box 1.

13   Darling to Linlithgow, 23 February 1928, Cambridge, Centre of South Asian Studies, University of Cambridge, Malcolm Darling Papers, Box 1.

14   Darling to Viceroy's office, 1946–47, Cambridge, Centre of South Asian Studies, University of Cambridge, Malcolm Darling Papers, Box 2:8.

15   Malcolm Darling, 'The Indian Peasant in the Modern World', *Asiatic Review* 38, no. 133 (1942): 49–65.

16   'India and the Four Freedoms' Transcript of discussion between Wickham Steed, Sir Malcolm Darling, Lord Hailey, Capt. Quintin Hogg, and Sir Ramaswami Mudalair, Overseas Eastern Transmission, 25 October 1943, Cambridge, Centre of South Asian Studies, Malcolm Darling Papers, Box 3:2, pp. 2–4.

17   See relevant paperwork for these assignments in Boxes 3:6, 6:1, and 6:2, Cambridge, Centre of South Asian Studies, Malcolm Darling Papers.

18   Some of these speeches, articles, and publications by Darling include: 'The Zeiss Works, or What a Factory Should Be', *Irish Economist Quarterly Journal of Cooperative Thought and Progress* 8, no. 3, (1923); 'Luigi Luzzatti', *Bombay Cooperative Quarterly* 5, no. 3 (1921); 'The Cattedre Ambulanti of Italy and the Training of the Peasant', *Agricultural Journal of India* 22, no. 4 (1927); 'The Economic Holding or the Family Farm', *Agricultural Journal on India* 22, no. 6 (1927); 'Presidential Address', *Indian Journal of Economics* 8, no. 30 (1928): 477–96; 'Planner and Peasant in India', *Yearbook of Agricultural Cooperation* (1958); 'Cooperation and India's Second Five Year Plan', *Review of International Cooperation* 52, no. 1 (1959); *Report on Certain Aspects of the Cooperative Movement in India* (New Delhi: Government of India Planning Commission, 1957); 'Cooperation and the Village Community', *Review of International Cooperation* 8, no. 9 (1952); 'The Indian Peasant in the Modern World',

Asiatic Review 8, no. 133 (1942): 49–65; 'All India Rural Credit Survey', *International Cooperative Alliance Review* (June 1955); Presidential Address of Mr M. L. Darling, Financial Commissioner Punjab, Delivered at the 21st Session of the U.P. Cooperative Conference held at Lucknow on 30 and 31 January 1937; 'The Indian Village and Democracy', *Journal of the Royal Society of the Arts* 91, no. 4645 (1943); 'Cooperative Farming in Italy', *Yearbook of Agricultural Cooperation* (1953); Presidential Address by Sir Malcolm Darling: Proceedings of the First Conference of the Indian Society of Agricultural Economics, Delhi, 24 and 25 February 1940.

19   Text of radio broadcast 'The Peasant and Politics' by Malcolm Darling, 2 February 1951, Cambridge, Centre of South Asian Studies, Malcolm Darling Papers, Box 3:1.

20   Text of Darling's speech delivered at The Commonwealth Conference on Agricultural Cooperation at Oxford, 23 to 28 July 1951, Cambridge, Centre of South Asian Studies, Malcolm Darling Papers, Box 1.

21   Punjab Information Bureau, *Rural Uplift in Gurgaon*, Punjab Archives (Lahore, 1928).

22   F. L. Brayne, *The Remaking of Village India* (Oxford: Oxford University Press, 1929).

23   Mahtama Gandhi, 'Village Improvement', *Young India*, 14 November 1929.

24   On missionary activity in colonial India related to economic development, see Gary R. Hess, 'American Agricultural Missionaries and Efforts at Economic Improvement in India', *Agricultural History* 42, no. 1 (1968): 23–34.

25   Note on Gurgaon development, London, British Library, Brayne Papers, MSS Eur. F152/29.

26   F. L. Brayne, *The Peasant's Home and Its Place in National Planning* (London: Village Welfare Association, 1949), p. 1.

27   Brayne, *The Peasant's Home*, p. 2.

28   Brayne, *The Peasant's Home*, p. 3.

29   Brayne, *The Peasant's Home*, p. 4

30   Brayne, *The Peasant's Home*, p. 6

31   F. Brayne, *Village Uplift in India* (Allahabad: Pioneer Press, 1927), p. 3.

32   Brayne, *Village Uplift in India*, p. 46.

33   Brayne, *The Peasant's Home*, p. 7

34   Brayne, *The Peasant's Home*, p. 11.

35   Brayne, *The Peasant's Home*, p. 16.

36   See Brayne's correspondence on a village course in religious education with The Council of Christian Education, Methodist Episcopal Church in Southern Asia, December 1933, London, British Library, Brayne Papers, MSS Eur F152/35. See also Brayne's correspondence on schools with Reverend King, St Stephen's College, Delhi, October 1931 on schools, London, British Library, Brayne Papers, MSS Eur F152/28.

37   F. Brayne, *The Neglected Partner* (London: Village Welfare Association, 1949).

38   F. Brayne, *Better Villages* (Oxford: Oxford University Press, 1937). The foreword was written by Sir Sikandar Hayat.

39   Brayne, *Village Uplift in India.*

40   F. Brayne, *New Weapons for Old Enemies: How Malaria can be Defeated by Paludrine, DDT and Gammexane* (London: Village Welfare Association, 1948).

41   Tom Kessinger, *Vilayatpur: 1848–1968: Social and Economic Change in a North Indian Village* (Berkeley: University of California Press, 1974), p. 133.

42   'Peacocks Calling', Unpublished Memoirs of Bill Cowley, Cambridge, Centre of South Asian Studies, p. 62.

43   C. F. Strickland, 'The Spread of Cooperation in the Punjab', *Agricultural Journal of India* (1918).

44   Presidential Address of Mr M. L. Darling Financial Commissioner Punjab, delivered at the 21st session of the UP Cooperative Conference held at Lucknow, 30 and 31 January 1937, Cambridge, Centre of South Asian Studies, Malcolm Darling papers, Box 1, p. 23.

45   Presidential Address of Mr M.L. Darling Financial Commissioner Punjab, delivered at the 21st session of the UP Cooperative Conference held at Lucknow, 30 and 31 January 1937, Cambridge, Centre of South Asian Studies, Malcolm Darling papers, Box 1, p. 19.

46   Malcolm Darling, 'The Indian Peasant in the Modern World', *Asiatic Review* 38, no. 133 (1942): 49–65, 49.

47   Malcolm Darling, 'The Peasant Strength of India', *Asia* (March 1941), p. 119.

48   Presidential Address, Sir Malcolm Darling: Proceedings of the First Conference of the Indian Society of Agricultural Economics held at Delhi, Feb. 24th and 25th, 1940, Cambridge, Centre of South Asian Studies, Malcolm Darling papers, Box 1, p. 8.

49   Malcolm Darling to Alice Darling, Feb. 22nd, 1933, Cambridge, Centre of South Asian Studies, Malcolm Darling papers, Box 1:16.

50   H. Calvert, *The Wealth and Welfare of the Punjab: Being Some Studies in Punjab Rural Economics* (Lahore: Civil and Military Gazette Press, 1922), p. 55.

51   Calvert, *The Wealth and Welfare of the Punjab,* pp. 368–70.

52   Darling, *Rusticus Loquitur,* p. 4.

53   All three succeeded Marshall in teaching economics or economic history at Cambridge. See a discussion in Clive Dewey, *Anglo-Indian Attitudes: The Mind of the Indian Civil Service* (London: Hambledon Press, 1993), p. 140.

54   See details in Darling, 'Luigi Luzzatti'.

55   Notes written by Darling, Cambridge, Centre of South Asian Studies, Malcolm Darling papers, Box 1.

56   Notes written by Darling, Cambridge, Centre of South Asian Studies, Malcolm Darling papers, Box 1.

57   Notes written by Darling, Cambridge, Centre of South Asian Studies, Malcolm Darling papers, Box 1.

58   Notes written by Darling, Cambridge, Centre of South Asian Studies, Malcolm Darling papers, Box 1.

59 Notes written by Darling, Cambridge, Centre of South Asian Studies, Malcolm Darling papers, Box 1.

60 Notes written by Darling, Cambridge, Centre of South Asian Studies, Malcolm Darling papers, Box 1.

61 Notes written by Darling, Cambridge, Centre of South Asian Studies, Malcolm Darling papers, Box 1.

62 Darling's Diary 1930–31, Cambridge, Centre of South Asian Studies, Malcolm Darling papers, Box 2:1, p. 31.

63 Malcolm Darling, 'Report on the Commonwealth Conference on Agricultural Cooperation at Oxford – July 23 to 28, 1951', *Asiatic Review* 38, no. 133 (1942), p. 2.

64 Darling, 'Ethics and Economics'.

65 Presidential Address of Mr M. L. Darling, Financial Commissioner Punjab, Delivered at the 21st session of the UP Cooperative Conference held at Lucknow, Jan. 30 and 31, 1937, Cambridge, Centre of South Asian Studies, Malcolm Darling papers, Box 1.

66 Notes by Darling, Cambridge, Centre of South Asian Studies, Malcolm Darling papers, Box 1.

67 Notes by Darling, Cambridge, Centre of South Asian Studies, Malcolm Darling papers, Box 1.

68 See Prem Chand Lal, *Reconstruction and Education in Rural India in the Light of the Programme Carried on at Sriniketan, the Institute of Rural Reconstruction Founded by Rabindranath Tagore* (London: G. Allen & Unwin Ltd, 1932), for a discussion.

69 Extract from diary, 1930s, Cambridge, Centre of South Asian Studies, Malcolm Darling papers, Box 2:5, p. 14.

70 Notes by Darling, Cambridge, Centre of South Asian Studies, Malcolm Darling papers, Box 1.

71 Notes by Darling, Cambridge, Centre of South Asian Studies, Malcolm Darling papers, Box 1.

72 Diary of tour, Wisdom and Waste 1930–31, Cambridge, Centre of South Asian Studies, Malcolm Darling papers, Box 2:1.

73 Diary: Wisdom and Waste, Cambridge, Centre of South Asian Studies, Malcolm Darling papers, Box 2:2, p. 4–5.

74 Miscellaneous notes, Cambridge, Centre of South Asian Studies, Malcolm Darling papers, Box 1, p. 20.

75 Malcolm Darling, 'Presidential Address', *Indian Journal of Economics Conference Number* 8, no. 3 (1928): 477–96.

76 Darling, 'Presidential Address'.

77 Presidential Address of Mr M.L. Darling Financial Commissioner Punjab, delivered at the 21st session of the UP Cooperative Conference held at Lucknow, Jan. 30 and 31, 1937, Cambridge, Centre of South Asian Studies, Malcolm Darling papers, Box 1.

78 Darling, 'Presidential Address'.

79　Miscellaneous notes, Cambridge, Centre of South Asian Studies, Malcolm Darling papers, Box 4:1, p. 20.

80　Presidential Address of Mr M.L. Darling Financial Commissioner Punjab, delivered at the 21st session of the UP Cooperative Conference held at Lucknow, Jan. 30 and 31, 1937, Cambridge, Centre of South Asian Studies, Malcolm Darling papers, Box 1, p. 12.

81　Miscellaneous notes, Cambridge, Centre of South Asian Studies, Malcolm Darling papers, Box 1.

82　Miscellaneous notes, Cambridge, Centre of South Asian Studies, Malcolm Darling papers, Box 1.

83　E. M. Forster, *A Passage to India* (New York: Harcourt, Brace and Company, 1924), p. 9.

84　Brayne to Darling, 21 April 1934, Cambridge, Centre of South Asian Studies, Malcolm Darling papers, Box 1.

85　Brayne to Darling, 21 April 1934, Cambridge, Centre of South Asian Studies, Malcolm Darling papers, Box 1.

86　See, for instance, 'The Suppression of Corruption', *Civil and Military Gazette*, Lahore, 3 October 1916, Islamabad, National Archives; and 'The Lyallpur Bribery Case', *Civil and Military Gazette*, 17 June 1916, Islamabad, National Archives.

87　Diary for October–November 1945, Cambridge, Centre of South Asian Studies, Malcolm Darling papers, Box 2:7.

88　April Darling's diary of ride across North India with Malcolm Darling, 1946–47, Cambridge, Centre of South Asian Studies, Malcolm Darling papers, Box 2:8, p. 43.

89　Evidence of Mr F. L. Brayne, Deputy Commissioner Gurgaon before the Royal Commission on Agriculture, 22 Feb. 1927, London, British Library, Brayne Papers, MSS Eur. F152/29.

90　Evidence of Mr F. L. Brayne, Deputy Commissioner Gurgaon before the Royal Commission on Agriculture, 22 Feb. 1927, London, British Library, Brayne Papers, MSS Eur. F152/29.

91　'Difficulties', London, British Library, Brayne Papers, MSS Eur. F152/41.

92　'Difficulties', London, British Library, Brayne Papers, MSS Eur. F152/41.

93　Punjab Civil Secretariat to Mohd Afzal Khan, PCS, Publicity Officer, Rural Reconstruction Dept. Lahore, 29 December 1939, London, British Library, Brayne Papers, MSS Eur. F152/41.

94　Brayne to a fellow officer, 23 July 1943, London, British Library, Brayne Papers, MSS Eur. F152/41.

95　Malcolm Darling to Lord Linlithgow, 28 Feb. 1928, Cambridge, Centre of South Asian Studies, Malcolm Darling Papers, Box 1.

96　Wisdom and Waste: Notes and Diaries, Cambridge, Centre of South Asian Studies, Malcolm Darling papers, Box 2:2, p. 10.

97 Diary 1930, Cambridge, Centre of South Asian Studies, Malcolm Darling papers, Box 2:1, p. 31.

98 Wisdom and Waste: Notes and Diaries, Cambridge, Centre of South Asian Studies, Malcolm Darling papers, Box 2:2, p. 23.

99 Darling, 'The Cattedre Ambulanti of Italy and the Training of the Peasant'.

100 Miscellaneous papers, Cambridge, Centre of South Asian Studies, Malcolm Darling papers, Box 2:7.

101 Diary for November–December 1945, Cambridge, Centre of South Asian Studies, Malcolm Darling papers, Box 2:7.

102 Quoted by Darling in his speech delivered at The Commonwealth Conference on Agricultural Cooperation at Oxford, 23 to 28 July 1951, Cambridge, Centre of South Asian Studies, Malcolm Darling papers, Box 1.

103 Diary for November–December 1945, Cambridge, Centre of South Asian Studies, Malcolm Darling papers, Box 2:7.

104 Sir Dennis Fitzpatrick, governor of the Punjab, note dated 23 September 1893, quoted in Dewey, *Anglo-Indian Attitudes*, p. 199.

105 Diary for November–December 1945, Cambridge, Centre of South Asian Studies, Malcolm Darling papers, Box 2:7.

106 Brayne to Hubert Calvert, 3 January 1933, quoted in Dewey, *Anglo-Indian Attitudes* p. 53.

107 Darling to Brayne, 3 September 1941, quoted in Dewey, *Anglo-Indian Attitudes*, p. 80.

6 | COLONIALISM AND THE DISCOURSE ON DEVELOPMENT

All knowledge that is about human society, and not about the natural world, is historical knowledge, and therefore rests upon judgment and interpretation. This is not to say that facts or data are nonexistent, but that facts get their importance from what is made of them in interpretation ... for interpretations depend very much on who the interpreter is, who he or she is addressing, what his or her purpose is, at what historical moment the interpretation takes place.

—Edward W. Said, *Covering Islam*[1]

The Indian Government being minded to discover the economic condition of their lands, sent a Committee to inquire into it; and saw that it was good...

Now this is the position
Go make an inquisition
Into their real condition
As swiftly as ye may.
Ay, paint our swarthy billions
The richest of vermilions

—Rudyard Kipling, *The Masque of Plenty*[2]

Cooperation, legislation, and the drive towards rural reconstruction in the Punjab comprised the immediate response to the problem of rural indebtedness in the province. From the Alienation of Land Act and the cooperative credit societies, a much wider push towards 'rural reconstruction' emerged, which encapsulated various ideas of reform as discussed in Chapter 3. Another development was the beginning of a discourse on rural affairs that was centred on statistical inquiry and intensive data gathering in the province. This culture of knowledge starting in the 1920s was significant for several reasons:

firstly, it emerged in a political climate where the government needed to show greater knowledge of its rural subjects after the Montagu–Chelmsford reforms. The research agenda and scope of the studies were also defined and limited by political considerations. Second, it signalled a global move towards statistical inquiry in agricultural life with similar questions being studied elsewhere. Such inquiries were the precursor to two fields of study that became more developed by the 1950s and 1960s: peasant studies and development studies. Third, the inquiries did not challenge the official narrative on various socio-economic issues and instead confirmed many existing colonial biases. And finally, in keeping with an argument made elsewhere in the book, the inquiries reaffirm the limited memory of development studies, in that they remain largely forgotten and unused. This chapter develops these points by discussing the emergence of this new culture of research during the interwar period.

At some level, the academic output on rural welfare may seem noteworthy for its abundance with countless books, journals, pamphlets, and newspaper articles being published in the first half of the twentieth century. On the other hand, the highly prolific nature of this research also points to a more problematic issue: as the discussion on rural indebtedness became increasingly intellectualized, the reports, books, and other publications became ends in themselves rather than vehicles for change in the rural areas. In the Punjab, this transition took place not just in the publication of academic journals and books by 'experts' but also through an organization set up by the government to inquire into socio-economic issues, that is, the Punjab Board of Economic Inquiry, established in 1919.

This chapter skirmishes through the overpopulated academic domain focusing on rural welfare in the Punjab to glean the major themes and limitations of the research output. A dominant focus is on the publications of the Punjab Board of Economic Inquiry for their lifelike depictions of rural life, produced after intensive data gathering on the part of investigators. While issues of sampling and representativeness prevent easy generalizations to be made from the studies, they still provide useful insights into economic life in the Punjab as well as a critique of the emerging culture of economic research. The Board conducted a series of inquiries, some running longitudinally over many years, which collected microeconomic data on individual households, villages, and districts in the Punjab. The data contained in the publications based on this research is fine-grained and microscopic enough to allow a closer peek into the daily economic life of the Punjab peasant. Curiously enough, most of the data or conclusions recommended by the inquiries did not feed into policymaking in the Punjab directly. Chhotu Ram was perhaps the only politician who referred to a few publications of the Board in his speeches. He used the evidence of the Punjab Banking Enquiry report on faulty weights and measures to criticize the moneylenders,[3] befriended F. L. Brayne, and popularized his ideas of village uplift, or 'Dehat Sudhar'.[4]

This chapter assesses the scope, findings, and implications of the new culture of research and how it can inform the debate on indebtedness and socio-economic reform in the Punjab more broadly. The inquiries, in their minuteness of detail, also provide insights into how power was distributed in rural areas and the practical constraints on implementing economic reform at the micro level. In addition, several themes which have dominated the historiography of the Punjab can be challenged and advanced by analysing the reports of the Board, that is, those pertaining to soldiers allow a fresh perspective on the impact of military recruitment in the province. It is evident that the findings from these reports do not question the official position on major economic debates, including indebtedness in any substantive way. Using a careful selection of prosperous peasants, sometimes cultivating government farms, stylized accounts of prosperity are presented as representative of the province, which evades the discussion of inequality and indebtedness. This allows one to examine and question the limits of the research agenda and its purpose. Finally, the content, style, and mere production of this culture of research allow one to trace an intellectual genealogy of peasant studies and development studies.

A New Research Culture and 'Rural Reconstruction'

The locus for conducting various encyclopaedic inquiries into the lives of Punjabi cultivators, soldiers, and industrial workers was the Punjab Board of Economic Inquiry. The Board was set up in 1919 under orders of the Punjab government to conduct inquiries on the agricultural conditions of the Punjab. W. H. Myles, Professor of economics at the University of the Punjab, discussed the establishment of the Board in 1925 as follows: 'The Government of the Punjab is quite prepared to admit how ignorant we are on many matters of economic importance and is desirous that enlightenment should be brought by careful, accurate and scientific investigation. The method by which it has sought to attain this end is somewhat new and novel.'[5] In 1919, a committee was established to inquire into the economic conditions of cultivators in the Punjab.

> It was recognized that much of the valuable material daily being collected by Government officers in the course of their work did not receive the publicity it deserved, and there was further most noticeable lack of cooperation between the official and the non-official investigator ... the idea therefore underlying the foundation of the Board was that it would be

a distinct advantage to institute a permanent agency for undertaking and coordinating investigation of an economic nature in the province and to associate in this body both officials and representative public men whose work brought them into close contact with economic conditions in the province.[6]

The Board was initially conceived of as an organization to investigate rural areas but was later split into two sections: rural and urban. Lala Harkishen Lal, the Minister of Agriculture, became the Chairman of the Joint Board, and the two Financial Commissioners were the respective heads of the two sections. The Board consisted of 26 members in 1925 – some were members ex-officio, some Government nominees, and some nominated by representative institutions, for example, the Punjab University, the banking institutions of Lahore, and the press. In its first meeting in December 1919, it outlined its functions as follows:

1. to lay down lines of economic investigation
2. to coordinate the results of economic inquiries
3. to encourage and direct economic study and research
4. to publish economic material

The timing of its establishment is significant. With the passage of the Montagu–Chelmsford reforms, there was a need for gathering more information on economic concerns of the population. Initially, the Board was composed of volunteers, which posed problems. By the mid-1920s, it had also run into financial difficulties, and the government declared it a non-official body. However, from the onset it carried out detailed economic investigations into various issues. Nested within a hundred publications of the Punjab Board of Economic Inquiry are intimate portrayals of everyday life in colonial Punjab from the 1920s to the 1940s. A century earlier, imperial anthropological studies of the Punjab by Baden-Powell and later Ibbetson had been powerful tomes, influencing not only the annexation and administration of the Punjab but also shaping the worldviews of Oxbridge graduates who were posted in the province. With the increasing stability of British rule in the province, the political need for comprehending an alien context dimmed, even as the earlier contributions by Ibbetson assumed biblical status in colonial officers' education. In a few instances, policy questions occasioned the need for a deeper engagement with the populace, and the issue of peasant indebtedness led a district officer, S. S. Thorburn, to gather data on individual families, later published in his book *Mussulmans and the Moneylenders* in 1884, discussed earlier. The subsequent passage of the Punjab Alienation of Land Act at the turn of the century was less determined by Thorburn's detailed findings, however, and more by the aligned political and economic interests of powerful landlords and the colonial state. The nature of imperial rule also changed with the rising tide of nationalism and emergence of local political leadership. There was now a greater focus on social and economic issues, in appearances if not in practice. As the politicians from the Unionist Party based their politics around economic issues, it was expedient for the government to be seen to investigate economic life in the province.

The turn towards statistical inquiry indicated a broader interest in quantitative investigation globally, a trend that would nourish the emergence of development economics with its fundamental dependence on numerical data. While census and famine records had established the tradition of collecting large-scale data, the motives there may have more to do with a modern state making its subjects 'legible' as discussed by James Scott in his book *Seeing like a State*.[7] The novelty of the research produced by the Board was how the inquiries were pinned by specific questions, often at a small scale, which resulted in the production of filigree accounts of economic life at the individual and household levels. This surfeit of information was matched by a general 'anonymity' that is characteristic of the publications – the subjects of the inquiry are rarely, if ever, identified and are discussed in an abstract fashion. This may be to give a dispassionate, academic tone to the inquiry, but the choice is laden with other concerns: it signifies the object of the inquiry is not to contribute to the improvement in the conditions under study but to present them in neat, scientific, and meticulous detail for consumption within the academy. This was an exercise in abstract inquiry that was not driven by a state imperative like the census or the famine records; instead, it was part of a culture of research that would be a closed circle of sorts, infrequently influencing government policy.

While the Punjab had no institution like the Labour Bureau in Bombay or an Industrial Intelligence Office in Bengal, it was the first province to have a research organization like the Board, a model which was seen as relevant for replication on the national level. It is curious, however, that from the very outset there was no explicit mention of how the findings from the various inquiries were to be translated into policies, feed into legislative discussions, or improve governance. Instead, the Board became a hub for a few officers interested in the issues who commissioned intensive and painstaking inquiries. These ultimately did not influence colonial administration or affect the extractive nature of the colonial state. It is telling that the champions and patrons of the organization were precisely those officers most moved by the plight of the Punjabi peasant and eager to undertake measures for reform and redress. Even as it represented a sidelining of their aims, it also set a precedent for the theory and practice of 'development studies', which became an academic angling for fine-grained microeconomic data, sophisticated statistical analysis, robust estimation and comparisons, months of work culminating in careful articulation, but whose ultimate destiny was as a formatted academic publication consumed more by an intellectual connoisseur than a practitioner. The family budgets series, for instance, suffered delays in publication during the Second World War with the reports from the war years published after 1945 due to a shortage of paper during the hostilities. It was clearly not a priority area, especially as the British realized that a colonial exit was imminent.

In all, the Board published 100 reports and pamphlets, ranging from series of family budgets, village surveys, and farm accounts, to one-off inquiries on particular economic issues – for example, the economic value of goats in the Punjab, the economics of gut-making, and the relationship between fertility and economic status. The publications of the Board can be broadly divided into rural, urban, and general reference categories. Among the rural inquiries were series of village surveys (from the 1920s), farm accounts (from the 1920s), and family budgets of cultivators (from the 1930s). The initial plan was to select a village in each of the 29 districts of the Punjab for an in-depth study based on daily data collection over a year. Ultimately, however, 12 such studies were published by the Board.

Similarly, the farm accounts series, which was published annually for data based on 1926–27 to 1944–45, examined farms in various districts and maintained logs of their cultivation expenses and incomes. Two earlier studies by the Board had examined farm accounts in the canal colonies and Hoshiarpur as well. Perhaps the most interesting series is the one based on family budgets of cultivators. The first such publication was based on data collected on tenant cultivators on a government seed farm in Lyallpur in 1932–33. Later, the scope of the inquiry was expanded and annual summaries of all financial dealings as well as other items, for instance, hours worked, and so on, were published for data till 1942–43. Other rural publications included two that studied the cost of production of crops in the late 1920s and late 1930s, respectively, three publications on the size and distribution of agricultural holdings in the Punjab, four on mortgages and sales of land, eight related to milk supply and issues involving cattle, four on food prices and the consumption of food, five related to markets and marketing practices, two analysing war economy during the Second World War, and four investigating miscellaneous issues, including sales of gold and ornaments and the relationship between fertility and social and economic status. By choosing open-ended topics that did not question any of the inequalities in rural areas, the Board was able to generate reports replete with information that had little political consequences and yet fulfilled the official imperative of conducting economic inquiries in the province.

Inquiries conducted by the urban section of the Board analysed particular industries, including tanning, lac, iron foundry, and cotton. An annual series of seven publications studying the period between 1936 and 1942 examined the cost of living for the urban working class. Other publications examined the condition of rickshaw men, poor artisans, and the impact of prices on various social strata. Reference books and periodicals published by the Board included monthly surveys of economic conditions (between 1945 and 1947), an annual review of economic conditions (1945–46), guides to economic literature on the Punjab and government reports and statistics, as well as series of agricultural statistics of the Punjab (1901–45) and vital statistics of the Punjab (1901–40).[8] In 1924, it also published a 'Questionnaire for Economic Inquiries'[9] for anyone interested in carrying out their own studies on rural economy. The questions related to cropping and cultivation, irrigation, holdings, effects of tenancy, land revenue indebtedness, mortgages, sales, purchases and industry, price of land, yields, rents, expenses of cultivation, and consumption. In none of the inquiries were any revolutionary changes proposed or any critique of government policy attempted. In the case of industrial inquiry, there was no attempt to ascertain the potential of developing heavy industry, and the Board content itself with cataloguing the various cottage industries.

An important issue emerges from a perusal of the publications of the Board of Economic Inquiry as well as other literature on economic issues being published in the Punjab at the same time. The Board conducted intensive inquiries, gathering microeconomic data, but the families chosen for study were not necessarily representative and were better off in their respective communities. This is discussed later in the chapter in the section on village surveys and family budgets. However, the question of accuracy of Indian agricultural statistics is one that has a larger import. Even at the beginning of the twentieth century, John Maynard Keynes questioned the accuracy of Indian statistics and the need to appoint trained statisticians.[10] Keynes felt that the 'great bulk of statistics relating to agriculture, price and wages' were 'open to criticism'.[11] A note from the imperial secretariat in 1934 also stated:

> The way in which the primary statistics of India are collected…. It is the hopeless inefficiency at the bottom, even more than the failure to collate them properly, that renders many of the statistics of India of so little value. In Sind, for example, there is nominally a census of agricultural livestock taken every four or five years. Actually there is no expenditure made on this census, and the figures are evolved by the village accountant out of his own inner consciousness. He takes the figures of the last census, assumes they must have been correct at the time they were produced, and adds or subtracts what he, only too justly thinks is a figure which will not evoke comment. The figures of the preceding census were … arrived at in exactly the same way, and if the present figures have any relation whatever to the

truth, the fact is to be attributed to providence working in a more than usually mysterious way.[12]

Scholars working on the Punjab in the post-colonial era have continued this criticism of statistical information and its limited accuracy.[13] This undermines the value of the quantitative information contained in reports published during this period but does not prevent one from understanding other key features of the research culture – for instance, repetition, the lack of focus on welfare (for example, the reports do not focus on the prevalence of illiteracy, disease, or inequality), confirmation of the official view on key economic issues, such as indebtedness, and propensity to gather data from stylized families or villages that produced a detailed but not representative image.

These inquiries were produced in a climate of academic research conducted on the economy of the Punjab. Aside from the periodical reports published by the provincial government which covered all aspects of administration from agriculture, census, communications, education, utilities, factories, health, crime, law, and trade, there were reports of special commissions and committees appointed to study specific questions. These included the Punjab Banking Enquiry Committee, the Royal Commission on Agriculture in India, the Punjab Colonies committee, the Royal Commission on Opium, and the Punjab indebtedness committee. Local publishing houses also published various books and journals that analysed several economic issues from indebtedness and education to the tea industry, and so on. In fact, the Board of Economic Inquiry published a comprehensive list of this surrounding economic literature in 1941 in a publication titled *A Bibliography of Economic Literature Relating to the Punjab.*[14]

Meanwhile, in Great Britain, the Indian Village Welfare Association was founded in 1931 to propagate ideas of rural development that were collectively termed as 'rural reconstruction'. The Association published pamphlets, organized broadcasts, and also arranged three 'Easter Schools' for persons engaged in or proposing to undertake rural work in India.[15] Around 100 people, English and Indian, attended the school every year, including probationers of the Indian Civil Service (ICS). While ideas of rural development were being propagated all over India in the 1920s and 1930s, the Punjab was at the forefront of the campaign to implement such projects. A Rural Community Board was established in the province, as were District Community Councils in each district. C. F. Strickland, an ICS officer who was heavily involved in rural reconstruction as well as cooperation, described them as follows:

> When a fair, a Health Week, or a school football tournament provides an opportunity for a meeting of all welfare agencies, propaganda is conducted on an rganized programme with Scout songs, dramas and films, ploughing

demonstrations, baby shows and cattle shows. There is reason to hope that in such a case the unity of reconstruction work will be borne in both on the peasantry and on the earnest but preoccupied officers who, having habitually more to do than they can ever accomplish may not unnaturally resent being dragged away from their touring duty to help in a 'stunt'. A 'stunt' of this kind, if followed up by further teaching and demonstration through a village welfare association of a cooperative better living society will make a more perceptible dint on the peasant's mind than any number of harangues by a single agency on a single topic.[16]

In 1933, F. L. Brayne was appointed the Commissioner of rural reconstruction in the Punjab after his pioneering work in Gurgaon. His initiatives enforced compulsory education for boys in 4,000 out of 33,000 villages in the Punjab, and 170,000 Punjabi children became members of the Junior Red Cross (out of a total India-wide membership of 250,000). Red Cross bands and Scout troops were 'heard in song and seen in drama; they clean villages, aid in health weeks, and turn the mind of the child from his own interests or those of a section of the community towards the common good. There are 1,800 rural libraries, and village games clubs promoted by the Education Department are multiplying'.[17] Rural reconstruction maintained ties with missionary organizations, and a rural reconstruction centre was proposed for the YMCA in Vanieke, Amritsar.

Other regions of India took up rural reconstruction in various degrees. Efforts were partially successful in the United Provinces though there was no central coordinating organization. In Bengal, a commissioner of rural reconstruction was appointed in the 1930s to draw up a plan for rural welfare of the province. Matters were more promising in Bombay where Sir Frederick Sykes drew up a 'Village Improvement Scheme'. The limitations of the schemes were apparent to the practitioners themselves as Strickland remarked:

> It should be clear from such an account that welfare work, while carried on with energy and devotion by a host of public servants and private individuals, is being done in a disjointed and often very ineffective manner, simply because they are working independently of one another.... The suggestion therefore which we would offer to rural reformers (we would particularly address ourselves to members of the IVWA in India or those who have attended an IVWA Easter School) is that the voluntary local associations working in any rural district should meet together.[18]

These practical activities relating to rural reconstruction were accompanied by an outpouring of academic and promotional literature. This included a series of publications, the *Oxford Pamphlets in Indian Affairs,* which focused on various socio-economic issues.[19] At the same time, statistical inquiry was being encouraged by the colonial government, and in 1939, the Indian Statistical Conference was held at the Forman Christian College, Lahore. The chief guest on the occasion was the governor of the Punjab, Sir Henry D. Craik, and he was received by Mr Manohar Lal, the Minister of Finance in the Punjab government. The secretaries at the event were Dr N. K. Bose and Prof. P. C. Mahlanobis, later architect of economic planning in Nehruvian India.[20] There was also a wide-ranging literature on rural welfare in India being published at this time that included publications by F. L. Brayne, M. L. Darling, as well as works by other authors.[21] Additionally, newspapers carried relevant articles on economic thought and issues.[22] Missionaries wrote extensively on socio-economic issues in India.[23] In addition, there were a range of academic journals focusing on economic issues in India, particularly relating to agriculture and rural life. The output of the Board of Economic Inquiry thus fed into this academic market more than it percolated to policymakers. The increasingly 'scientific' and hyper-detailed nature of the investigations led to new forms of inquiry that became a standard form of research for many decades. Chief among these were 'village studies', discussed in greater detail as follows.

Village Surveys and the Limitations of Statistical Data

In 1940, the Punjab covered an area of 99,089 sq. miles with 202 towns and 35,256 villages.[24] It had a population of 28.4 million, which was predominantly rural (numbering 24 million). These figures exclude the North-West Frontier Province, which was separated from the Punjab in 1901, and also figures for Delhi around which an imperial enclave was formed in 1911. Since its inception, several inquiries conducted by the Board aimed at ascertaining how different classes of Punjabi society earned and spent their income. Village surveys were undertaken under which investigators from the Board took up residence in the village under investigation for a year and kept daily accounts of numerous variables. The information was then processed by statisticians of the Board and, under the supervision of officials, translated into yearly publications.

Village surveys carried out by Board investigators helped establish a trend of conducting village studies that continued in the post-colonial era. In the 1950s and 1960s, there were three major ways in which village studies were carried out in South Asia. Anthropologists conducted them to understand the relationships between different social groups, political scientists used them to develop theories of collective behaviour, and the government commissioned them as economic planning in India and Pakistan entailing a component of village or rural development.[25] Surprisingly enough, these dissertations showed little awareness of the earlier colonial attempt at conducting similar surveys. Perhaps the two most famous studies were Zekiye Elgar's *A Punjabi Village in Pakistan*,[26] published as a book in 1960, and Tom Kessinger's *Vilayatpur*, published in 1974. Elgar was a protégé of Margaret Mead, and the book was based on her doctoral work at Columbia University. Kessinger's *Vilayatpur* became a classic, even as it attracted criticism for its use of village sources.[27] Earlier still, scholars at various American and local universities had conducted village studies and submitted them as doctoral dissertations – for example, E. D. Lucas published his *The Economic Life of a Punjab village* in 1934. In the post-colonial era, some scholars sought to study the same villages again – for example, in the case of Rohtak, Malcolm Darling had conducted a detailed study of the drought-stricken district in 1931. Man Singh Mathur visited six of the villages Darling had studied earlier in 1966 to compare the current conditions with the colonial account.[28]

In a more general sense, the interest in peasant studies continued all over the world from the 1950s onwards. Discussing the case of Egypt, Timothy Mitchell showed how the field of peasant studies linked closely with the colonial rule of Egypt.[29] He also shows how an account of Egyptian peasantry published in 1938 was plagiarized by a leading American academic in the 1970s, signalling both the continued popularity of intimate accounts of peasant life and the various political purposes they serve. While the account in 1938 was written to support a colonial critique of the peasant's way of life (the author Ayrout writes how the peasant 'preserves and repeats but does not originate anything'[30]), while in the 1970s, Mitchell believes it served American interests vis-à-vis the Egyptian military and Cold War politics to resurrect the essentialized description of the peasant. In a similar way, the detailed inquiries into rural life in the Punjab confirmed many colonial biases – for instance, regarding the prosperity of the province and, second, the wanting character of its peasantry.

The global move towards statistical inquiry of microeconomic questions was also shared by the International Labour Organisation (ILO), established in 1919. From the 1920s onwards, the ILO had embarked on a programme of publications, including official bulletins, the monthly *International Labour Review*, series of documents investigating various questions related to labour, as well as a newspaper. Its members included developing countries (such as India) and from the 1930s onwards, it was active in the collection and exchange of information on a diverse range of economic issues.[31] However, in 1949, it experienced a change in policy and in a post-colonial age; it was decided that the 'experience accumulated by the organisation in the first thirty years of its existence could be used to the greatest advantage if it were made available immediately to the developing countries through the provision of technical assistance in the countries themselves'.[32] Many erstwhile colonial officers, including Malcolm Darling, who had been dealing with the ILO since the 1920s, became its employees, and the organization was also linked with the technical assistance programme of the United Nations, sending its 'experts' on productivity missions to developing countries, including India and Pakistan, from the 1950s onwards.[33] In this way, there were both practical and intellectual continuities between the statistical research of late colonialism and 'technical assistance' of early postcolonialism.

Apart from the link between statistical inquiry, multilateral organizations, and development studies, another aspect of the research carried out by the Board of Economic Inquiry was its reliance on statistics and the questionable reliability of the same. This issue is addressed by examining the village surveys carried out by the Board in greater detail. Village surveys formed part of a series that examined 12 villages in the Punjab, eight of which are in current-day India and the remaining four in Pakistan. Surveys were published for the following villages (villages located in West Punjab, current day Pakistan are in bold; the districts are in parentheses):

1. Gaggar Bhana (Amritsar)
2. Gijhi (Rohtak)
3. Tehong (Jullundur)
4. **Kala Gaddi Thamman (Chak 73 G.B.) (Lyallpur)**
5. Naggal (Ambala)
6. **Gajju Chak (Gujranwala)**
7. Bhadas (Gurgaon)
8. **Bhambu Sandila (Muzaffargarh)**
9. Suner (Ferozpure)
10. Jamalpur Sheikhan (Hissar)
11. **Durrana Langana (Multan)**
12. Launa (Kangra)

I discuss the four from Pakistan in greater detail below for two reasons. First, they represent a range of economic conditions: from the prosperous village in the canal colony of Lyallpur to a village near the industrial centres of the province to two villages in south Punjab, a region known for its chronic poverty and underdevelopment. Second, it has been possible to follow up on some of these villages and to contrast their present circumstances with the accounts in the village reports, which present some an interesting, if somewhat crude, comparison. The account of daily life, consumption, and markets in these village surveys allows a reconstruction of rural life under the colonial government on a microeconomic level. The methodology and findings are used to discuss the limitations of the research in general.

Description of the Villages

The four villages in question are Kala Gaddi Thamman (or Chak 73 G.B. as it was otherwise called) in the Lyallpur district, Gajju Chak in the Gujranwala district, Bhambu Sandila in the Muzaffargarh district, and Durrana Langana in the Multan district.

The first, Kala Gaddi Thamman, lay in a prosperous tract of the Chenab colony, which was described in the *Chenab Colony Gazetteer*, 1904, as a 'country of extreme desolation where no crops would grow and where nomad tribes called *janglis* grazed their cattle'. By the time the inquiry was conducted in 1926, it was a 'land of smiling villages and the most prosperous tract in the province'. The essentialized description points to the official bias and the underlying intent to emphasize the benevolent nature of colonial rule. Canal irrigation had been introduced in the area in 1892 and the district of Lyallpur established in 1910. The colony was divided into squares of land covering an area of 27.8 acres, which were then awarded to colonists. Cultivators, usually in the prime of life, from east and central Punjab were brought to the tract initially as crown tenants and later with hereditary rights of occupancy. The village was named after the three villages in Gurdaspur district from where the settlers hailed: Kalewala, Gaddian, and Thamman.[34] Kala Gaddi Thamman was situated about 11 miles south of Lyallpur and was chiefly inhabited by Sikh Jats. In 1927, the total population of the village was 920. The majority were Sikh (520), and the remainder Muslims (100), Christians (170), Vedic Dharamis (56), Mazhabis (4), Chamars (8), and Hindus (62).

In 2015, the village of Kala Gaddi Thamman was visited, and the following observations made. At this point, there was no Hindu or Sikh in the village, and the population was entirely Muslim apart from six Christian families numbering 25 individuals. In the same year, apart from two cultivators whose land exceeds 100 *kanals*, that is, 12 acres, all the other cultivators had less than 100 *kanals* of land. The situation had thus altered since the time of the colonial inquiry with the fragmentation of holdings. In the colonial inquiry, indebtedness was high in the village amounting to 96,000 rupees. There were no moneylenders in the village in 2015, and the cultivators borrowed money using their agricultural passbooks from the Agriculture Development Bank in the form of agricultural loans. Sixty per cent of the cultivators borrowed from the agricultural bank to meet their financial needs.

The total population of the village is around 4,000. The *chak* has a Basic Health Unit, that is, a hospital, as well. There is a primary school for boys where around 150 or 200 pupils study. There is a middle school for girls as well where 200–50 girls study. There are no cooperative credit societies in the village. There was no memory of the colonial survey of the village among the administrators though some recalled the Hindu and Sikh population of the village and how they migrated away in 1947. The socio-economic indicators in the village were poor.

Durrana Langana, the second village, was located in the Multan district where one-third of the land was owned by large landowners, leading to a different political economy than that of the canal colonies. Apart from the feudal lords, the *kirars* (Hindu moneylenders and traders) and *pirs* (religious saints) wielded great influence in the area. Durrana Langana was an agglomeration of habitations scattered around wells, and three quarters of the village estate were owned by two landlords, Malik Ahmad Bakhsh Dehar and Malik Khuda Bakhsh Dhar. They were considered 'enlightened' landlords, having attended school, and were favourably disposed to the usage of new seed varieties in cotton and wheat, while also having a reputation for assisting their tenants.[35] The landlords ran a *langar* in the village where free meals were provided, and travellers provided free food and accommodation. In Durrana Langana, the total population in 1936 was 1,670, out of which 1,559 were Muslim and 111 Hindus.[36] The main occupation of the village was cultivation, and 159 families (948 persons) were directly connected with it. The mode of cultivation was a combination of well and canal irrigation.

Gajju Chak, the third village, was located in the Gujranwala district. It was a small village of 43 households and located around eight miles from the Gujranwala city. In 1931, the population of the village was 229, comprising 209 Muslims and 20 Christians. The majority of the populace were engaged in cultivation and described in the report thus:

> A cultivator in Gajju Chak usually does nothing aside from cultivation. Occasionally he says his prayers but the major portion of his spare time he spends in resting, smoking, gossiping, visiting friends and relatives and in such pastimes as cock-fighting. Even when conditions are abnormal and the outlook gloomy, he simply waits for a better future, and may perhaps devote more care to preparation for the next harvest.[37]

In most respects, the village was fairly representative of central Punjab with poor sanitation, low literacy, high indebtedness, primitive methods of cultivation, and an apathetic population. Canal irrigation and cooperation had both been introduced in the village but with little impact. According to the investigator of the Board:

A deadening lethargy exists even though the village is situated near a town and one or two people have seen the world outside the village. Religion has a strong hold on people, there being two mosques in the village and the missionary spirit in one of the sects is evidenced from the assistance given in the education of a boy at an institution fairly far away.[38]

The fourth village, Bhambu Sandila, was located in the Muzaffargarh district in the south of Punjab, a district known for its chronic poverty and backwardness. The inquiry was conducted in 1931–32 and published in 1935. Unlike the rest of the district, the village had no major landlord and was entirely composed of small proprietors. The total area of the village was 1,362 acres, and the population, entirely Muslim, numbered 548 in 1931. The only non-Muslims associated with the village were six Hindu shopkeepers who lived outside the village. These Hindus were influential in the village, however, as they controlled over half the village area through mortgages and their trading and moneylending activities.[39] Due to large increase in population, the size of land holdings had shrunk, and 171 out of the 327 landowners had holdings less than one acre in size. Generally speaking, it was not possible to support oneself through cultivation on one's own holding alone.[40]

Comparisons among these four villages enable a nuanced examination of how similar institutional formations in bureaucratic and administrative machinery translated into diverse lived experiences for the populations of the villages. In particular, it can be seen that the existing distribution in the ownership of land determined how power was distributed in the rural landscape. It is also interesting to note the degree to which existing anthropologies of castes in the Punjab were referred to (and reaffirmed) in the investigations by the Board in their village inquiries. So, for instance, the tenant cultivators in Kala Gaddi Thamman in the Lyallpur district are described as the industrious, thrift Sikh Jat of central Punjab, benefiting fully from the colonial gift of canal irrigation, whereas the cultivators in south Punjab were hopeless and indolent. In Muzaffargarh, distinctions were drawn between the Hindus and Muslims as follows: 'On the holdings of the former (that is, Hindus) are found good cattle, decent brick building, fruit trees and such intensive crops as cane, pepper and vegetables while on the latter (that is, Muslims) half-starved worn-out cattle, mud huts and no better crops than indifferent wheat.'[41] Overall the population of Muzaffargarh was discussed in unflattering terms by the colonial officers, with Malcolm Darling describing them thus: 'In no other district in the Punjab is the peasant so listless, feckless and depressed and nowhere else is his standard of living so low ... in this district we see rural life at its worst.'[42]

Investigators of the Board were schooled in these colonial stereotypes and categories and reproduced them in their descriptions and analyses. The inquiries are also noticeable for a lack of criticism of official policies or recommendations for the government to improve conditions. What emerged then was a dense account of daily village life interpreted through the lens of existing colonial biases and stereotypes. The reports were as thick with information as they were devoid of critique of the government. Instead, the peasant's lifestyle was criticized (unless he were a thrifty, hardworking Jat) in line with the official narrative on debt. Occasionally, historical arguments were made criticizing Sikh rule or geographical arguments blaming topography and climate for economic backwardness.

The Political Economy and Confirmation of Biases

The village studies can be used to make several points about the research agenda and findings of the Board of Economic Inquiry. In the description of rural feudal structures, the landlords are mentioned in flattering terms, partly because they enabled the investigators of the Board to live in the village for months on end to collect the data. In a few cases, the landlords were criticized. For example, in Muzaffargarh, the investigator noted that the landlords were

> no blessing to the countryside as they are more concerned with intrigues of all kinds than in decent farming and are mostly in debt through extravagance and mismanagement.... Instead of being the leaders of the people in progress they are a check to all advance, spending their days lolling on a charpoy, listening to gossip and scandal with an occasional outing after game.[43]

However, the criticism was accompanied by a quote from Malcolm Darling, and so, in a way, the Board was again confirming the viewpoint of a colonial official rather than attempting an independent critique of rural political economy. Darling had described the situation in Muzaffargarh thus:

> There are good landlords, of course, but they are few and far between. There are, it is said, only five percent who do not in one form or another oppress their tenants, for instance by taking more than their share at the division of the produce, by letting their horses graze in their fields, by impounding their fowls when guests have to be fed, or by running cases against good men who leave them and harassing them till they return.[44]

Echoing colonial policy, the moneylenders were also roundly criticized in all the surveys as well as other inquiries conducted by the Board into market practices in the Punjab. In the village survey for Bhambu Sandila, the moneylenders had 'all the vices of their fraternity; in fact much more so since it is far too common a sight in the tract to see the poor cultivator deprived of all his harvest on the threshing floor to meet the exactions of the moneylender who seems to be omnipresent whenever there is a chance to extract something on account'.[45] The investigator goes on to say:

> Once a man is in the moneylender's clutches, the latter employs all the wiles and artifices of his profession to keep the borrower in his toils. If the debtor is a man of substance much latitude is given and no demand is made until the amount becomes bigger than he can pay even if he wishes to, which is, however rare. It is only when the civil gaol looms in sight that the borrower resigns himself to the tender mercies of the moneylender and tacitly agrees to live as his serf henceforth. He then becomes indifferent so long as he is not troubled beyond being required to affix his thumb impression to the necessary documents.[46]

However, in other inquiries, some additional concerns were raised. In Gajju Chak, six Muslim moneylenders lent money while using land as security with possession, which allowed them to cultivate it cheaper than if they had to rent it. The other sources of borrowing were non-agriculturist moneylenders from other villages, two cooperative credit societies, and the government. In 1927, only four out of the 43 families in the village were free from debt. The cooperative credit societies had been established in 1921 and 1926 and had 30 members at the time of the inquiry. The rate of interest on government loans was only 6 per cent, but villagers complained of the slow process and the bribes that had to be given to junior staff to secure them. The cooperative societies charged 12.5 per cent per annum, while the agriculturist moneylenders either asked for security of land or gave interest-free loans for religious reasons. Non-agriculturist moneylenders from other villages generally charged 25 per cent per annum or 12 per cent. Around 23 per cent of all loans were taken from the non-agriculturist moneylenders despite the high rates because of the borrower's desire for secrecy.[47] The criticisms of cooperatives in terms of bribes and corruption were, however, not taken up and do not figure in any of the reports for the working of cooperative societies.

In Durrana Langana, Multan, in 1936, 231 out of 310 families were indebted, while in 1925, the corresponding number was 141 out of 265 families. The average debt per indebted family had fallen from 589 rupees in 1925–26 to 227.9 rupees in 1936. 'The non-agriculturist Hindu moneylenders including the commission agents and milk-sellers of Multan and the village shopkeepers were the chief lenders having Rs 41,459 (78.7 percent of the total debt) due to them'[48] while the village cooperative society accounted for only 2.6 per cent of the debt. It was seen that the passage of the Punjab Alienation of Land Act had consolidated the position of the landlords by preventing non-agriculturists from acquiring land easily.[49] This evidence was also not mentioned in official discussions on the Alienation of Land Act.

Markets and Consumption

One issue on which the Board investigated an issue that later led to a policy change was the condition of weights and measures in markets. In the inquiries of the Board of Economic Inquiry, the villages all depicted different relationships with the market. For Durrana Langana, the nearest market was in the Multan city where produce was taken on camels which were the only mode of transport.[50]

In Gajju Chak, the major commercial crops grown included wheat, gram, cotton, and rice. The nearest major market was located eight miles away at the Gujranwala city, but only a small fraction of produce was sold there with the majority being sold in the village itself. Villagers preferred to sell in the village to save conveyance costs and because of the distrust with which market agents, *artias*, were viewed. A cooperative commission shop in Gujranwala allowed villagers to sell at better prices and charged less for the service than the *artias*.[51] While purchases made outside the village were paid for in cash, those from the *bania* or local sellers were usually on credit and settled through the periodic sale of agricultural produce.[52] There was little local industry – the village had no potter and only two carpenters, women did the ginning and spinning, and most of the cloth used was homespun.

The Board of Economic Inquiry undertook a series of inquiries into market practices in the Punjab, including the condition of weights and measures. An issue of concern in the cotton and grain markets was often the lack of regulation in markets. Other regions like Bombay and Berar had passed legislations and bye-laws, but the Punjab lacked such a regulatory environment. While the formal responsibility for ensuring correct market practices lay with the District Boards, no acts or bye-laws were introduced by the Board when an inquiry was conducted into market practices in the Punjab by the Board in 1930–31. At the time of the inquiry, there was little regulation of prices, compliance with standard weights, and imposition of other fees and charges. The study in question examined 25 markets of agricultural produce in 17 districts of the Punjab. The findings with regard to weights and measures were particularly damning, with only 50.8 per cent of stamped and only 12 per cent of unstamped weights found to be accurate. The ambiguous policy implications or governmental responsibility for the lack of regulation are reflected in E. D. Lucas's remarks prefacing the report: 'One mistake made by the public in the province is to look to the government to remedy all evils, many of the evils described herein can only be remedied by the force of an enlightened and active public opinion.'[53] In fact, the governor of the Punjab blocked a proposal put forward in the Punjab Legislative Council to improve the conditions of weights and measures used in the province based on this report. As discussed in Chapter 2, it was only in the late 1930s when, under the initiative of Chhotu Ram, a law was passed to improve trading practices for farmers.

A major concern was the use of faulty weights and measures in the markets. There was no system for the periodic examination of weights and scales in use, and since many cultivators were not able to weigh their produce on their own before bringing it to the market, this made them vulnerable to fraud. For example, none of the 38 cultivators in Sargodha or 45 in Dinga Bahauddin had weighed their products beforehand.[54] The situation was marginally better in Ludhiana and Ferozepure: 90 out of 130 sellers had weighed at home in Ludhiana, whereas 110 out of 150 in Ferozepure had done so. The hand scale was used for weighing grain in all the markets except those in Multan where a platform scale was used instead.[55]

Another inquiry, published in 1936, focused on the condition of weights and measures in the Punjab and gathered data in thirteen areas of the province. The Government of India had appointed the Weights and Measures Committee in 1913–14. This committee visited seven districts in the Punjab, collected 81 written statements, and interviewed 216 people, finding that the majority favoured the imposition of a uniform system of weights and measures.[56] In 1923, the provincial governments introduced bye-laws that defined standard weights and measures, and these were later adopted by local bodies in the province. Nineteen towns, 12 *mandis*, 50 factories, and 180 villages were visited by investigators from the Board between 1927 and 1931.[57] Some of the investigators employed were from the cooperative societies department.

The results of the inquiry showed that out of 2,027 cultivators questioned, 710 (35.1 per cent) sold their produce in the *mandi*, 580 (28.6 per cent) sold theirs in the village, 491 (24.2 per cent) sold in the city, and 106 (6.2 per cent) sold to the factories or their agents.[58] Out of 1,926 people, 30 per cent had weighed their produce before selling it, 11 per cent had measured it, while 59 per cent had neither weighed not measured it and relied on the market estimate.[59]

It was found that 51.2 per cent of all weights were accurate.[60] Twenty-nine out of 210 shops examined had all correct weights, while 54 had none.[61] The percentage of stamped weights that were found to be accurate was as follows:

Mandi and factory: 53.9 per cent
City: 56.8 per cent
Village: 41.2 per cent

For unstamped weights, the percentage that was accurate was as follows:

Mandi: 16.7 per cent
City: 4.3 per cent
Village: 5.8 per cent

An additional inquiry by the Board focused only on the factors affecting the price of wheat in the Punjab. The districts studied were Amritsar, Jullundur, Lyallpur, and Okara. Some of the conclusions of the report were decidedly suspect. For example, regarding price changes in Amritsar, it was remarked: 'It was noticed that in Amrtisar the appearance of even a cloud in the sky, or a change in the direction of the wind, had repercussions in prices.'[62] At the time of the inquiry, India was one of the largest wheat producers in the world, ranking third largest in terms of area sown after the USSR and the USA. The Punjab had the largest percentage of area under wheat cultivation (29 per cent), followed by Uttar Pradesh (25 per cent). Wheat acreage in the Punjab had almost doubled during colonial rule, increasing from 4,710 acres in 1867–68 to 9,175 acres in 1932.[63] *Artias*, the middlemen, again dominated the wheat trade in all four of the districts studied, though cooperative shops had part of the trade in Okara and Lyallpur.[64] There was also an active futures market in wheat, with the astute speculating to great profit in the futures trade.[65] Alongside this modern trade were the traditional technologies. For example, donkeys, carts, and camels were still the main mode of transport for taking the wheat from the farm to the market.[66] This account of the wheat trade, like the inquiries on market practices, did not evoke any policy response despite the obvious suggestions that could have been made to improve the trade in the commodity.

Remedies for Development

Underdevelopment in the four villages was diagnosed differently by the investigators of the Board. In every case, however, the backwardness was attributed to factors not related to the government. Gajju Chak in the Gujranwala district was described as having 'dirty lanes, filthy surroundings and narrow low houses' without any recommendations for better administration. Bhambu Sandila's poverty was blamed on its marriage customs: the investigator reported that there were eight instances in the village where people married women for whom they first obtained divorces from their husbands by paying cash or giving land. Intermarriage and an aversion to emigration were further blamed for the weak physique and listlessness of the populace. Initiative, drive, and effort were identified with the religion and caste. For example, for Hindu Aroras (that is, the *kirars*), it was said: 'If cultivation is anywhere above average, if fruit trees are growing along the water-courses or if an experiment is being tried, it is ten to one that there is a kirar in the background directing and supervising the work.'[67]

The south of the Punjab was also associated with poor health and education. The influenza epidemic of 1918 killed 50 per cent of the rural population through a lack of knowledge of preventive measures and an insufficiency of medical supplies.[68] Literacy in Muzaffargarh was very low: 6.3 per cent of the male population was literate, 0.4 per cent of the female, and 3.7 per cent overall. Furthermore, the prospects for improving education seemed remote with the grinding poverty making school unaffordable for the majority. Gajju Chak in the Gujranwala district was also largely illiterate, with only three men able to read and write. A school was located a mile away from the village, but only seven boys from the village attended it. Through the influence of the Ahmadi community, there was one boy attending school in Qadian in the Gurdaspur district, but overall the district lagged behind others as seen in the literacy rates in Table 6.1.[69]

The standard of living varied in the villages, with some lacking bare necessities, often reflective of the overall financial condition of the district. In Muzaffargarh, there were only two metalled roads leading to impediments in communication. A large part of the district was a desert, and this was home to date palms – dates forming the staple diet for many locals for a third of the year.[70] Despite the poor socioeconomic conditions, the peasant hardly ever emigrated, causing Malcolm Darling to remark:

> Yet the amazing thing is that no people in the Punjab are less inclined to leave their homes.... Living on his well, isolated from his fellows and invariably marrying the daughter of a neighbor, he sees nothing of any district but his own. He neither enlists nor emigrates, and, unless faced with starvation, will hardly move from one tehsil to another. Cut off from the rest of the

Table 6.1   Literacy rates in six districts in the Punjab

District of Inquiry	Percentage of Literate Population
Amritsar	21.15
Lyallpur	15.65
Jullundur	4.38
Rohtak	1.77
Ambala	12.20
Gujranwala	4.67

Source: Anchal Das, *An Economic Survey of Gajju Chak, A Village in the Gujranwala District of the Punjab*, Village Surveys–6 (Lahore: Punjab Board of Economic Inquiry, 1934), pp. iii–iv.

world but desert and hill, the people are caged in their surrounding, and, like birds born in captivity, have no desire for anything else.[71]

The situation was exacerbated by the perceived indolence of the locals and a high rate of crop failure. On average, 58 per cent of the sown area had failed. Darling goes on to say:

> A crop can almost always be sown and almost always be lost; and what this means to cultivators who are always in debt can easily be imagined. It would matter less if in a good year store were laid by for a bad, but an incurable thriftlessness prevents this being done ... it is contrary to their habits to keep ready money by them. If a man makes a few more hundred rupees than his expenses, he will not keep any part of it for a bad year. He at once buys more land or more bullocks, or more ornaments for his wife. He will do anything rather than keep the cash.[72]

Living conditions were poor with the peasant family and animals often sharing the same room. Because of the high level of indebtedness, produce was not taken to the markets but seized by the creditor, leaving a little for the family to subsist on and sometimes not even that.[73] However, the village was also characterized by its generous hospitality captured in the local proverb, 'Not even an enemy should go away when the baking plate is put on the fire'. In none of these cases is the role of the government highlighted in improving living conditions. Instead, the villagers' lifestyle or the terrain of the region are blamed for the poor socio-economic conditions.

The outlook was said to be brighter in Kala Gaddi Thamman, Lyallpur, where education for boys was compulsory and expenditure on marriages not exceptionally high. The fact that settlers had been brought in from central Punjab seemed to loosen the hold of tradition, and its location in the major wheat-producing area allowed it to be directly connected to the international grain market. This contrasted sharply with the inward-looking villages of south Punjab that seemed unable to break from the oppression of the local power brokers. However, this confirmed the colonial perception that the canal colonies and the cultivators there were more progressive, whereas those from the south of Punjab were not.

Farm accounts were maintained since 1923–24 but contained information on income and expenditure of cultivation alone and did not examine other dimensions like spending on ceremonies, education, debt, and so on. More illuminating from understanding consumption are a series of family budgets and household budgets initially collected for four tenant-cultivator families in the Lyallpur district in 1932–33. These families were then followed for the next 10 years in annual reports on their income and expenditure. At the same time, other families were added to the initial sample so that the scope of the investigations became somewhat representative of the province. The same tendency for in-depth investigation saw the deployment of investigators from the Board for a year in the respective village, observing village life and maintaining daily logs for the computation of the various costs, incomes, purchases, and transactions by each family. The level of detail of these inquiries is truly remarkable with information collected on calorie count, daily sugar consumption, number of days worked, and so on. I followed up on the cultivators and farm to the present day, and the colonial and contemporary findings are presented as follows.

Family Budgets

The series on family budgets was initiated with the study of four families of tenant-cultivators in the Lyallpur district. In some ways, the series is representative of the inherent biases and limitations of the research the Board carried out. The first series of observations was recorded in 1932–33 and from thereon, annual records were kept till 1942–43. The tenants cultivated land on the Government Seed Farm, Risalewala, a government farm of 802 acres, which was also used for crop experiments in cotton and sugarcane. The following year, two more families on the farm were included in the observation. In 1936–37, five more families were added: one in Jullundur, two in Hoshiarpur, one in Amritsar, and one in Rohtak. In 1938–39, 15 families from the Kangra district were added to the analysis. These families provided an interesting contrast as their holdings were quite small, and their income had to be supplement by joining government service or the army. In 1941–42, a separate inquiry was conducted on 30 families in the Murree suburban zone in the Rawalpindi district.

The system of cultivation in use at the farm was one in which the cultivator received a share of the land yield and received stock, tools, and seed from the government. The investigator from the Board kept a daily opening and closing inventory, daily cash, kind and labour accounts, and weekly milk and fuel accounts. Out of the four families, three were Arain and one Jat. All four were Muslim and had holdings of around 27 acres each, cultivated using two pairs of bullocks on the half-*batai* system. The size of the holding was considerably larger than the provincial average at the time, which was around 8.7 acres. The findings from these reports can therefore not be seen as representative of the average farmer. In the first year, 64.3 per cent of the expenditure was on food, and the next highest category, dress, employed 20.7 per cent.[74]

It is apparent that these families of cultivators were quite stylized in that they were not indebted and were cultivators on a government farm, so they did not pay a revenue demand like most cultivators. It is curious therefore that they were chosen to be the object of inquiry, and this signals the inherent bias of the Board to showcase success stories. Lyallpur, with a population of 42,922, was also one of the most prosperous districts of the Punjab, having benefited hugely from canal irrigation. In some respect, the cultivators represent the optimum scenario for a tenant cultivator in the Punjab, and so the fact that only one out of the four families were able to balance their budget through cultivation alone in 1933[75] is striking. With respect to their income and social status, the tenants were midway between ordinary tenants and the peasant proprietors in the canal colonies. Among Punjabi farmers on the whole, they were a little above average in their earnings. Their living conditions were not ideal and E. D. Lucas, Acting Secretary, commented on their dwellings thus:

> The mud huts of these tenants are low-roofed, windowless, airless and miserable abodes ... in the winter nights, December to February, they are so ill-clad that a closely shut mud box (as someone called these huts) is their chief protection against the bitter cold. There is a village primary school but except for one boy from the family of tenant A, it is not patronized by these families. The Arain is a hard-hearted, hardworking small-scale cultivator and he sees no prospect of returns from the present scheme of education.... In fact he is afraid that his boys may thus learn to shun the hard toil, dirt and sweat of the farm.[76]

The standard of living of the farmers, as evidenced by other measures, was woeful. Twenty-two out of 37 boys of school-going age in the village attended school, while only two girls did. Among the families studied, one out of three boys attended and none of the girls went to school.[77] In the following years, education would continue to be the lowest item of expenditure for the families, occupying around 0.3 per cent of their total expenditure. In 1933–34, two more families were added to the survey, and out of the six families, four were completely illiterate.

The inquiries analysed various aspects of consumption, including how much sugar was consumed, as an indicator of prosperity. Comparisons were also made along other dimensions, some of which are illustrated in Table 6.2 and Table 6.3.

The data on consumption, income, and spending of the farmers assists in ascertaining the extent of penetration of the market. For example, in 1935–36, the families purchased all their rice, meat, vegetables, fruit, and salt from outside the farm.[78]

As part of the research for this book, the area of the Lyallpur (now Faisalabad) district that was the site of the Risalewala farm was visited to see if any of the families of the colonial period were still living there. It was learnt that the lands had been allotted to new tenants in 1947 after some Sikh tenants migrated to India. Despite

Table 6.2   Sugar consumption per capita in the world

	(in lbs.)
USA	89.14
United Kingdom	93.37
Denmark	95.57
Europe	36.83
India	22.30

Source: Kartar Singh, *Family Budgets of Four Tenant Cultivators in the Lyallpur District 1932–33*, publication no. 40 (Lahore: Punjab Board of Economic Inquiry, 1934), p. 11.

Table 6.3   Comparison (percentages) of food consumed

	China	Risalewala	USA
Grains	89.8	75.1	38.7
Animal Products	1.0	14.9	39.2
Vegetables	8.9	0.3	9
Fruits	0.1	0.3	3
Sugar	0.2	9.2	10.1

Source: Kartar Singh, *Family Budgets of Four Tenant Cultivators in the Lyallpur District 1932–33*, publication no. 40 (Lahore: Punjab Board of Economic Inquiry, 1934), p. 15–18.

a thorough search, local administration had no recollection or knowledge of the inquiry by the Board in the colonial period, though they were able to provide other records of peasants on the farm and their details since the early twentieth century. The area is still owned by the government though, and in 1962 the Ayub Agricultural Institute was established there. The land of the Risalewala farm was taken over by the provincial government, along with the tenants. The institute habilitated the tenants in alternate locations outside the institute, and some left the lands themselves. However, 25 tenants are still cultivating the institute's 176 acres. Now their economic condition is very different: they do not live in mud huts and are not obliged to sell their produce to government. Most are resident in houses in adjacent localities. However, 20 per cent are living on government land in *pucca* houses in the periphery. They also keep livestock – youth are given employment opportunities in the institute. The living conditions overall were abysmal.

Previously, tenants and the institute used to distribute the produce in a 50–50 ratio. However, now tenants get 60 per cent and the institute gets 40 per cent of the produce. The tenants are provided seed free of cost from the institute; however, expenses for insecticide and fertilizer are split 50–50. Tenants sell their crops in the open market. The institute carries out crop experiments and is not conducting any inquiries regarding family budgets of the tenants. There was no memory or record of the colonial investigations either.[79]

Soldiers in the Punjab

Several other inquiries undertaken by the Board studied various social groups in Punjabi society, ranging from soldiers to rickshaw drivers to educated and unemployed youth. Much has been written on the Punjab as a military province, with 400,000 of the 563,091 recruits of the British Indian army hailing from the province in 1919. Meanwhile, imperial anthropologies consistently bracketed the Punjabis as a martial race possessing the physical and mental attributes to make good soldiers.[80] In the interwar period, a major imperial concern was the maintenance of loyalty in the imperial army and particularly in the Punjab where the majority of soldiers hailed from. For this purpose, a merging of civil-military bodies occurred in the formation of District Soldiers Boards. These boards were initially set up to resettle soldiers after the first World War but 'eventually became established institutions in the districts, representing the interests of the military classes'.[81] There was a sustained official interest in the condition of soldiers, and the Board of Economic Inquiry also conducted a relevant inquiry in this regard.

The inquiry was commissioned by the board during 1934–38, a period of low agricultural prices before the war, and analysed soldiers' savings and how these were spent. The Punjab has been regarded as a military province with various land grants and other privileges accorded to the army. While most of these perks were reserved for commissioned officers, non-commissioned ranks, that is, soldiers, were also given a few benefits. Chief among these was an amount given by the Military Department to the soldier when he left service. In popular culture, any connection with military service was automatically associated with some wealth, and the welcome home of a soldier is described thus:

> A young soldier returning home with a wad of notes in his belt is a welcome sight to his relatives and friends. If he arrived with a scrap or two of paper consisting of fixed deposit receipts, cash certificates or a savings bank pass book, his welcome might be less hilarious but he would have more chance of keeping his money intact until he could find a way of laying it out to the best advantage. How easy would all this work be if only we had established a Punjab legion at the end of the Great War on the lines of the famous British Legion![82]

Soldiers were considered to have a higher standard of living: 'Among the things which usually mark an ex-military man from others in the village are neater dress, a better type of house, the use of chairs, crockery and a wrist watch.'[83]

The inquiry in question contained data from 1934–38 on soldiers from the infantry and cavalry which were numerically the largest divisions of the Indian Army. The ranks investigated were all non-commissioned: sepoys, *sowars*, and other non-commissioned officers. The interviewees were all those who had been pensioned, transferred to reserve, or discharged between 1934 and 1938. While 1,000 people were interviewed and asked to fill out a questionnaire, the ultimate findings from the report relied on 216 records, which were considered to be the most reliable and complete.

In June 1939, there were 127,556 pensioners in the Punjab. The largest numbers were in the Rawalpindi (16,725) and the Jhelum (12,961) districts. The 216 respondents whose answers formed the basis of this study were either sepoys in the infantry (101) or *sowars* (29) in the cavalry, while the rest belonged to other ranks. Nineteen had left the service for reasons that prevented them from receiving a pension, while a further six had taken gratuity instead of pension. The remaining earned monthly incomes from the army ranging between 3 rupees and 17 rupees, with an average income of 85 rupees per year.

In terms of educational attainment, 157 of the sample had never attended school, 27 had passed the primary school exam, 16 had completed middle school, and five had the matriculation certificate. The youngest member of the sample was 23 years old, while the oldest was 50.

The total savings of the soldiers amounted to 73,922 rupees. The average amount saved per head was 342 rupees, with the highest being saved by the Gurkhas, 885 rupees. About 50 per cent had left the army with amounts ranging between 200 rupees and 400 rupees. Of the total savings of 73,922 rupees, 865 rupees were held in cash by 20 people at the time of interview, and another 12 had 2,919 rupees in their post office accounts. The others spent whatever they had brought from the army, about half of them within six months of their return to the village, and hardly 20 per cent had any balance to carry next year.

So, after subtracting cash and deposits, the total savings were 70,138-6-0 rupees and broke down as shown in Table 6.4.

Most of the debt had been incurred for marriage or house-building expenses, but there was no data provided for this. Other such inquiries had found that in some cases debt resulted from tax or revenue payments owed to the government, but this theme was not addressed in this inquiry which is a serious omission. One Muslim Rajput of Banyani (Rohtak) paid to his creditor all the 108 rupees he received on transfer

Table 6.4 Breakdown of total savings

Item		Amount	Percentage
1.	Repayment of debt	13,798-8-0	19.7
2.	House	12,572-14-0	17.9
3.	Animals, carts, and sheds	10,976-8-0	15.6
4.	Land and agricultural transactions	10,050-0-0	14.4
5.	Ceremonies, litigation, and festivities	7,902-15-0	11.3
6.	Household and recurring requirements	5,073-11-0	7.2
7.	Business	1,720-0-0	2.0
8.	Miscellaneous	1,392-0-0	2
9.	Unspecified	6,659-14-0	9.5

Source: Roshan Lal Anand, *Soldiers' Savings and How They Use Them: Being a Study of the Ways in which the Punjab Soldier Uses the Money He Receives on Leaving the Army*, publication no. 68 (Lahore: Punjab Board of Economic Inquiry, 1940).

to Reserve, in payment of a debt incurred on his marriage in 1932 (the marriage had cost him 500 rupees).[84] Only 27 cases of expenditure on marriage were recorded – partly because most of the men interviewed had been married for a while and had children not yet of marriageable age.[85] Some still ran into debt, however. For example, in Kangra, a 'Rajput spent Rs 600 on his marriage out of which Rs 300 were given in cash to the bride's guardians. This ran him into debt and in order to pay it back he accepted a gratuity of Rs 300 instead of a monthly pension of Rs 3. At the time of interview he was 36 years old and acknowledged that had it not been for the debt, he would have preferred the pension.'[86]

Overall, the report recommended giving the soldiers the retirement benefit in the form of a savings account or cash certificates to prevent them from spending it too soon and too unwisely. The report distinguished between productive, mid-way, and unproductive expenditure. However, the definition of productive, mid-way, or unproductive expenditure was not given. So, as was the case with earlier official inquiries into indebtedness, there was an element of judgment and a criticism for all 'social expenditure'. Contrary to the dominant image of an entrenched military elite, the inquiry shows the poverty and financial struggle of the ordinary soldier, giving a voice to a marginalized figure in Punjabi society. However, given the tendency to not question government policy, the issue of the relationship between debt and land revenue was not addressed. Overall, the inquiries of the Board, despite the richness of the data and value of the subject under study, remained inconsequential, however, and were only consumed for their intellectual merit while ignoring any practical implications of the research.

Conclusion

The Punjab Board of Economic Inquiry emerged in the early twentieth century as a research organization to investigate economic conditions in the province. At the time, academic journals in Economics were also being published in India along with several indigenous research centres. During the first half of the twentieth century, other organizations like the Gokhale Institute (established in 1930) emerged, championing their own ideas for socio-economic reform. There was also a spread of eugenicist ideas like those of P. C. Mahlanabois, a pioneer in statistical research in India.[87] In some ways, these local initiatives echoed colonial biases against certain castes and classes in the subcontinent. Indebtedness was one problem where these deeply held prejudices found expression in research, policy, and actions by the state, and in writings by local intellectuals. This chapter analysed the findings of a major institution, the Punjab Board of Economic Inquiry, not only with reference to indebtedness but also its investigations into rural areas more generally. Local critiques went beyond the official line though. For example, the Khaksar movement, a fascist-style organization, was as similarly popularizing its vision of rural economic resurgence as the Communist party in the Punjab was seeking to expand its influence.

It emerges that, first, the scope and nature of inquiries being conducted was crucial for understanding the role of the Board and similar research institutes and publications. The aim was not to inform policy meaningfully; instead, the gathering of data became an end in itself. This is despite the potential of the inquiries to enrich contemporaneous debates in rural poverty. The way that the sample was chosen was not for the sake of determining conditions in the most backward or poor villages but instead where data could be obtained more easily – for example, on a government farm or in an area of sympathetic landlords. Often the data collection entailed daily account keeping by an investigator of the Board who took up residence there. However, there was little uptake of this painstakingly gathered data by government officials, except to reaffirm existing colonial prejudices and opinions. Despite the operations of the Board, many officials continued to regard such research as unnecessary, and a proposal to establish an agricultural research institute in Delhi was vehemently opposed by the government.[88]

At the same time, these filigree inquiries allow us to gauge a sense of everyday economic life in the Punjab at the time. It signalled probably one of the earliest attempts to study individual budgets and village economies, a trend that continued to flourish with the emergence of the community development initiatives of the 1950s and 1960s. Village studies became a fashionable doctoral dissertation topic well into the 1970s, even as most studies retained little historical memory of earlier efforts.

The collection of statistical data and its use in reports was a trend that became the hallmark of technocrats or experts dispatched to developing countries later. While the questions may have changed, the output of multilateral organizations may also be critiqued for selective samples, ideological presuppositions, and a weak link with government policy and implementation. At the same time, the academic culture and consumption of reports by donor agencies continues. The fetishization of the local and the community also carries on, and the case study remains an active area of research. The irony is the innovative way in which these ideas are presented with no recognition of the individual, household, and district-level inquiries conducted decades ago by the Board of Economic Inquiry.

Notes

1   Edward W. Said, *Covering Islam* (New York: Pantheon Books, 1981), p. 154.

2   Rudyard Kipling, 'The Masque of Plenty', *The Collected Poems of Rudyard Kipling* (Ware: Wordsworth Editions Ltd, 1994), p. 37.

3   Madan Gopal, *Sir Chhotu Ram: A Political Biography* (New Delhi: B.R. Publishing Corporation, 1977), pp. 167–68.

4   Prem Chowdhry, *Punjab Politics: The Role of Sir Chhotu Ram* (Delhi: Vikas, 1984), pp. 234–37.

5   W. H. Myles, 'The Board of Economic Inquiry, Punjab', *Indian Journal of Economics* 5, no. 3 (1925): 246–49.

6   Myles, 'The Board of Economic Inquiry, Punjab',.

7   James Scott, *Seeing Like a State: How Certain Schemes to Improve the Human Condition Have Failed* (New Haven: Yale University Press, 1988).

8   See Cyril P. K. Fazal, *A Bibliography of Economic Literature Relating to the Punjab* (Lahore: Punjab Board of Economic Enquiry, 1941); Dial Das, *Vital Statistics of the Punjab 1901–40* (Lahore: Dial, 1943); Cyril P. K. Fazal, *A Guide to Punjab Government Reports and Statistics* (Lahore: Punjab Board of Economic Enquiry 1939); and Gulshan Rai, *Agricultural Statistics of the Punjab 1901–2 to 1935–6* (Lahore: Punjab Board of Economic Enquiry, 1937).

9   Punjab Board of Economic Inquiry, *Questionnaire for Economic Inquiries* (Lahore: Punjab Board pf Economic Enquiry, 1924).

10 Anand Chandavarkar, *Keynes and India: A Study in Economics and Biography* (London: Macmillan, 1989), p. 17.

11 Chandavarkar, *Keynes and India*, p. 40.

12 Quoted in Clive Dewey, 'Patwari and Chaukidar: Subordinate Officials and the Reliability of India's Agricultural Statistics', in *The Imperial Impact: Studies in the Economic History of Africa and India*, edited by C. Dewey and A.G. Hopkins, pp. 280–314 (London, 1978), p. 280.

13 See, for instance, Carl E. Pray, 'The Economics of Agricultural Research in British Punjab and Pakistani Punjab, 1905–1975', *Journal of Economic History* 40, no. 1 (1980): 174–76; and Carl E. Pray, 'The Impact of Agricultural Research in British India', *Journal of Economic History* 44, no. 2 (1984): 429–40.

14 Fazal, *A Bibliography of Economic Literature Relating to the Punjab.*

15 C. F. Strickland, *The Progress of Rural Welfare in India* (London: Oxford University Press, 1934), p. 3.

16 Strickland, *The Progress of Rural Welfare in India*, p.11.

17 Strickland, *The Progress of Rural Welfare in India*, p. 12.

18 Strickland, *The Progress of Rural Welfare in India*, p. 37.

19 These included: A. J. Appasamy et. al., *The Cultural Problem*, Oxford Pamphlets on Indian Affairs (London: Oxford University Press, 1942); K. M. Panikkar, *Indian States*, Oxford Pamphlets on Indian Affairs (London: Oxford University Press, 1942); A. Appadorai, *Democracy in India*, Oxford Pamphlets on Indian Affairs (London: Oxford University Press, 1942); S. Natarajan, *Social Problems*, Oxford Pamphlets on Indian Affairs (London: Oxford University Press, 1942); Radhakamal Mukerjee, *The Food Supply*, Oxford Pamphlets on Indian Affairs (London: Oxford University Press, 1942); T. Vijayaraghavacharya, *The Land and Its Problems*, Oxford Pamphlets on Indian Affairs (London: Oxford University Press, 1943); Suniti Kumar Chatterji, *Languages and the Linguistic Problem*, Oxford Pamphlets on Indian Affairs (London: Oxford University Press, 1943); John B. Grant, *The Health of India*, Oxford Pamphlets on Indian Affairs (London: Oxford University Press, 1943); Seton Lloyd, *Iraq*, Oxford Pamphlets on Indian Affairs (London: Oxford University Press, 1943); Verrier Elwin, *The Aboriginals*, Oxford Pamphlets on Indian Affairs (London: Oxford University Press, 1943); K. G. Saiyadain et. al., *The Educational System*, Oxford Pamphlets on Indian Affairs (London: Oxford University Press, 1943); B. S. Guha, *Racial Elements in the Population*, Oxford Pamphlets on Indian Affairs (London: Oxford University Press, 1944); Harold Glover, *Soil Erosion*, Oxford Pamphlets on Indian Affairs (London: Oxford University Press, 1944); F. L. Brayne, *Winning the Peace*, Oxford Pamphlets on Indian Affairs (London: Oxford University Press, 1944); Seth Drucquer, *Broadcasting*, Oxford Pamphlets on Indian Affairs (London: Oxford University Press, 1945); A. M. Heron, *Mineral Resources*, Oxford Pamphlets on Indian Affairs (London: Oxford University Press, 1945); Bimal C. Ghose, *Industrial Location*, Oxford Pamphlets on Indian Affairs (London: Oxford University Press 1945); F. P. Antia, *Transport*, Oxford Pamphlets on Indian Affairs (London: Oxford University Press, 1946); Claude Batley, *Architecture* (London, 1946); Percival Spear, *National Harmony*, Oxford Pamphlets on Indian Affairs (London: Oxford University Press, 1946); W. R. S. Satthianadhan and J. C. Ryan, *Cooperation*, Oxford Pamphlets on Indian Affairs, no. 39 (London: Oxford University Press, 1946); and T. K. Critchley, *Australia and New Zealand*, Oxford Pamphlets on Indian Affairs (London: Oxford University Press, 1946).

20 See the complete list of delegates and an account of the opening ceremony of the conference in Henry Duffield Craik, 'Opening Ceremony of the Indian Statistical Conference: Second Session, 1939', *Indian Journal of Statistics* 4, no. 4 (1940): 603–06.

21 See, for instance, A. P. Pillay, *Welfare Problems in Rural India* (Bombay: DB Taraporevala Sons and Co., 1932); E. Thompson, *The Reconstruction of India* (London: Faber and Faber, 1930); C. F. Strickland, *Review of Rural Welfare Activities in India* (London: Village Welfare Association, 1932); Miriam Young, *Seen and Heard in a Punjab Village* (London: Student Christian Movement Press, 1931); Lord Linlithgow, *The Indian Peasant* (London: Faber and Faber, 1932); and G. Keating, *Agricultural Progress in Western India* (London: Longmans, Green and Co., 1921).

22 See the article 'Indian Economics', *Civil and Military Gazette*, 4 November 1916; and an essay on the war of capital and labour, 'Sarmaya aur Mehnat ki Jang', *Zamindar*, 28 August 1912.

23 See, for instance, Rev. J. C. Heinrich, *The Psychology of a Suppressed People* (London: George Allen and Unwin Ltd, 1937), a book by a missionary on the poor and untouchables.

24 Dial Das, *Vital Statistics of the Punjab 1901–40, publication no. 80*, Punjab Board of Economic Inquiry (Lahore, 1943).

25 Hugh Tinker, 'Authority and Community in Village India', *Pacific Affairs* 32, no. 4, (1959): 354–75.

26 Zekiye Elgar, *A Punjabi Village in Pakistan* (New York: Edwin Mellen Press, 1964).

27 See a review of the book, Clive Dewey, 'Annals of Rural Punjab', *Modern Asian Studies* 10, no. 1 (1976): 131–38; and Kessinger's response, Tom Kessinger, 'Indian Village Records and Historical Village Studies. A Reply to C. Dewey, "Annals of Rural Punjab"', *Modern Asian Studies* 11, no. 4 (1977): 615–22.

28 Man Singh Mathur, 'Rural Change in Perspective', *Economic and Political Weekly* 3, no. 5 (1968): 259–65.

29 See Timothy Mitchell, *Rule of Experts: Egypt, Techno-Politics, Modernity* (Berkeley: University of California Press, 2002).

30 Quoted in Mitchell, *Rule of Experts*, p. 129.

31 See David A. Morse, *The Origin and Evolution of the I.L.O. and its Role in the World Community* (New York: State School of Industrial and Labor Relations, Cornell University, 1969).

32 Morse, *The Origin and Evolution of the I.L.O.*, p. 46.

33 Sir Malcolm Darling was one such expert sent by the ILO to Pakistan in the 1950s to study labour conditions there. Other examples include Sir Roger Thomas, erstwhile ICS officer, who became an adviser to the Government of Pakistan in the 1950s and 1960s on agricultural issues. His private papers contain an account of the various missions: Sir Roger Thomas papers, London, British Library, Mss Eur. F235.

34 Randhir Singh, *An Economic Survey of Kala Gaddi Thamman (Chak 73 G.B.): A Village in the Lyallpur District of the Punjab*, Punjab Board of Economic Inquiry Village Survey No. 4 (Lahore, 1932), p. iii.

35 R. K. Seth and Faiz Illahi, *An Economic Survey of Durrana Langana, a Village in the Multan District of the Punjab*, Punjab Board of Economic Inquiry Village Surveys–11 (Lahore, 1938), p. iii.

36 Seth and Illahi, *An Economic Survey of Durrana Langana*, p. x.

37 Anchal Das, *An Economic Survey of Gajju Chak, A Village in the Gujranwala District of the Punjab*, Punjab Board of Economic Inquiry Village Surveys–6 (Lahore, 1934), p. vi.

38 A. Das, *An Economic Survey of Gajju Chak*, p. xv

39 Abdur Rahim Khan, *An Economic Survey of Bhambu Sandila, A Village in the Muzaffargarh District of the Punjab*, Punjab Board of Economic Inquiry Village Surveys–8 (Lahore, 1935), p. xv.

40 Khan, *An Economic Survey of Bhambu Sandila*, p. 7.

41 Khan, *An Economic Survey of Bhambu Sandila*, p. vi.

42 Malcolm Darling, *Rusticus Loquitur: The Old Light and the New in the Punjab Village* (London: Oxford University Press, 1930), p. 276.

43 Khan, *An Economic Survey of Bhambu Sandila*, p. xiii.

44 Darling, *Rusticus Loquitor*, p. 286.

45 Seth and Illahi, *An Economic Survey of Durrana Langana*, p. xiv.

46 Seth and Illahi, *An Economic Survey of Durrana Langana*, p. xviii.

47 A. Das, *An Economic Survey of Gajju Chak*, p. xi.

48 Seth and Illahi, *An Economic Survey of Durrana Langana*.

49 A. Das, *An Economic Survey of Gajju Chak*, p. 154.

50 Seth and Illahi, *An Economic Survey of Durrana Langana*, p. 266

51 A. Das, *An Economic Survey of Gajju Chak*, p. xii.

52 A. Das, *An Economic Survey of Gajju Chak*, p. xiii.

53 L. Dawar, *Market Practices in the Punjab: Being a Study of the Practices Affecting the Producer in the Grain and Cotton Markets, Together with the Rules and Regulations Governing Similar Practices under the Bombay and Berar Market Legislation*, Punjab Board of Economic Inquiry (Lahore, 1934), p. iv.

54 Dawar, *Market Practices in the Punjab*, p. 47.

55 Dawar, *Market Practices in the Punjab*, p. 51.

56 W. H. Myles, *Condition of Weights and Measures in the Punjab: Being the Result of Investigations in Thirteen Areas in the Province*, publication no. 42 (Lahore: Punjab Board of Economic Inquiry, 1936), p. ii.

57 Myles, *Weights and Measures in the Punjab*, p. iii.

58 Myles, *Weights and Measures in the Punjab*, p. vi.

59 Myles, *Weights and Measures in the Punjab*, p. vi

60 Myles, *Weights and Measures in the Punjab*, p. viii

61 Myles, *Weights and Measures in the Punjab*, p. 19

62 I. D. Mahendru, *Some Factors Affecting the Price of Wheat in the Punjab: Being an Examination of the Conditions in the Amritsar, Jullundur, Lyallpur and Okara Mandis Together with a Description of the Market Transactions as Regards Wholesale Dealings in Wheat*, Punjab Board of Economic Inquiry (Lahore, 1937), p. v.

63 Mahendru, *The Price of Wheat in the Punjab*, p. 6.

64 Mahendru, *The Price of Wheat in the Punjab*, p. 37.

65 Mahendru, *The Price of Wheat in the Punjab*, p. 102.

66 Mahendru, *The Price of Wheat in the Punjab*, p. 25.

67 Darling, *The Punjab Peasant in Prosperity and Debt*, p. 105.

68 Khan, *An Economic Survey of Bhambu Sandila*, p. xi.

69 Figures from A. Das, *An Economic Survey of Gajju Chak*, pp. iii–iv.

70 Khan, *An Economic Survey of Bhambu Sandila*, p. xi.

71 Darling, *The Punjab Peasant in Prosperity and Debt*, p. 98.

72 Darling, *The Punjab Peasant in Prosperity and Debt*, pp. 99–100.

73 Khan, *An Economic Survey of Bhambu Sandila*, p. xix.

74 Labh Singh, *Family Budgets 1937–38 of Ten Cultivators in the Punjab, Being the Sixth Year's Accounts of Six Cultivators on the Risalewala Farm near Lyallpur and Second Year's Accounts of Four Owner: Cultivators in the Hoshiarpur, Amritsar and Rohtak Districts*, Punjab Board of Economic Inquiry (Lahore, 1939), p. 4.

75 Kartar Singh, *Family Budgets of Four Tenant Cultivators in the Lyallpur district 1932–33*, publication no. 40, Punjab Board of Economic Inquiry (Lahore, 1934), p. iii.

76 K. Singh, *Family Budgets of Four Tenant Cultivators in the Lyallpur district 1932–33*, p. iii.

77 K. Singh, *Family Budgets of Four Tenant Cultivators in the Lyallpur district 1932–33*, p. 20.

78 Labh Singh, *Family Budgets 1935–36 of Six Tenant Cultivators in the Lyallpur District, Being the Fourth Year's Accounts of Some Cultivators on the Risalewala Farm near Lyallpur*, Punjab Board of Economic Inquiry (Lahore, 1938), p. 19.

79 Fieldwork visit to Risalewala, Faisalabad district, June 2015.

80 See Catherine Coombs, 'Partition Narratives: Displaced Trauma and Culpability among British Civil Servants in 1940s Punjab', *Modern Asian Studies* 45, no. 1 (2011): 201–24.

81 See a detailed discussion in Tai Yong Tan, 'Maintaining the Military Districts: Civil-Military Integration and District Soldiers' Boards in the Punjab, 1919–1939', *Modern Asian Studies* 28, no. 4 (1994):. 833–74.

82 Roshan Lal Anand, *Soldiers' Savings and How They Use Them: Being a Study of the Ways in which the Punjab Soldier Uses the Money He Receives on Leaving the Army*, publication no. 68, Punjab Board of Economic Inquiry (Lahore, 1940), p. iii.

83 Anand, *Soldiers' Savings and How They Use Them*, p. 19.

84 Anand, *Soldiers' Savings and How They Use Them*, p. 18.

85 Anand, *Soldiers' Savings and How They Use Them*, p. 22.

86 Anand, *Soldiers' Savings and How They Use Them*, p. 22.

87 See P. C. Mahalanobis, 'Analysis of Race-Mixture in Bengal', *Journal of the Asiatic Society of Bengal*, no. 23 (1927): 301–33.

88 See details of the controversy in Azim Husain, *Mian Fazl-i-Husain: A Political Biography* (New York: Longmans, Green & Co., 1946), pp. 216–20.

Postscript

To those new states whom we welcome to the ranks of the free, we pledge our word that one form of colonial control shall not have passed away merely to be replaced by a far more iron tyranny ... to those people in the huts and villages of half the globe struggling to break the bonds of mass misery, we pledge our best efforts to help them help themselves, for whatever period is required – not because the communists may be doing it, not because we seek their votes but because it is right. If a free society cannot help the many who are poor, it cannot the few who are rich. To our sister republics south of our border we offer a special pledge – to convert our good words into good deeds – in a new alliance for progress – to assist free men and free governments in casting off the chains of poverty.

—President John F. Kennedy, inaugural address, 20 January 1961

Ideas of rural reconstruction or cooperation did not pass away with colonial rule but endured in South Asia under new nomenclature and frameworks. This postscript discusses the legacy of British policies of development in the Punjab, even though the lineage is marked by a discontinuity: while programmes of community developed and funded by the Americans took root in both India and Pakistan from the 1950s onwards, there was little recognition of the earlier colonial flirtation with similar ideas. Instead, community development was presented as a novel way of eradicating 'third world poverty' and continues to be recast in various deifications of the local as an 'innovative' cure for underdevelopment. This ahistorical persistence of ideas of community is neither accidental nor benign: at the heart of all valorization of 'grassroots' development is an abdication of responsibility at the structural level and a transfer of blame to the poor. Much like the colonial schemes of rural uplift, the community development programmes are also premised on self-help and a fundamental criticism of the outlook and habits of the peasant or citizen as the root cause of indebtedness or poverty.

Both India and Pakistan embarked on large-scale community development programmes in the 1950s and 1960s, with the financial support of the United States. In some ways, these programmes built on the earlier colonial experiments in rural reconstruction, though without acknowledging this historical precedent. In both countries, the programmes met with ultimate failure, rather like the colonial case. Furthermore, just like the forgotten colonial experiments, the community development movements of the 1950s and 1960s remain largely forgotten, as for India and Pakistan the period is remembered as the era of Nehruvian planning and dam-building and Ayub's rapid industrialization and the green revolution, respectively. This amnesia regarding the failure of community development programmes, or the earlier colonial version, allows the approaches to retain a tenacity and legitimacy as an answer to underdevelopment that they ill-deserve. This postscript discusses the emergence of development studies and recounts the failure of post-colonial attempts at community development, as well as the fate of the cooperative experiments in the Punjab.

However, even the failed programmes of the 1950s and 1960s do not represent the finale. Ideas of community-based development, including microfinance, continue to remain popular to this day as antidotes to poverty. Between 2004 and 2014, the World Bank spent around 85 billion dollars on community-based or community-driven development.[1] With its faith in local cultures and a suspicion of the regulatory state, such ideas appeal to both the right and the left. The lack of historical memory of previous attempts at community development and their failure is a major reason why there remains a therapeutic aura around such programmes.[2] F. L. Brayne and Malcolm Darling were emphasizing rural uplift or rural reconstruction in the 1930s, and at the time 'their activity was regarded by higher authority as a heresy practiced by crazy district officers.'[3] In other quarters, the efforts were seen as revolutionary and inspirational.[4] Brayne's Gurgaon experiment was highly localized and intensive and also ultimately unsuccessful. It was based fundamentally on the idea that the peasant's worldview and habits needed to be reformed.[5] The following sections discuss the theoretical relationship between colonialism and development studies, and the equally ineffectual post-colonial attempts at community development and cooperation, while summarizing the main arguments of the book.

Some Introductory Thoughts on Colonialism and Development Studies

Development economics, or development studies, is generally considered to be a 'post-colonial' discipline with newly independent states channelling the nationalist impulse to devise growth strategies and plans of industrialization throughout the 1950s and 1960s. This did not occur *in vacuo* as the United States embarked on a large-scale programme of foreign aid in the same period alongside the technical assistance programme of the United Nations and other multilateral organizations. Development thus became an ameliorative science bent on undoing the extractive wrongs of colonialism. Some scholars have argued that the new foreign aid and technical assistance regime, couched in Cold War politics, was hardly without direct benefit to the donor countries,[6] but there has been little recognition of the colonial roots of assisted development. Instead, development studies were conceived of as a forward-looking subject, answering questions that had not been asked before and proposing solutions that were novel. History was therefore not the inspiration for development studies; history was instead the extractive colonial force that needed to be unwritten. This section explores the intellectual genealogy of the field of development studies, in terms of theory and methodology, and what the colonial experience meant for the discipline.

The term 'development' was first used in a socio-economic sense by Karl Marx and others in the nineteenth century, but the adjective 'underdeveloped' has a much recent origin. It was first used in a paper by an employee of the International Labour Organisation (ILO), William Benson, in an article titled 'The Economic Advancement of Underdeveloped Areas' in 1942.[7] In December 1948, the United Nations General Assembly adopted a pair of resolutions: 'Economic Development of Underdeveloped Countries' and 'Technical Assistance for Economic Development', signalling the start of a post-colonial era of development led by international organizations. The first popular usage of the word 'underdeveloped' was by the American President, Harry Truman, in 1949, as part of Point Four in his inaugural speech. Truman said: 'Fourth, we must embark on a brave new programme for making the benefits of our scientific advances and industrial progress available for the improvement and growth of underdeveloped areas.' The introduction of the adjective 'underdeveloped' and later the noun 'underdevelopment' changed the meaning of the word 'developed' or 'development' for the two were inextricably linked. Earlier usage of the term development, for example, by Vladimir Lenin in his work on the development of capitalism in Russia (1899) or Joseph Schumpeter's *Theory of Economic Development* (1911), had discussed development as an 'intransitive phenomenon which simply happens'.[8] The coinage of the word 'underdeveloped' gave development a 'transitive meaning',[9] replacing the colonizer–colonized dichotomy with the developed–underdeveloped one. According to Rist, the difference, however, was that the former was based on opposition with inevitable confrontation, while the latter was based on mutual benefit. Development and underdevelopment shared a symbiotic relationship, and development studies emerged as a field of inquiry where the diagnosis and cure for underdevelopment were to be found.

Despite these recent origins, the novelty of ideas of development economics has been questioned in a general sense. Gerald Meier, a leading development economist of the twentieth century, wrote: 'Much of the development theory of today is already to be found in the writings of the eighteenth century, especially in those of Hume (1748), Steuart (1767) and Smith.'[10] Others such as William Barber have written on classical political economy and its application in India.[11] These connections were also emphasized in scholarship during the 1950s and 1960s on neocolonialism, such as Paul Baran's seminal *The Political Economy of Growth*,[12] and later works on structuralism and dependency theory by scholars like Raul Prebish, Hans Wolfgang Singer, and Gunnar Myrdal. The Soviet Industrialization debate from the 1920s was also significant and focused on macroeconomic policies to advance national growth in underdeveloped economies. Overall, this scholarship focused on various macroeconomic themes such as industrialization, the structure of the international economy, and uneven trade relations, and how they engaged the post-colonial state in 'neocolonialism'.[13] However, the connection between microeconomic schemes of development and colonialism has not been studied deeply. Exceptions are *Colonizing Egypt*[14] and *Rule of Experts*[15] by Timothy Mitchell, which discuss the emergence of peasant studies as well as the rise of technocrats, but connections between development studies and colonialism need to be analysed further.

A useful example for understanding the links between colonialism in India and the development of economic thought is through the life of John Maynard Keynes who worked at the India Office at the start of his career. Keynes published numerous books on Indian finance and had a long intellectual engagement with the economic problems of the country despite never visiting it.

> [Keynes] belonged to a generation to which the Indian Empire and the problems of the British Government of India stood as a great challenge luring many of the intelligent men of the age into its service.... India in effect functioned as a vast social laboratory where economic and juridical changes and reforms could be implemented and observed with minimal political constraints despite the unavoidable deference to custom and status in a traditional society.[16]

Keynes also continued to advise on Indian economic affairs in the post-colonial era. As a professor at Cambridge, he and Alfred Marshall mentored a generation of graduates who would serve in India as imperial bureaucrats (including Malcolm Darling[17]) as well as Indian students who pioneered economic and statistical inquiry in the country. The latter included P. C. Mahalanobis mentioned earlier, who became Director of the Indian Statistical Institute and an architect of national planning in post-colonial India, and Sir Manohar Lal, an economist who later served as Finance Minister in the Punjab government (1935–40). Keynes also supported the cooperative movement in India, as discussed in Chapter 4, despite a lack of results. The greatest impact was through the careers of his mentees who became civil servants in India. For a few officers like Darling and Brayne, India represented an intellectual or a moral challenge that inspired plans for rural reconstruction borne out of an intimate knowledge of peasant life. Punjab thus became the site of schemes of community development decades before they were championed by international organizations, and an examination of the initiatives historicizes and pegs ideas of community and development studies in a genealogy starting from colonialism.

This is also significant because the discipline of development economics was not regarded as a serious economic sub-field for many years, as economists felt that developing economies were merely the sites for case studies or the application of theories and models developed in the West. They were not seen as crucibles from which original models or theories emerged. Hans Singer, a leading development economist, recalls a conversation with Joseph Schumpeter in 1947 when he told him that he (Singer) would be working with the United Nations on the problems of underdeveloped countries. Schumpeter replied, 'But I thought you were an economist!'[18] It was only after the development of mathematical growth models in development economics in the 1950s and 1960s that the field acquired some credibility in the increasingly quantified discipline of economics. However, the problem with the development of mathematical models was that their abstraction and assumption resulted in basic prescriptions, which fuelled the growth mania in developing economies throughout the 1950s and 1960s.[19] On the other hand, the community development movement proceeded from more humble roots and was pushed with a political agenda to battle communism in the era of the Cold War. When the growth models became increasingly criticized and eventually discredited by the 1970s, due to their links with increasing inequality, a move towards human development approaches emerged. Community development programmes, however, remained popular despite being ineffective, yet their colonial origins, the repeated experiments in this direction, and their limitations remain grossly under-studied.

This book examined a trial of the ideas of community development in colonial Punjab to question both ideas of community development and theories of path dependence and institutional continuity. It did not stop at excavating the experimental evidence but also suggested why the approaches continue to be popular. It is not simply a case of amnesia. Rather, both institutional explanations of underdevelopment and community development approaches share an important feature: they absolve the status quo from blame. Institutional explanations castigate an inherited colonial 'system' that is largely immutable by definition, whereas community development programmes task the poor individual with self-help and the burden of lifting himself or herself out of poverty. In both cases, the ruling elite or power structures remain free of blame. Hence, an examination of both approaches in a period of colonial rule not only furthers an understanding of the local history of the Punjab but also critiques development theory.

Community Development and Cooperation after 1947

The community development movement started from the 1930s to the 1960s and touched much of the world. By 1960, the United Nations estimated that over 60 countries possessed large-scale community development programmes: nearly half of them were nationwide in extent.[20] In India, the community development programme began on 2 October 1952, Gandhi's birthday. The programme started as a pilot in Etawah, Uttar Pradesh, in 1947 and, after its perceived success, was scaled to the national level.[21] It was funded by the United States and initially covered 16,500 villages. Within a decade, it expanded to 446,000 villages (253.2 million inhabitants) all over India under what came to be known as *panchayat raj*. By 1965, it covered every village in India (in terms of population this equalled over 10 per cent of the world's population).[22] In Pakistan, the movement started a bit later, in 1953, under the Village-AID programme, again through funding from American foreign aid agencies.[23]

An American architect, Albert Mayer, led the project in Etawah, and the chief idea was to make the villagers responsible for their development by having them design and implement welfare schemes.[24] Even as Nehru emerged as the champion of dams and large-scale planning, he placed community development at the centre of a campaign called 'democratic decentralization' to counter the centralizing process. *Panchayat raj*, which was the nationwide successor of the Etawah project, was thus based on village councils, local elections, and devolution. Nehru termed community development as 'by far the most revolutionary thing we have undertaken'[25] and the 'the dynamo providing the motive force'[26] of the first five-year plan.

In Pakistan, the Village-AID (Village Agricultural and Industrial Programme) was launched also with American financial support in 1953 and later followed by the West Pakistan Rural Works Programme under the Ayub regime in the 1960s.[27] The Village-AID programme was described in the first five-year plan (1955–60) as follows: 'The Village-AID programme is of crucial importance as the means for bringing better living standards and a new spirit of hope (and) confidence to the villagers where, according to the 1951 census, 90 per cent of the people of the country live.'[28] The idea was to improve conditions through the 'initiative and energy of village people themselves, cooperating and pooling their own resources'. It was envisioned as a nationwide community development programme and between 1955 and 1960, 25.5 crore rupees were spent on it. During this period, 150,000 agricultural demonstration plots were set up, 1,000 miles of canals were dug, 3,000 miles of unmetalled roads were built, and 4,000 miles of old roads were repaired. Much like *panchayat raj* in India, the second five-year plan in Pakistan (1960–65) saw the introduction of a system of 'Basic Democracies that built on the endeavours at community development by political devolution. The Village-AID programme was formally discontinued in 1962 without even a formal evaluation and replaced by the Basic Democracies and Rural Works Programme (1962–69). During the same period, Ayub Khan also sponsored the Korangi Township, a community development programme aimed at resettling refugee slum dwellers.[29] All these attempts at rural development met with bureaucratic opposition and internal rivalries between departments.[30]

An important feature of the community development programme in Pakistan was the role of Akhtar Hameed Khan, a former Indian Civil Service (ICS) officer, who established the Academy for Rural Development in Comilla (former East Pakistan, current-day Bangladesh) in 1958. Khan was familiar with colonial efforts at rural reconstruction and criticized them, saying 'it cost government next to nothing and it achieved little more than nothing'.[31] Akhtar Hameed Khan became the architect of the 'Comilla approach' to rural development, which grew out of an intensive community development project in the region. While discussing the Comila academy, Khan wrote: 'Luckily the Comila Academy got the patronage of both Ayub Khan and the Harvard advisers. Ayub Khan protected me when the moneylender-contractor lobby asked him to drive me away because according to them I was a disguised communist who was working against Pakistan.'[32] The Academy carried out research and training in community development, and Khan would later found the Orangi Pilot Project, another attempt at community development, in Karachi in the 1980s. The salient feature of Khan's approach was the rejection of an outside expert in rural development. Khan wrote: 'In the light of our research, we discarded the orthodox notions of an outsider, a missionary or guide-philosopher friend, or a multipurpose worker, or an agricultural assistant, coming to convert or rescue or reclaim the village. Instead we found that it was more fruitful to rotate village representatives between the nascent urban centre and their rural habitations.'[33]

Meanwhile, the cooperative movement in the Punjab also persisted in the post-colonial era. In March 1948, the Government of Pakistan decided to launch a scheme to popularize agriculture on cooperative lines, starting with the most favourable areas. For this purpose, the Thal colony, a new canal colony in the Punjab, was selected where ex-service men and refugees from India were resettled. In the Multan district as well, cooperative societies were established and in all over 200 cooperative farming societies were formed with members totalling 11,765 families,[34] and, in February 1959, a Credit Inquiry Commission was appointed to appraise the state of credit facilities in rural areas, especially in anticipation of proposed land reforms.[35] 'These societies helped members in the economic as well as social fields. Through them the members purchased seed and other of their agricultural and domestic requirements. They further aimed at providing dwelling houses, laying roads, lighting and drainage facilities. Thus they were put in the process of becoming full-fledged cooperative farming societies.'[36] From 1953 to 1956, the government enlisted the services of Professor Schiller, an FAO expert for cooperative farming, in the Punjab under the United Nations Technical Assistance Programme to develop cooperatives.[37] Schiller advocated 'individual farming on cooperative lines' in the Punjab, which was 'an arrangement whereby the small farmers, instead of working separately with inadequate resources on small plots of land scattered haphazardly, can cultivate cooperatively in proper farming units, permitting the adoption of improved farming methods which would raise the level of productivity and so ensure a higher income than before.'[38]

The Failure of the Programmes

Despite the rhetoric and patronage of the programmes at the highest levels, community development programmes in both India and Pakistan failed to achieve much. In India, they became a bureaucratic leviathan lacking genuine grassroots participation.[39] The final straw was Nehru's death in 1964. Nehru had been the foremost champion of community development, but his successor, Lal Bahadur Shastri, directed the community developers to focus exclusively on increasing agricultural production, and, after him, Indira Gandhi brought the ministry of community development under the ministry of agriculture in 1966, further decreasing its importance and power. She slashed funding for the programme, and the balance between centralization and decentralization that Nehru had tried to maintain instead gave way to authoritarianism under Indira Gandhi.

In Pakistan as well, both the Village-AID and the Rural Works Programme ultimately failed to achieve much. Critics of the programme pointed out that:

It is one of the inner contradictions of the Community Development Programme that the people directing the programme represent the interests and classes which stand to lose their status, privilege and power if the programme succeeds. Today political and economic power is concentrated in the hands of the westernized elite and specially the government servants. Democratisation of society is bound to reduce this power and the advantages that accrue from it.[40]

The Village-AID programme had close similarities with Brayne's work in Gurgaon in that the village worker was the outside agent acting as 'educator-organiser-planner-friend-philosopher-guide'.[41] Both the Village-AID and Rural Works programmes were shelved due to a lack of results.

Aside from the immediate factors leading to the collapse of the community development programmes in India and Pakistan, several more general trends can be observed about the approach in general. Ideologically, community development programmes mirrored the colonial attempts at rural reconstruction in that a foreign vision of improvement was implemented in the rural areas at an intimate level. Even though the ultimate success of the programme was linked with the villagers' effort and enthusiasm, they were not the architects of the vision, except in Akhtar Hameed Khan's Comilla project where he explicitly rejected prescriptions from outside. Partha Chatterjee has attributed the obsession with economic development among post-colonial governments in South Asia as a continuation of an 'enlightenment epistemology' that had motivated colonial officials to similarly prescribe for the peasant.[42] However, this view of community development as an example of a larger drive towards modernization in developing countries is not entirely convincing.

One problem with viewing community development as part of a holistic agenda of modernization, industrialization, and development is the deep ideological conflicts between modernizers and theorists supporting community development. Modernization theorists focused on deficiencies in developing countries – the absence of democratic institutions, capital, technology, and so on, and then prescribed ways to acquire these.[43] They championed large-scale industrialization, urbanization, and growth, accusing community development supporters to be 'cultists about participation'.[44] The sociologist W. E. Moore observed that community developers were behaving like 'peasant lovers, who have a somewhat distorted notion of peasant communities and certainly a distorted notion of the general level of health, material well-being and general satisfaction on the part of the local people'.[45]

Even within India, not everyone was enamoured of the community development approach, with one of the detractors being B. R. Ambedkar. Ambedkar argued that the village was the site where caste hierarchies were the strongest and untouchables faced the most galling discrimination. He wrote, 'What is the village but a sink of localism, a den of ignorance, narrow mindedness and communalism?'[46] The community development programmes shied away from addressing the structural inequalities of rural society, instead going for cosmetic makeovers and self-examination on the part of peasants. Ambedkar felt that this ignored the inherent biases and injustice of rural life.

Another reason behind the failure of the community development programmes was the lack of political backing. In the Indian case, while the first five-year plan had openly advocated for the approach, the vision of the second plan was provided by P. C. Mahlanobis, a physicist and passionate modernizer. He believed that the development of heavy industry must be given paramount importance and wanted to emulate Soviet and Chinese styles of economic planning. In such a schema, community development automatically fell to the sidelines.

In Pakistan, the various tiers of bureaucratic machinery clashed over the implementation of the Village-AID and later the Rural Works programme. After 1947, the Civil Service of Pakistan (the descendants of the ICS) was supplemented by various technical departments for agriculture, irrigation, power, and so on, and the two strands of bureaucracy could not work amicably to implement the programme.[47] Rural development in the colonial case had been allowed to continue as long as it did not antagonize the local political elite – the main concern of the colonial bureaucracy was the maintenance of law and order. However, with independence, economic development itself became a primary aim of the government and the same complacency was no longer possible. Ayub Khan's regime openly sought to change the rural structure by introducing land reforms, but these were not well-implemented, and on the ground, with an ineffective bureaucratic machinery, the programme did not manage to effect real change. On the contrary, rural elites managed to enrich themselves through community development – for example, roads built under the programme benefited the wealthy.[48] In both India and Pakistan, none of the structural inequalities stemming from debt, patriarchy, and caste were challenged. In India, community councils were captured by village headmen, caste leaders, and landlords, and the *panchayat* councils had little say in the agenda to be implemented.[49] So much so that an in-depth study of the Indian community development programme by Swedish economist Gunnar Myrdal concluded that its net effect had been to 'create more, not less, inequality'.[50]

Finally, the failure of community development approaches to substantially alter conditions provokes one to explore alternatives: what *has* been successful in improving economic conditions in rural areas? In 1962, T. Epstein published a study of two villages in South India. In one of the villages, a canal had been constructed, while in the other there was none. The village without the canal was the one to experience social and economic change as in the irrigated village, the existing elite capitalized on the new opportunities and became more elaborate than before. In the dry village, the villagers were forced to look outside and change occurred through emigration and other entrepreneurial behaviour.[51] This links back to Darling's book about the poverty of the Punjab peasant emerging from the prosperity of the province, but whereas Darling blamed the peasant for his lack of thrift, it can be argued that there were higher stakes for the Punjabi elite in maintaining and expanding their privilege.

Conclusion

> A poverty curtain has descended right across the face of our world, dividing it materially and philosophically into two different worlds, two separate planets, two unequal humanities – one embarrassingly rich and the other desperately poor.
>
> —Mahbub ul Haq, *The Poverty Curtain*[52]

> What has been will be again, what has been done will be done again; there is nothing new under the sun.
>
> —*Ecclesiastes 1:9*

Colonial efforts at rural uplift in the Punjab in the 1930s rested on a belief that the peasant should lift himself out of poverty by reforming his habits and outlook. Such an approach was a convenient one for the imperial bureaucracy that did not want to antagonize local politicians through any structural change and yet wanted to appear committed to some programme of socio-economic reform. Henry Calvert, an Indian Civil Service officer, at the forefront of efforts at rural reconstruction in the Punjab in the 1930s emphasized the role of the peasant's outlook as follows:

> It may be stated that the main causes of poverty of the Punjab are to be found in the history of the province. It should be sufficiently obvious that if that mass of the people in any country are poor, it must be because they are not doing what is necessary to make them rich; they are not using the factors of wealth in sufficient degree.... Chief amongst all faults and

defects is the absence of what Mr Moreland calls the Will to live Better, the determination to improve the human lot by human labour ... it has been said that whereas the ambition of the man in the west is to acquire comfort and amusements, that of the East is to acquire dignity and leisure and there is much truth in this. The Indian prefers to repress his wants rather than exert himself to satisfy them. It is the intense desire for more material comfort that is the moving force to increasing wealth. A people who do not want material things and who believe in stifling human desire will never have great industries and will always be poor.[53]

Post-colonial attempts at community development and cooperation inherited this fundamental assumption about the ultimate responsibility for poverty resting with the peasant. At the same time, community developers valorized the villager instead of the modernist vision that saw large-scale planning as the panacea for underdevelopment. With ultimate blame for poverty also came the absolute faith that the peasant was the agent of sustained progress. Despite the rhetoric and heavy investment in nationwide community development programmes in India and Pakistan in the 1950s and 1960s, the programmes achieved little and had to be abandoned. What is curious, however, is the persistence in development studies of ideas of 'grassroots development', which are repeatedly seen as something new and innovative with no history. The latest among these cures, microfinance, is hailed as a revolutionary idea and yet substantially it does not differ much from the state-sponsored cooperatives in the Punjab in the early twentieth century.

In the 1990s, Amitai Etizioni popularized ideas of communitarianism,[54] and later Hilary Clinton published *It Takes a Village* in 1996,[55] both espousing the virtues of developing local communities. Meanwhile, the World Bank maintained an active interest in programmes of community development despite its own reports finding no evidence of success. After reviewing nearly 500 studies of participatory development and decentralization, Ghazala Mansuri and Vijayendra Rao, two leading economists at the World Bank, concluded that community-directed development had 'modest results, benefits that skewed significantly toward local elites and greater difficulty in encouraging the durable formation of egalitarian communities'.[56] The continued popularity of the approach is only possible within an ahistorical framework and a preference for maintaining structural continuity. By placing the blame on the poor, the rich are dropped from the equation and their role in creating or engendering poverty is ignored.

The same can be said of institutionalist approaches to development that also remain in vogue. By blaming an inherited colonial system and an impassive structure, the failure of development interventions is accepted and rationalized. And so both forms of discourse and prescription go hand in hand: community development or localized approaches blame the individual, and institutionalist approaches blame the past. In neither case is a more nuanced understanding of the close connections and overlaps examined: development programmes and projects are incubated within the institutional and bureaucratic structure and implemented through it. The failure of the programmes may have more to do with the ideological assumptions and interests of the implementers in maintaining the status quo in power structures than in attributing the failure to a colonial past. The existence of community development during a period of colonial rule therefore challenges this bifurcation of blaming either history (in the case of institutionalist approaches) or individuals (in the case of community development). Rural reconstruction or village uplift in the Punjab indicated that it was bureaucratic opposition, a lack of funds, and an unwillingness to challenge structural inequalities that caused the programme to fail.

The examination of the simultaneous development of institutions and an agenda of rural reconstruction in the Punjab in the early twentieth century allows a complex and multi-faceted appreciation of problems of rural development, while at the same time simplifying the reasons for failure. At a basic level, this book has challenged the chronology of institutional development preceding economic development and instead presented the historical antecedents of contemporary prescriptions of economic reform. An appreciation of how and why similar initiatives failed in the early twentieth century not only yields a greater understanding of the limitations of community development but also challenges the catch-all concept of 'institutions' that are blamed with an astonishing lack of clarity on where the precise faults or constraints lie.

Second, this book has attempted to weave together a more complex understanding of the colonial impact on the Punjab than the binary depictions in existing historiography. Punjab was neither a supreme beneficiary nor a site of extreme extraction, but instead a bit of both. As a site for microeconomic interventions in poverty reduction, it was a laboratory that catalyzed a global movement towards community – one that ill-acknowledges its colonial roots and is instead generally seen as a post-colonial, US-sponsored drive.

Third, the book challenges the salience of 1947 as a turning point in the economic history of the Punjab. Instead, it shows how economic policy and political influence were being shaped and distributed from the interwar period onwards and the moment of Partition signalled transition more than rupture. Two structural continuities are important: first, the political elite, mostly from the Unionist Party, who were influencing institutional and legislative reform from the 1920s and 1930s and can thus be seen as architects of the corrosive institutional inheritance so favoured as a cause of underdevelopment by institutional theorists. It is in the individual continuity of self-interested political influence rather than an abstract persistence of institutional structure that one can step beyond the terminology to appraise the colonial legacy. Second, with the emergence of colonial officials like Brayne and Darling who sought to implement personalized visions of economic reform, without any official directive to do so, a new class of technocrats or foreign experts was born; this also germinated in the interwar period and the incubating structures were well in place by then. Post-colonial states were thus birthed into a world thick with technocracy, and expert handmaidens ushered them into an era of technical assistance, foreign aid, community development, and the science of development economics. The missionary faith of Brayne and the circumspect intellectualism of Darling may have been commercialized into theories and models applied to poor countries universally, but a backward glance at the trajectory of the ideas reveals little evolution. Anchoring the ideas in space and time allows one to appreciate the colonial impact. Much is made of institutions as colonial inheritance, but of the weightless history of community development, scarcely a mention is made. This book has attempted to redress the balance a little.

Notes

1 Daniel Immerwahr, *Thinking Small: The United States and the Lure of Community Development* (Cambridge, MA: Harvard University Press, 2014), p. 13.

2 For a critical appraisal of rural development approaches in general, see S. H. Deshpande, 'All-Sided Approach to Rural Development: How Valid Is It?' *Economic and Political Weekly* 3, no. 16 (1968): 638–43; and John Harriss (ed.), *Rural Development, Theories of Peasant Economy and Agrarian Change* (London: Hutchinson, 1982).

3 Hugh Tinker, 'Authority and Community in Village India', *Pacific Affairs* 32, no. 4 (1959): 354–75.

4 See the review of Brayne's books by H. R. C. Hailey, 'Review', *Economic Journal* 40, no. 157 (1930): 136–37.

5 B. B. Mukherjee, 'Brayne's Gurgaon Experiment: Rural Welfare in India', *Social Forces* 8, no. 2 (1929): 253–4.

6 See Naved Hamid, *Foreign Aid: A Trap?* (Lahore: Progressive Publishers, 1972), pp. 26–33, for a discussion of foreign aid given to Pakistan in the 1950s and 1960s and its benefits to donor countries.

7 Gilbert Rist, *The History of Development: From Western Origins to Global Faith* (London: Zed Books, 2014 [1997]), p. 72. On the origins of the terminology, see also H. W. Arndt, 'Economic Development: A Semantic History', *Economic Development and Cultural Change* 29, no. 3 (1981): 457–66.

8 Rist, *The History of Development*, p. 73.

9   Rist, *The History of Development*, p. 73.

10 Gerald M. Meier, 'The Progressive State in Classical Economics', in Gerald M. Meier (ed.), *From Classical Economics to Development Economics* (London: St Martin's Press, 1994), pp. 5–27.

11 See, for instance, William J. Barber, *British Economic Thought and India, 1600–1858* (Oxford: Oxford University Press, 1975) and William J. Barber, 'British Classical Economists and Underdevelopment in India' in Meier (ed.), *From Classical Economics to Development Economics*, pp. 51–67.

12 Paul Baran, *The Political Economy of Growth* (New York: Monthly Review Press, 1957).

13 For a summary, see Shahrukh Rafi Khan, *A History of Development Economics Thought: Challenges and Counter-Challenges* (Oxford: Oxford University Press, 2014).

14 Timothy Mitchell, *Colonising Egypt* (Cambridge: Cambridge University Press, 1988).

15 Timothy Mitchell, *Rule of Experts: Egypt, Techno-Politics, Modernity* (Berkeley: University of California Press, 2002).

16 Anand Chandavarkar, *Keynes and India: A Study in Economics and Biography* (London: Macmillan, 1989), p. 3.

17 Darling was an officer in the Indian Civil Service who became an authority on peasant indebtedness in the Punjab. His life and works are described in detail in Chapter 3.

18 Hans W. Singer, 'Early Years (1910–38)', in Alan Cairncross and Mohinder Puri (eds.), *Employment, Income Distribution and Development Strategy: Essays in Honour of H. W. Singer* (London: Macmillan, 1976), pp. 1–14.

19 See Arthur W. Lewis, 'Development and Distribution', in Cairncross and Puri (eds.), *Employment, Income Distribution and Development Strategy*, pp. 26–42.

20 Immerwahr, *Thinking Small*, p. 9.

21 Walter C. Neale, 'Indian Community Development, Local Government, Local Planning, and Rural Policy since 1950', *Economic Development and Cultural Change* 33, no. 4 (1985): 677–98.

22 Immerwahr, *Thinking Small*, p. 78.

23 Shoaib Sultan Khan, *Rural Development in Pakistan* (New Delhi: Vikas, 1980), p. 2.

24 For a discussion of the American involvement in community development programmes in India, see Alice Thorner, 'Nehru, Albert Mayer and Origins of Community Projects', *Economic and Political Weekly* 16, no. 4 (1981): 117–20.

25 Immerwahr, *Thinking Small*, p. 10.

26 Immerwahr, *Thinking Small*, p. 82.

27 See a summary of rural development in Pakistan in Khwaja Amjad Saeed, *The Economy of Pakistan* (Oxford: Oxford University Press, 2006), pp. 48–51.

28 Government of Pakistan, First Five Year Plan, National Planning Board (Karachi, 1957), p. 16

29 For a critical appraisal of this programme, see Markus Daechsel, 'Sovereignty, Governmentality and Development in Ayub's Pakistan: The Case of Korangi Township', *Modern Asian Studies* 45, no. 1 (2011): 131–57.

30 See details in Khan, *Rural Development in Pakistan*, p. 3.

31 Khan, *Rural Development in Pakistan*, p. 2.

32 Akhtar Hameed Khan, *Orangi Pilot Project: Reminiscences and Reflections* (Oxford: Oxford University Press, 1996), p. 39.

33 Akhtar Hameed Khan, 'The Ghost of Comilla', *Integrated Rural Development Review* I, no. 1 (1975): 76–85.

34 A. K. Khalid, *The Agrarian History of Pakistan* (Lahore: Allied Press, 1998), p. 283.

35 In 1956–57, in West Pakistan, the Credit Enquiry Commission found that out of the 10,985 societies, 2,421 or a quarter, were in D-class – that is, they were defunct and on the verge of liquidation, while another 2,194 societies were in C-class or nearly defunct. In March 1972, the Cooperative (Reform) Order was promulgated by the government of Zulfiqar Bhutto. However, less than 10 per cent of total rural credit was disbursed by cooperatives by this point. See S. M. Akhtar, *Economic Development of Pakistan* (Lahore: Publishers United Ltd, 1986), p. 69.

36 Khalid, *The Agrarian History of Pakistan*, p. 283.

37 Khalid, *The Agrarian History of Pakistan*, p. 283.

38 Khalid, *The Agrarian History of Pakistan*, p. 285. See also Otto Schiller, *Individual Farming on Cooperative Lines* (Lahore: Punjab Cooperative Union, 1961).

39 Immerwahr, *Thinking Small*, p. 93

40 Masih-uz-Zaman quoted in Jack D. Mezirow, *Dynamics of Community Development* (New York: Scarecrow Press, 1963), p. 149.

41 Shahid Javed Burki, 'West Pakistan's Rural Works Programme: A Study in Political and Administrative Response', *Middle East Journal* 23, no. 3 (1969): 321–42.

42 Immerwhar, *Thinking Small*, p. 69.

43 For a discussion of modernization versus the dependency perspective, see John Isbister, *Promises Not Kept: Poverty and the Betrayal of Third World* (Bloomfield: Kumarian Press, 2006), p. 31.

44 See Immerwahr, *Thinking Small*, p. 63 for details of academic debates in the 1950s and 1960s between the two camps.

45 Immerwahr, *Thinking Small*, p. 63.

46 Ambedkar made these remarks in the Constituent Assembly on 4 November 1948, quoted in George Mathew, *Status of Panchayati Raj in the States of India 1994* (New Delhi: Concept Publishing Company, 1995), p. 1.

47 For a detailed discussion, see Shahid Javed Burki, 'West Pakistan's Rural Works Programme: A Study in Political and Administrative Response', *Middle East Journal* 23, no. 3 (1969): 321–42.

48 This links back to scholarship on rural elites dominating the economy during the colonial period, see, for instance, D. A. Washbrook, 'Progress and Problems: South Asian Economic and Social History c. 1720–1860', *Modern Asian Studies* 22, no. 1 (1988): 57–96.

49   Walter C. Neale, 'Indian Community Development, Local Government, Local
     Planning, and Rural Policy since 1950', *Economic Development and Cultural Change*
     33, no. 4 (1985): 677–98.

50   Immerwahr, *Thinking Small*, p. 11.

51   T. Scarlett Epstein, *Economic Development and Social Change in South India* (Manchester:
     Manchester University Press, 1962) pp. 314–26.

52   Mahbub ul Haq, *The Poverty Curtain* (New York: Columbia University Press, 1976).

53   H. Calvert, *The Wealth and Welfare of the Punjab: Being Some Studies in Punjab Rural
     Economics* (Lahore: Civil and Military Gazette Press, 1922), p. 385.

54   See, for instance, Amitai Etzioni, *The Spirit of Community: Rights, Responsibilities and
     the Communitarian Agenda* (New York: Crown Publishers, 1993).

55   Hilary Clinton, *It Takes a Village* (New York: Simon & Schuster, 1996).

56   Immerwahr, *Thinking Small*, p. 176.

Glossary

bania	moneylender
barani	non-irrigated, dry
chapraasi	orderly
crore	an amount of money equalling ten million
insaf	justice
jama	revenue demand
Jat	an agricultural caste
kamin	village menial
Khatri	a moneylending caste
kisan	farmer
lakh	an amount of money equalling one hundred thousand
mandi	market
naib	assistant
riba	interest
sahukar	moneylender
zamindar	cultivator
zera'at pesha shaks	a person engaged in agricultural activity

BIBLIOGRAPHY

Newspapers

Civil and Military Gazette

Jat Gazette

The Pioneer

The Tribune

Zamindar

Manuscripts

British Library, London

Brayne papers, MSS Eur. F152

Fazl-i-Husain papers, MSS Eur. E 352

Sir Roger Thomas papers, MSS Eur. F235

Centre of South Asian Studies, Cambridge

Cowley papers including 'Peacocks Calling', Unpublished Memoirs of Bill Cowley, Cambridge, Centre of South Asian Studies

Malcolm Darling papers

Unpublished memoirs of Bill Cowley

Printed Primary Sources

Cambridge University Library

Annual report of the working of the Punjab Alienation of Land Act 13 of 1900 for the year ending 30th September 1901 (Lahore, 1902).

Report on the working of Debt Conciliation Boards in the Punjab from the dates of their inception up to the 31st December 1939.

Punjab Provincial Banking Enquiry Committee, 1929–30, vol. 1.

National Documentation Centre, Islamabad

Alan Mitchell, Esquire, I.C.S., Commissioner, Lahore Division, Simla to Deputy Commissioner's Office, Gujranwala, 7 August 1934, Islamabad, National Documentation Centre, File no. 83/C.

Annual report on the working of cooperative credit societies in the Punjab for the year ending 31st March 1905 (Lahore, 1905).

Annual report on the working of cooperative credit societies in the Punjab for the year ending 31st March 1906 (Lahore, 1907).

Annual report on the working of cooperative credit societies in the Punjab for the year ending 31st March 1907 (Lahore, 1908).

Annual report on the working of cooperative credit societies in the Punjab for the year ending 31st July 1908 (Lahore, 1909).

Annual report on the working of cooperative credit societies in the Punjab for the year ending 31st March 1909 (Lahore, 1910).

Annual report on the working of cooperative credit societies in the Punjab for the year ending 31st July 1910 (Lahore, 1911).

Annual report on the working of cooperative credit societies in the Punjab for the year ending 30th June 1911 (Lahore, 1912).

Annual report on the working of cooperative credit societies in the Punjab for the year ending 31st July 1912 (Lahore, 1913).

Annual report on the working of cooperative credit societies in the Punjab for the year ending 31st July 1913 (Lahore, 1914).

Annual report on the working of cooperative credit societies in the Punjab for the year ending 31st July 1914 (Lahore, 1915).

Annual report on the working of cooperative credit societies in the Punjab for the year ending 31st July 1915 (Lahore, 1916).

Annual report on the working of cooperative credit societies in the Punjab for the year ending 31st July 1916 (Lahore, 1917).

Annual report on the working of cooperative credit societies in the Punjab for the year ending 31st July 1917 (Lahore, 1918).

Annual report on the working of cooperative credit societies in the Punjab for the year ending 31st March 1918 (Lahore, 1919).

Annual report on the working of cooperative credit societies in the Punjab for the year ending 31st March 1919 (Lahore, 1920).

Annual report on the working of cooperative credit societies in the Punjab for the year ending 31st July 1920 (Lahore, 1921).

Annual report on the working of cooperative credit societies in the Punjab for the year ending 31st March 1921 (Lahore, 1922).

Annual report on the working of cooperative credit societies in the Punjab for the year ending 31st July 1923 (Lahore, 1924).

Annual report on the working of cooperative credit societies in the Punjab for the year ending 31st July 1924 (Lahore, 1925).

Annual report on the working of cooperative credit societies in the Punjab for the year ending 31st July 1925 (Lahore, 1926).

Annual report on the working of cooperative credit societies in the Punjab for the year ending 31st July 1926 (Lahore, 1927).

Annual report on the working of cooperative credit societies in the Punjab for the year ending 31st July 1927 (Lahore, 1928).

Annual report on the working of cooperative credit societies in the Punjab for the year ending 31st July 1928 (Lahore, 1929).

Annual report on the working of cooperative credit societies in the Punjab for the year ending 31st July 1929 (Lahore, 1930).

Annual report on the working of cooperative credit societies in the Punjab for the year ending 31st July 1932 (Lahore, 1933).

Annual report on the working of cooperative credit societies in the Punjab for the year ending 31st July 1936 (Lahore, 1937).

Annual report on the working of cooperative credit societies in the Punjab for the year ending 31st July 1937 (Lahore, 1938).

Annual report on the working of cooperative credit societies in the Punjab for the year ending 31st July 1938 (Lahore, 1939).

C. C. Garbett, Chief Secretary to Government, Punjab to All Deputy Commissioners in the Punjab, 5 November 1934, Islamabad, National Documentation Centre, Secret file No. 12467-34-9-S.B.

Communism (General Aspects), Government of Punjab Secret Pamphlet, 25 April 1934, Islamabad, National Documentation Centre, S-358.

Cuthbert King, Commissioner, Lahore Division to Deputy Commissioner, Lahore, 5 May 1943, Secret file, Islamabad, National Documentation Centre, S-361.

Notes on the Khaksar Movement 1940 (with Addendum 1940–4), Punjab Government Secret Document, Islamabad, National Documentation Centre, S-360.

The Ahrar Movement in the Punjab, 1931–38, Government of Punjab Secret Document, (Lahore, 1939) Islamabad, National Documentation Centre, S-358.

The Ahmadiyya Sect: Notes on the Origin, Development and History of the Movement up to the Year 1938, Government of Punjab Secret Document (Lahore, 1938), Islamabad, National Documentation Centre, S-359.

Punjab Archives, Lahore

Department of Revenue and Agriculture Proceedings 1901, Punjab Government, Lahore, Punjab Archives, File No. 1.

Department of Revenue and Agriculture Proceedings 1901, Punjab Government, Lahore, Punjab Archives, File No. 9.

Indian Legislative Council Debates, 27 September 1899, Lahore, Punjab Archives.

Letter no. 605 dated the 15th October 1908, from the Junior Secretary to the Financial Commissioner, Punjab, Lahore, Punjab Archives.

Memorandum to Lord Minto from Punjab Hindu Sabha, 24 June 1909, Lahore, Punjab Archives, Board of Revenue file 441/212 A.

Punjab Administration Report, 1849–51, Lahore, Punjab Archives.

Punjab Administration Report, 1872–73, Lahore, Punjab Archives.

Punjab Administration Report, 1880–01, Lahore, Punjab Archives.

Punjab Information Bureau, *Rural Uplift in Gurgaon*, Punjab Archives (Lahore, 1928).

Punjab Legislative Council Debates, vol. 12, 22 Feb. 1928, Punjab Archives, Lahore.

Punjab Legislative Council Debates, Lahore, Punjab Archives, vol. 12 (1928–29), p. 709.

Statement of Pandit Nanak Chand, Legislative Council Debates, Lahore, Punjab Archives, vol. 9 A (1926), p. 842.

British Library, London

Report of Punjab Colonies (Baillie) Committee 1907–8 (Lahore, 1908), London, British Library India Office Records, IOR/V/26/315/1.

Publications of the Punjab Board of Economic Inquiry

Anand, Roshan Lal. *Soldiers' Savings and How They Use Them: Being a Study of the Ways in which the Punjab Soldier Uses the Money He Receives on Leaving the Army*, publication no. 68 (Lahore: Punjab Board of Economic Inquiry, 1940), p. iii.

Das, Anchal. *An Economic Survey of Gajju Chak, A Village in the Gujranwala District of the Punjab*, Village Surveys–6 (Lahore: Punjab Board of Economic Inquiry, 1934).

Das, Dial. *Vital Statistics of the Punjab 1901–40*, publication no. 80 (Lahore: Punjab Board of Economic Inquiry, 1943).

Dawar, L. *Market Practices in the Punjab: Being a Study of the Practices Affecting the Producer in the Grain and Cotton Markets, Together with the Rules and Regulations Governing Similar Practices under the Bombay and Berar Market Legislation* (Lahore: Punjab Board of Economic Inquiry, 1934).

Fazal, Cyril P. K. *A Bibliography of Economic Literature Relating to the Punjab* (Lahore: Punjab Board of Economic Inquiry 1941).

———. *A Guide to Punjab Government Reports and Statistics* (Lahore: Punjab Board of Economic Inquiry, 1939).

Khan, Abdur Rahim. *An Economic Survey of Bhambu Sandila, A Village in the Muzaffargarh District of the Punjab*, Village Surveys–8 (Lahore: Punjab Board of Economic Inquiry, 1935).

Lucas, E. *Domestic budgets (1941–42) of Thirty Families in the Murree Suburban Zone, Rawalpindi District*, publication no. 87 (Lahore: Punjab Board of Economic Inquiry, 1946).

Mahendru, I. D. *Some Factors Affecting the Price of Wheat in the Punjab: Being an Examination of the Conditions in the Amritsar, Jullundur, Lyallpur and Okara Mandis Together with a Description of the Market Transactions as Regards Wholesale Dealings in Wheat* (Lahore: Punjab Board of Economic Inquiry, 1937).

Myles, W. H. *Condition of Weights and Measures in the Punjab: Being the Result of Investigations in Thirteen Areas in the Province*, publication no. 42 (Lahore: Punjab Board of Economic Inquiry, 1936).

Punjab Board of Economic Inquiry. *Questionnaire for Economic Inquiries* (Lahore: Punjab Board of Economic Inquiry, 1924).

Rai, Gulshan. *Agricultural Statistics of the Punjab 1901–2 to 1935–6* (Lahore: Punjab Board of Economic Inquiry, 1937).

Seth, R. K. and Faiz Illahi. *An Economic Survey of Durrana Langana, a Village in the Multan District of the Punjab*, Village Surveys–11 (Lahore: Punjab Board of Economic Inquiry, 1938).

Singh, Kartar. *Family Budgets of Four Tenant Cultivators in the Lyallpur district 1932–33*, publication no. 40 (Lahore: Punjab Board of Economic Inquiry, 1934), p. iii.

Singh, Labh. *Family Budgets 1937–38 of Ten Cultivators in the Punjab, Being the Sixth Year's Accounts of Six Cultivators on the Risalewala Farm near Lyallpur and Second Year's Accounts of Four Owner-Cultivators in the Hoshiarpur, Amritsar and Rohtak Districts* (Lahore: Punjab Board of Economic Inquiry, 1939), p. 4.

Singh, Labh. *Family Budgets 1935–36 of Six Tenant Cultivators in the Lyallpur District, Being the Fourth Year's Accounts of Some Cultivators on the Risalewala Farm near Lyallpur* (Lahore: Punjab Board of Economic Inquiry, 1938), p. 19.

Singh, Randhir. *An Economic survey of Kala Gaddi Thamman (Chak 73 G.B.): A Village in the Lyallpur District of the Punjab*, Village Survey No. 4 (Lahore: Punjab Board of Economic Inquiry, 1932).

Government Publications

Government of India, *Report on Certain Aspects of the Cooperative Movement in India* (New Delhi: Government of India Planning Commission, 1957).

Government of Pakistan, *First Five-Year Plan* (Karachi: National Planning Board, 1957).

Pamphlets

Antia, F. P. *Transport*, Oxford Pamphlets on Indian Affairs (London: Oxford University Press, 1946).

Appadorai, A. *Democracy in India*, Oxford Pamphlets on Indian Affairs (London: Oxford University Press, 1942).

Appasamy, A. J. et al. *The Cultural Problem*, Oxford Pamphlets on Indian Affairs (London: Oxford University Press, 1942).

Batley, Claude. Architecture, Oxford Pamphlets on Indian Affairs (London: Oxford University Press, 1946).

Brayne, F. L. *Winning the Peace*, Oxford Pamphlets on Indian Affairs (London: Oxford University Press, 1944).

Chatterji, Suniti Kumar. *Languages and the Linguistic Problem*, Oxford Pamphlets on Indian Affairs (London: Oxford University Press, 1943).

Critchley, T. K. *Australia and New Zealand*, Oxford Pamphlets on Indian Affairs (London: Oxford University Press, 1946).

Drucquer, Seth. *Broadcasting*, Oxford Pamphlets on Indian Affairs (London: Oxford University Press, 1945).

Elwin, Verrier. *The Aboriginals*, Oxford Pamphlets on Indian Affairs (London: Oxford University Press, 1943).

Ghose, Bimal C. *Industrial Location*, Oxford Pamphlets on Indian Affairs (London: Oxford University Press 1945).

Glover, Harold. *Soil Erosion*, Oxford Pamphlets on Indian Affairs (London: Oxford University Press, 1944).

Grant, John B. *The Health of India*, Oxford Pamphlets on Indian Affairs (London: Oxford University Press, 1943).

Guha, B. S. *Racial Elements in the Population*, Oxford Pamphlets on Indian Affairs (London: Oxford University Press,1944).

Heron, A. M. *Mineral Resources*, Oxford Pamphlets on Indian Affairs (London: Oxford University Press, 1945).

Lloyd, Seton. *Iraq*, Oxford Pamphlets on Indian Affairs (London: Oxford University Press, 1943).

Mukerjee, Radhakamal. *The Food Supply*, Oxford Pamphlets on Indian Affairs (London: Oxford University Press, 1942).

Natarajan, S. *Social Problems*, Oxford Pamphlets on Indian Affairs (London: Oxford University Press, 1942).

Panikkar, K. M. *Indian States*, Oxford Pamphlets on Indian Affairs (London: Oxford University Press, 1942).

Saiyadain, K. G. et al. *The Educational System*, Oxford Pamphlets on Indian Affairs (London: Oxford University Press, 1943).

Satthianadhan, W. R. S., and J. C. Ryan. *Cooperation*, Oxford Pamphlets on Indian Affairs, no. 39 (London: Oxford University Press, 1946).

Spear, Percival. *National Harmony*, Oxford Pamphlets on Indian Affairs (London: Oxford University Press, 1946).

Vijayaraghavacharya, T. *The Land and Its Problems*, Oxford Pamphlets on Indian Affairs (London: Oxford University Press, 1943).

Secondary Sources

Books

Ahmed, Waheed. *Diary and Notes of Fazl-i-Husain* (Lahore: Research Society of Pakistan, 1977).

———. *The Punjab Story, 1940–1947: The Muslim League and the Unionists: towards Partition and Pakistan* (Islamabad: National Documentation Wing, Cabinet Division, Government of Pakistan, 2009).

Akhtar, S. M. *Economic Development of Pakistan* (Lahore: Publishers United Ltd, 1986).

Alavi, Hamza, P. L. Burns, G. R. Knight, P. B. Mayer, and Doug McEachern. *Capitalism and Colonial Production* (London: Croom Helm, 1980).

Ali, Imran. *Punjab under Imperialism, 1885–1947* (Princeton: Princeton University Press, 1988).

Bagchi, Amiya Kumar. *The Political Economy of Underdevelopment* (Cambridge: Cambridge University Press, 1982).

Baran, Paul A. *The Political Economy of Growth* (New York: Monthly Review Press, 1957).

Barber, William J. *British Economic Thought and India, 1600–1858* (Oxford: Oxford University Press, 1975).

Barrier, Norman G. *The Punjab Alienation of Land Bill of 1900* (Durham, NC: Duke University Press, 1966).

Bayly, C. A. *Rulers, Townsmen and Bazaars* (Cambridge: Cambridge University Press, 1983).

Brayne, F. L. *Better Villages* (Oxford: Oxford University Press, 1937).

———. *New Weapons for Old Enemies: How Malaria Can Be Defeated by Paludrine, DDT and Gammexane* (London: Village Welfare Association, 1948).

———. *Socrates in an Indian Village* (London: Oxford University Press, 1929).

———. *The Neglected Partner* (London: Village Welfare Association, 1949)

———. *The Peasant's Home and Its Place in National Planning* (London: Village Welfare Association, 1949).

———. *The Remaking of Village India* (Oxford: Oxford University Press, 1929).

———. *Village Uplift in India* (Allahabad: Pioneer Press, 1927).

Calvert, Hubert. *The Wealth and Welfare of the Punjab: Being Some Studies in Punjab Rural Economics* (Lahore: Civil and Military Gazette Press, 1922).

Chandavarkar, Anand. *Keynes and India: A Study in Economics and Biography* (London: Macmillan, 1989).

Chowdhry, Prem. *Punjab Politics and the Role of Chhotu Ram* (Delhi: Vikas, 1984).

Clinton, Hilary. *It Takes a Village* (New York: Simon & Schuster, 1996).

Darling, Malcolm. *Apprentice to Power* (London: Hogarth Press, 1966).

———. *At Freedom's Door* (Oxford: Oxford University Press, 2011).

———. *Rusticus Loquitur: The Old Light and the New in the Punjab Village* (London: Oxford University Press, 1930).

———. *Some Aspects of Co-Operation in Germany, Italy and Ireland* (Lahore: Superintendent, Government Printing, Punjab, 1922).

———. *The Punjab Peasant in Prosperity and Debt* (Bombay: Oxford University Press, 1925).

———. *Wisdom and Waste in the Punjab Village* (Oxford: Oxford University Press, 1934).

Dewey, Clive. *Anglo-Indian Attitudes: Mind of the Indian Civil Service* (London: Hambledon Press, 1993).

Dickens, Charles. *A Tale of Two Cities* (New York: Barnes & Noble Classics, 2004 [1859]).

Easterly, William. *The Tyranny of Experts: Economists, Dictators and the Forgotten Rights of the Poor* (New York: Basic Books, 2014).

Elgar, Zekiye. *A Punjabi Village in Pakistan* (New York: Edwin Mellen Press, 1964).

Epstein, T. Scarlett. *Economic Development and Social Change in South India* (Manchester: Manchester University Press, 1962).

Etzioni, Amitai. *The Spirit of Community: Rights, Responsibilities and the Communitarian Agenda* (New York: Crown Publishers, 1993).

Fanon, Frantz. *The Wretched of the Earth* (London: Penguin UK, 2001 [1961]).

Forster, E. M. *A Passage to India* (New York: Harcourt, Brace and Company, 1924).

Gilmartin, David. *Empire and Islam: Punjab and the Making of Pakistan* (Berkeley: University of California Press, 1988).

Gopal, Madan. *Sir Chhotu Ram: A Political Biography* (New Delhi: B.R. Publishing Corporation, 1977).

Graeber, David. *Debt: The First 5000 Years* (New York: Melville House Publishing, 2011).

Hamid, Naved. *Foreign Aid: A Trap?* (Lahore: Progressive Publishers, 1972).

Haq, Mahbub ul. *The Poverty Curtain* (New York: Columbia University Press, 1976).

Harriss, John (ed.). *Rural Development, Theories of Peasant Economy and Agrarian Change* (London: Hutchinson, 1982).

Heinrich, Rev. J. C. *The Psychology of a Suppressed People* (London: George Allen and Unwin Ltd, 1937).

Hull, Matthew. *Government of Paper: The Materiality of Bureaucracy in Urban Pakistan* (Berkeley: University of California Press, 2012).

Husain, Azim. *Mian Fazl-i-Husain: A Political Biography* (New York: Longmans, Green & Co., 1946).

Ibbetson, Denzil. *Panjab Castes* (Lahore: Superintendent, Government Printing, Punjab, 1916).

Immerwahr, Daniel. *Thinking Small: The United States and the Lure of Community Development* (Cambridge, MA: Harvard University Press, 2014).

Isbister, John. *Promises Not Kept: Poverty and the Betrayal of Third World Development* (Hartford: Kumarian Press, 2003).

Jalal, Ayesha. *Democracy and Authoritarianism in South Asia: A Comparative and Historical Perspective* (Cambridge: Cambridge University Press, 1995).

———. *The Sole Spokesman: Jinnah, the Muslim League and the Demand for Pakistan* (Cambridge: Cambridge University Press, 1985).

Keating, G. *Agricultural Progress in Western India* (London: Longmans, Green and Co., 1921).

Kessinger, Tom G. *Vilayatpur, 1848–1968: Social and Economic Change in a North Indian Village* (Berkeley: University of California Press, 1974).

Khalid, A. K. *The Agrarian History of Pakistan* (Lahore: Allied Press, 1998).

Khan, Akhtar Hameed. *Orangi Pilot Project: Reminiscences and Reflections* (Oxford: Oxford University Press, 1996).

Khan, Shahrukh Rafi. *A History of Development Economics Thought: Challenges and Counter-Challenges* (Oxford: Oxford University Press, 2014).

Khan, Shoaib Sultan. *Rural Development in Pakistan* (New Delhi: Vikas, 1980).

Kipling, Rudyard. *The Collected Poems of Rudyard Kipling* (Ware: Wordsworth Editions Ltd, 1994).

Kundera, Milan. *The Unbearable Lightness of Being* (New York: Harper and Row, 1984).

Lal, Prem Chand. *Reconstruction and Education in Rural India in the Light of the Programme Carried on at Sriniketan, the Institute of Rural Reconstruction Founded by Rabindranath Tagore* (London: G. Allen & Unwin Ltd, 1932).

Linlithgow, L. *The Indian Peasant* (London: Faber and Faber, 1932).

Lucas, E. D. *The Economic Life of a Punjab Village* (Lahore: Civil and Military Gazette Press, 1935).

Major, Andrew J. *Return to Empire: Punjab under the Sikhs and British in the Mid-Nineteenth Century* (New Delhi: Sterling Publishers, 1996).

Malik, Iftikhar Haider. *Sikandar Hayat Khan* (1892–1942): *A Political Biography* (Islamabad: National Institute of Historical and Cultural Research, 1985).

Mathew, George. *Status of Panchayati Raj in the States of India 1994* (New Delhi: Concept Publishing Company, 1995).

Mezirow, Jack D. *Dynamics of Community Development* (New York: Scarecrow Press, 1963).

Mitchell, Timothy. *Colonising Egypt* (Cambridge: Cambridge University Press, 1988).

———. *Rule of Experts: Egypt, Techno-Politics, Modernity* (Berkeley: University of California Press, 2002).

Morse, David A. *The Origin and Evolution of the I.L.O. and Its Role in the World Community* (New York: State School of Industrial and Labor Relations, Cornell University, 1969).

Mukherjee, Mridula. *Colonialising Agriculture: The Myth of Punjab Exceptionalism* (New Delhi: SAGE Publications, 2005).

Myrdal, Gunnar. *Asian Drama: An Inquiry into the Poverty of Nations* (Harmondsworth: Penguin Books, 1968).

Naoroji, Dadabhai. *Poverty and Un-British Rule* (London: S. Sonnenschein & Co., 1901).

Nelson, Matthew. *In the Shadow of the Shariah: Islam, Islamic Law and Democracy in Pakistan* (New York: Columbia University Press, 2011).

North, Douglass. *Institutions, Institutional Change and Economic Performance* (Cambridge: Cambridge University Press, 1990).

Ostrom, Elinor. *Governing the Commons: The Evolution of Institutions for Collective Action* (Cambridge: Cambridge University Press, 1990).

Pillay, A. P. *Welfare Problems in Rural India* (Bombay: DB Taraporevala Sons and Co., 1932).

Popkin, Samuel L. *The Rational Peasant: The Political Economy of Rural Society in Vietnam* (Berkeley: University of California Press, 1992).

Puri, Nina. *Political Elite and Society in the Punjab* (New Delhi: Vikas, 1985).

Raman, Bhavani. *Document Raj: Writing and Scribes in Early Colonial South India* (Chicago: Chicago University Press, 2012).

Rist, Gilbert. *The History of Development: From Western Origins to Global Faith* (London: Zed Books, 2014 [1997]).

Roseberry, R. J., *Imperial Rule in Punjab: The Conquest and Administration of Multan, 1818–1881* (New Delhi: Manohar Publications, 1987).

Saeed, Khwaja Amjad. *The Economy of Pakistan* (Oxford: Oxford University Press, 2006).

Said, Edward W. *Covering Islam* (New York: Pantheon Books, 1981).

Saiyid, Dushka H. *Exporting Communism to India: Why Moscow Failed* (Islamabad: National Institute of Historical and Cultural Research, 1995).

Scott, James C. *Seeing Like a State: How Certain Schemes to Improve the Human Condition Have Failed* (New Haven: Yale University Press, 1998).

———. *The Moral Economy of the Peasant: Rebellion and Subsistence in Southeast Asia* (New Haven: Yale University Press, 1976).

Schiller, Otto. *Individual Farming on Cooperative Lines* (Lahore: Punjab Cooperative Union, 1961).

Sevea, Iqbal Singh. *The Political Philosophy of Muhammad Iqbal: Islam and Nationalism in Late Colonial India* (Cambridge: Cambridge University Press, 2012).

Soto, Hernando De. *The Mystery of Capital: Why Capitalism Triumphs in the West and Fails Everywhere Else* (New York: Bantam Press, 2000).

Stein, Burton, and Sanjay Subrahmanyam (eds.). *Institutions and Economic Change in South Asia* (Oxford: Oxford University Press, 1996).

Stokes, Eric. *The Peasant and the Raj: Studies in Agrarian Society and Peasant Rebellion in Colonial India* (Cambridge: Cambridge University Press, 1978).

Strickland, C. F. *The Progress of Rural Welfare in India* (London: Oxford University Press, 1934).

———. *Review of Rural Welfare Activities in India* (London: Village Welfare Association, 1932).

Talbot, Ian. *A History of Modern South Asia: Politics, States, Diasporas* (Yale: Yale University Press, 2016).

———. *Khizr Tiwana, the Punjab Unionist Party and the Partition of India* (Richmond: Taylor & Francis Ltd, 1996).

———. *Punjab and the Raj* (New Delhi: Manohar Publications, 1988).

Tanwar, Raghuvendra. *Politics of Sharing Power: The Punjab Unionist Party 1923–1947* (New Delhi: Manohar, 1999).

Tawney, Robert. *Land and Labour in China* (London: George Allen and Unwin Ltd, 1932).

Thompson, E. *The Reconstruction of India* (London: Faber and Faber, 1930).

Thorburn, S. S. *Mussalmans and the Moneylenders in the Punjab* (Edinburgh: William Blackwood & Sons, 1884).

Tomlinson, B. R. *The Economy of Modern India 1860–1970* (Cambridge: Cambridge University Press, 1993).

Ullah, Ata. *The Cooperative Movement in the Punjab* (London: George Allen & Unwin Ltd, 1937).

van den Dungen, P. H. M. *The Punjab Tradition: Influence and Authority in Nineteenth-Century India* (London: Allen & Unwin Ltd, 1972).

Young, Miriam. *Seen and Heard in a Punjab Village* (London: Student Christian Movement Press, 1931).

Chapters in Edited Books

Barber, William J. 'British Classical Economists and Underdevelopment in India'. In *From Classical Economics to Development Economics*, edited by Gerald M. Meier, pp. 51–67 (London: St Martin's Press, 1994).

Dewey, Clive. 'Some Consequences of Military Expenditure in British India: The Case of the Upper Sind Sagar Doab 1849–1947'. In *Arrested Development in India: The Historical Dimension*, edited by Clive Dewey, pp. 93–169 (Delhi: Manohar Publications, 1988).

Dewey, Clive. 'Patwari and Chaukidar: Subordinate Officials and the Reliability of India's Agricultural Statistics'. In *The Imperial Impact: Studies in the Economic History of Africa and India*, edited by C. Dewey and A. G. Hopkins, pp. 280–314 (London: Athlone Press, 1978).

Galiani, Sebastian, and Itai Sened. 'Introduction'. In *Institutions, Property Rights and Economic Growth: The Legacy of Douglass North*, edited by Sebastian Galiani and Itai Sened, pp. 1–10 (New York: Cambridge University Press, 2014).

Lewis, Arthur W. 'Development and Distribution'. In *Employment, Income Distribution and Development Strategy: Essays in Honour of H. W. Singer*, edited by Alan Cairncross and Mohinder Puri, pp. 26–42 (London: Macmillan, 1976).

Meier, Gerald M. 'The Progressive State in Classical Economics'. In *From Classical Economics to Development Economics*, edited by Gerald M. Meier, pp. 5–27 (London: St Martin's Press, 1994).

Shepsle, Kenneth A. 'Institutional Equilibrium and Equilibrium Institutions'. In *Political Science: The Science of Politics*, edited by Herbert Weisberg, pp. 51–55 (New York: Agathon Press, 1986).

Singer, Hans W. 'Early Years (1910–38)'. In *Employment, Income Distribution and Development Strategy: Essays in Honour of H. W. Singer*, edited by Alan Cairncross and Mohinder Puri, pp. 1–14 (London: Macmillan, 1976).

Articles

Acemoglu, D., J. Robinson, and S. Johnson. 'The Colonial Origins of Comparative Development: An Empirical Investigation', *American Economic Review* 102, no. 6 (2012): 3077–3110.

Acemoglu, Daron, and Simon Johnson. 'Unbundling Institutions', *Journal of Political Economy* 113, no. 5 (2005): 949–95.

Arndt, H. W. 'Economic Development: A Semantic History', *Economic Development and Cultural Change* 29, no. 3 (1981): 457–66.

Banerjee, Abhijit, and Lakshmi Iyer. 'History, Institutions and Economic Performance: The Legacy of Colonial Land Tenure Systems in India', *American Economic Review* 95, no. 4 (2005): 1190–1213.

Barrier, N. G. 'The Punjab Disturbances of 1907: The Response of the British Government in India to Agrarian Unrest', *Modern Asian Studies* 1, no. 4 (1967): 353–83.

Besley, Timothy, and Torsten Persson. 'The Origins of State Capacity: Property Rights, Taxation and Politics', *American Economic Review* 99, no. 4 (2009): 1218–44.

Bhattacharya, Neeladri, 'Lenders and Debtors: Punjab Countryside 1880–1940', *Studies in History* 1, no. 2 (1985): 305–42.

Burki, Shahid Javed. 'West Pakistan's Rural Works Programme: A Study in Political and Administrative Response', *Middle East Journal* 23, no. 3 (1969): 321–42.

Chander, S. 'Congress-Raj Conflict and the Rise of the Muslim League in the Ministry Period, 1937–39', *Modern Asian Studies* 21, no. 2 (1987): 303–28.

Chandra, Bipan. 'Colonialism, Stages of Colonialism and the Colonial State', *Journal of Contemporary Asia* 10, no. 3 (1980): 172–85.

Chowdhry, Prem. 'Social Support Base and Electoral Politics: The Congress in Colonial Southeast Punjab', *Modern Asian Studies* 25, no. 4 (1991): 811–31.

Coombs, Catherine. 'Partition Narratives: Displaced Trauma and Culpability among British Civil Servants in 1940s Punjab', *Modern Asian Studies* 45, no. 1 (2011): 201–24.

Craik, Henry Duffield. 'Opening Ceremony of the Indian Statistical Conference: Second Session, 1939', *Indian Journal of Statistics* 4, no. 4 (1940): 603–06.

Daechsel, Markus. 'Sovereignty, Governmentality and Development in Ayub's Pakistan: The Case of Korangi Township', *Modern Asian Studies* 45, no. 1 (2011): 131–57.

Darling, Malcolm L. 'All India Rural Credit Survey', *International Cooperative Alliance Review* (June 1955).

Darling, Malcolm L. 'Cooperation and India's Second Five Year Plan', *Review of International Cooperation* 52, no. 1 (1959).

———. 'Cooperation and the Village Community', *Review of International Cooperation* 8, no. 9 (1952).

———. 'Cooperative Farming in Italy', *Yearbook of Agricultural Cooperation* (1953).

———. 'Ethics and Economics', *Indian Journal of Economics* 8, no. 3 (1928): 492–95.

———. 'Luigi Luzzatti', *Bombay Cooperative Quarterly* 5, no. 3 (1921).

———. 'Planner and Peasant in India', *Yearbook of Agricultural Cooperation* (1958).

———. 'Presidential Address', *Indian Journal of Economics Conference* 8, no. 30 (1928): 477–96.

———. 'Report on the Commonwealth Conference on Agricultural Cooperation at Oxford – July 23 to 28, 1951', *Asiatic Review* 38, no. 133 (1942).

———. 'The Cattedre Ambulanti of Italy and the Training of the Peasant', *Agricultural Journal of India* 22, no. 4 (1927).

———. 'The Economic Holding or the Family Farm', *Agricultural Journal on India* 22, no. 6 (1927).

Darling, Malcolm L. 'The Indian Peasant in the Modern World', *Asiatic Review* 38, no, 133 (1942): 49–65.

Darling, Malcolm L. 'The Indian Village and Democracy', *Journal of the Royal Society of the Arts* 91, no. 4645 (1943).

———. 'The Peasant Strength of India', *Asia* (March 1941).

———. 'The Zeiss Works, or What a Factory Should Be', *Irish Economist Quarterly Journal of Cooperative Thought and Progress* 8, no. 3 (1923).

Deshpande, S. H. 'All-Sided Approach to Rural Development: How Valid Is It?' *Economic and Political Weekly* 3, no. 16 (1968): 638–43.

Dewey, Clive. 'Annals of Rural Punjab', *Modern Asian Studies* 10, no. 1 (1976): 131–38.

Galor, O., and O. Moav. 'From Physical to Human Capital Accumulation: Inequality and the Process of Development', *Review of Economic Studies* 71, no. 4 (2004): 1001–26.

Gandhi, Mahatma. 'Village Improvement', *Young India*, 14 November 1929.

Gill, Anita. 'Interlinked Agrarian Credit Markets: Case Study of Punjab', *Economic and Political Weekly* 39, no. 33 (2004): 3741–51.

Habib, Irfan. 'Colonisation of the Indian Economy,' *Social Scientist* 3, no. 32 (1975): 23–53.

Hailey, H. R. C. 'Review', *Economic Journal* 40, no. 157 (1930): 136–37.

Hess, Gary R. 'American Agricultural Missionaries and Efforts at Economic Improvement in India', *Agricultural History* 42, no. 1 (1968): 23–34.

Islam, M. Mufakharul. 'The Punjab Land Alienation Act and the Professional Moneylenders', *Modern Asian Studies* 29, no. 2 (1995): 271–91.

Kessinger, Tom. 'Indian Village Records and Historical Village Studies. A Reply to C. Dewey, "Annals of Rural Punjab"', *Modern Asian Studies* 11, no. 4 (1977): 615–22.

Khan, Akhtar Hameed. 'The Ghost of Comilla', *Integrated Rural Development Review* 1, no. 1 (1975): 76–85.

Khan, Imdad Ali. 'Allama Iqbal and National Development: An Analysis of His Socio-Political Thoughts', *Journal of Rural Development and Administration* 28, no. 3 (1996): 45–57.

Mahalanobis, P. C. 'Analysis of Race-Mixture in Bengal', *Journal of the Asiatic Society of Bengal*, no. 23 (1927): 301–33.

Malik, Iftikhar H. 'Identity Formation and Muslim Party Politics in the Punjab, 1897–1936: A Retrospective Analysis', *Modern Asian Studies* 29, no. 2 (1985): 293–323.

Mathur, Man Singh. 'Rural Change in Perspective', *Economic and Political Weekly* 3, no. 5 (1968): 259–65.

Mukherjee, B. B. 'Brayne's Gurgaon Experiment: Rural Welfare in India', *Social Forces* 8, no. 2 (1929): 253–54.

Mukherjee, Mridula. 'Some Aspects of Agrarian Structure of Punjab 1925–47', *Economic and Political Weekly* 15, no. 26 (1980): 46–58.

Myles, W. H. 'The Board of Economic Inquiry, Punjab', *Indian Journal of Economics* 5, no. 3 (1925): 246–49.

Nath, Raja Narendar. 'Address to the Non-Agriculturist Conference at Dera Baba Nanak', *The Tribune*, 28 April 1936.

———. 'The Punjab Agrarian Laws and Their Economic and Constitutional Bearings', *Modern Review* 65 (January 1939): 29–36.

Neale, Walter C. 'Indian Community Development, Local Government, Local Planning, and Rural Policy since 1950', *Economic Development and Cultural Change* 33, no. 4 (1985): 677–98.

Pray, Carl E. 'The Economics of Agricultural Research in British Punjab and Pakistani Punjab, 1905–1975', *Journal of Economic History* 40, no. 1 (1980): 174–76.

———. 'The Impact of Agricultural Research in British India', *Journal of Economic History* 44, no. 2 (1984): 429–40.

Robb, Peter. 'Bihar, the Colonial State and Agricultural Development in India, 1880–1920', *Indian Economic and Social History Review* 25, no. 2 (1988): 205–35.

Robb, Peter. 'British Rule and Indian Improvement', *Economic History Review* 34, no. 4 (1981): 507–23.

Rodrik, Dani. 'Institutions for High-Quality Growth: What They Are and How to Acquire Them,' *Studies in Comparative International Development* 35, no. 3 (2000): 3–31.

Sharma, Shalini, 'Communism and "Democracy": Punjab Radicals and Representative Politics in the 1930s', *South Asian History and Culture* 4, no. 4 (2013): 443–64.

Sharma, S., and S. Chamala. 'Moneylender's Positive Image: Paradigms and Rural Development', *Economic and Political Weekly* 38, no. 17 (2003): 1713–20.

Strickland, C. F., 'Cooperation and the Rural Problem of India', *Quarterly Journal of Economics* 43, no. 3 (1929): 500–31

———. 'The Spread of Cooperation in the Punjab', *Agricultural Journal of India* (1918).

Talbot, Ian. 'Planning for Pakistan: The Planning Committee of the All-India Muslim League 1943–46', *Modern Asian Studies* 28, no. 4 (1994): 875–89.

Tan, Tai Yong. 'Maintaining the Military Districts: Civil-Military Integration and District Soldiers' Boards in the Punjab, 1919–1939', *Modern Asian Studies* 28, no. 4 (1994): 833–74.

Thorner, Alice. 'Nehru, Albert Mayer and Origins of Community Projects', *Economic and Political Weekly* 16, no. 4 (1981): 117–20.

Tinker, Hugh. 'Authority and Community in Village India', *Pacific Affairs* 32, no. 4 (1959): 354–75.

Washbrook, David A. 'Law, State and Agrarian Society in Colonial India', *Modern Asian Studies* 15, no. 3 (1981): 649–721.

———. 'Progress and Problems: South Asian Economic and Social History c. 1720-1860', *Modern Asian Studies* 22, no. 1 (1988): 57–96.

Unpublished Dissertations

Dewey, Clive. 'The Official Mind and the Problem of Agrarian Indebtedness in India, 1870–1910'. Unpublished Ph.D. dissertation, University of Cambridge, 1973.

INDEX